THE
B
SHINES BRIGHTER

THE
B
SHINES BRIGHTER

✦

THE BISBEE HIGH SCHOOL
LEGACY

HADLEY HICKS

DRAWINGS BY
SAM MOORE, BHS '56

iUniverse, Inc.
New York Lincoln Shanghai

THE B SHINES BRIGHTER
THE BISBEE HIGH SCHOOL LEGACY

iUniverse, Inc.

For information address:
iUniverse, Inc.
2021 Pine Lake Road, Suite 100
Lincoln, NE 68512
www.iuniverse.com

ISBN: 0-595-32831-8

Printed in the United States of America

"Because of you, the B shines brighter."
These words were spoken by Coach Waldo M. Dicus to the nine seniors on the
1951 Bisbee High School football team just before we took the field for the
annual "Copper-Pick" battle against our archrival, the Douglas High
School *Bulldogs*. These words seem appropriate for the title of a
book of memories contributed by many, many former
Bisbee High students of three decades.

Contents

(Webster dictionary: "gleanings. To collect or gather anything little by little. Gatherings")

ACKNOWLEDGEMENTS

So many people played a huge role in the writing of this book. I have already mentioned **Dale Hancock**, **Junie Hamrick Schaub**, and **Ed Swiec** who started these hundreds of emails rolling. Those three, plus a couple of others I forget, planted the idea in me to try to write a book. If I could remember who they were, I'd personally thank them.

My precious wife, **Nancy** was such an encouragement to me. She was the one who said "Go for it!" when I broached the subject of writing a book. Nancy was my "detail" person. She handled the many financial and technical aspects of working with the publishers.

My son, **Mike** did not like my original title. He suggested *The B Shines Brighter.*

My brother, **Bill**, suggested I put the word "Bisbee" in the title. Thus, *The Bisbee High School Legacy.*

My daughter-in-law, **Jean** was one of my proofreaders, technical advisor, and one who laughed heartily at all the right places. She spent many hours preparing the manuscript for publication.

My other proofreader, **Lynnette Wuthnow,** a former English teacher who shuddered at the language we used in Bisbee.

I couldn't have gotten this book finished without the aid of **Terry Robson,** Sterling Unified Public Schools Computer Coordinator. He made numerous trips to my house to "un-do" the frequent computer glitches I caused.

Kathy Phillips, my Bisbee connection. Kathy did much running around Bisbee getting information for me.

Sam Moore, volunteered to draw the cartoons for 63% of my royalties. I couldn't pass on a good deal like that.

Of course, in the back of my mind, thoughts that my children and grandchildren would someday read the book encouraged me. They are:

Susie and Dennis McDonald, Jason and Megan, Camp Verde, Arizona.

Mike and Jean Hicks, Michael and Taylor, Inman, Kansas.

Steve and Lori Hicks, Joanna, Luke, and Elizabeth, Camp Verde, Arizona.

Kristin and Scott Randolph, Harrison and Addisyn, Sterling, Kansas.

Anthony and Mieka Stecker, Annika and Adrie, Spirit Lake, Iowa.

I would be negligent not to mention the hundred or so Bisbeeites who so enthusiastically participated in the *email marathon* that is still going full blast as I write. I am sorry that I could not get every story and remembrance in the book. The biggest problem, besides the computer, was *what to leave out!*

Thank you all so very much.

iUniverse, the publishers, have been great to work with. They are strictly "upper Vista"!

I am so very thankful to my Lord and Savior, Jesus Christ, for blessing me with the health and energy to get this done.

Hadley Hicks
808 N. Sherwood
Sterling, Kansas
67579
hhicks@sterling.edu
620-278-3680

INTRODUCTION

"Organizing all of these stories into a book will be a wonderful
challenge and a best seller for lovers of finding the way back home."

Susan Ridgway, BHS, '67

You need to understand that this is a book about *memories*. It is not meant to be
a book about *facts*.

There are many contributors to this book and if one of the contributors
"remembers" an event a certain way, then that is the way the event will be
described. If two contributors describe the same event from different view points,
then both views will be reported and the reader can choose which one is the more
entertaining; or the more plausible.

It needs to be understood by readers who are not familiar with the copper
mining town of Bisbee, it is really three cities and numerous "suburbs" all rolled
into one unique town…. *Bisbee.* Bisbee proper is tucked in a canyon in the Mule
Mountains in Southern Arizona. From the northern city limit "up the canyon",
to the southern city limit "down the canyon", down Slag Dump Hill to be exact,
is approximately three-four miles before Bisbee merges into the city limits of
Lowell. Lowell widens out to encompass numerous "suburbs". Lowell spawns a
number of these "suburbs" scattered to the four compass points, until the third
city, Warren, is reached. Approximately three to five miles separate Lowell and
Warren. Six miles further south of Warren, on the Mexican border, are the two
Naco's; Naco, Arizona and Naco, Senora, Mexico. Naco, Arizona was the home
of The Warren Country Club, swimming pool, and the Bisbee Water Works.
Naco, Sonora, Mexico, "across the line", was the home of numerous curio shops,
bars, and whorehouses. It was not politically correct in those days to call them
"houses of prostitution", or, "houses of ill-repute"; they were simply, "whore
houses".

From the northern most city limit of Bisbee, to the southern most city limit of
Warren, we are looking at approximately ten miles, more or less. "More" if you
were skating, walking, or cruising with buddies. It was not uncommon to take

three-four hours to navigate the entire distance between the three cities. There were many turning off places...people to see...places to go; sometimes it took all night. When "Slag Dump Hill" became "Citation Avenue", the entire distance was often covered in minutes. Karl Kaleel, BHS '50, holds the "old" record of 5.7 minutes going home to Bisbee from Warren.

Depending on the people involved, the mode of transportation, and the degree of urgency to get home, that very common task of *getting home* was often an adventure.

As Susan Ridgway, BHS '67, so poetically said, this book is, **".... for lovers of finding the way back home."**

These memories will help you "find your way back home."

MAP OF BISBEE

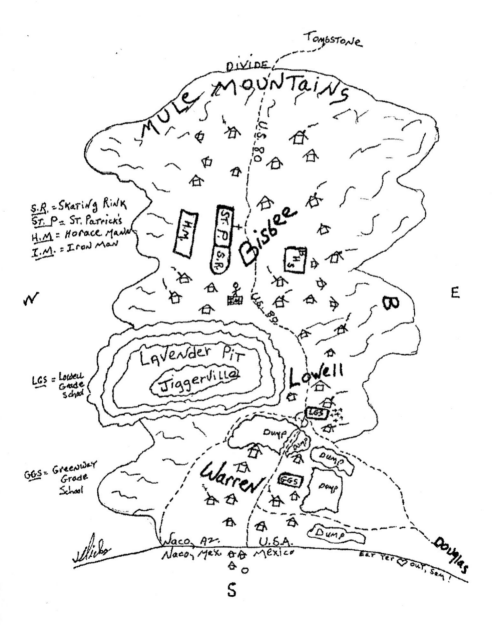

S.R. = Skating Rink
St. P. = St. Patrick's
H.M. = Horace Mann
I.M. = Iron Man

LGS = Lowell Grade School

GGS = Greenway Grade School

Tombstone

DIVIDE

MULE MOUNTAINS

Bisbee

Lavender Pit
Jiggerville

Lowell

Warren

Dump

Naco, Az.
Naco, Mex.   U.S.A.
Mexico

Douglas

Eat Yer ♡ out, Sam!

N   E

S

FOREWORD

EARL HINDMAN, 1942–2003

"Earl Hindman's journey began on Oct.20 1942, in the Copper Queen Hospital in the mining town of Bisbee, Arizona. We lived in a small settlement on the outskirts of Bisbee. The settlement was started to provide housing for the 'Jigger Bosses' of the Calumet and Arizona Company, the only serious rival to the Copper Queen Consolidated, and was named Jiggerville."

Thus began the story of the life and death of "The Man Behind the Fence" as told by Dean Shields, sister of Earl Hindman. Hindman gained fame as *Wilson*, the next door neighbor to Tim Taylor in the popular TV series, *Home Improvement*. Hindman was recognized all over America as, "The Man Behind the Fence". His death on October 29, 2003 triggered numerous questions from Bisbeeites all over the country. Some remembered him and some did not. Most were vague at best as to where the heck *Jiggerville* was!

That's the Hindman kid. He likes to look over fences.

It seems that Ed "Pappy" Swierc, Bisbee High School graduate 1953, got the ball rolling when he emailed a response to numerous inquiries to Dale Hancock, BHS graduate 1957, who then forwarded the letter to Junie Hamrick Schaub, BHS graduate 1965. One email led to another, which led to another, until at present there are over 100 Bisbeeites who have been in contact with one another, sharing memories of their days in Bisbee.

As Dale Hancock, '57 wrote:

"We have a little email circle going having Bisbeeites sharing memories and stories of Bisbee. It was a special place and time for all of us. Maybe you will connect with some friends or hear stories about people that you knew. We would like all to participate and share.... as you look at the email list at the top of the page and know of others who should be included, let us know and we will add them to the list. You can then forward messages to them and have them put us on their list...we would like to hear the stories...but most of all we would like to reflect on the friendships, good times, funny times, exciting times, different times, or whatever...so please join in. It has already started to roll...but, let's get a good list of Bisbee friend's email addresses so we can all read and share."

Dale continues, ".... send the Bisbee connections and email addresses you have that I do not, and let's get a memory email circle going. We can share good times of our special hometown that we can return to only in our memories. Bisbee has changed as has the rest of the world...but not those special times and friendships; they do not change...we can expand our old Bisbee network and have fun...."

Thanks; Dale, Junie, and Ed. for getting the ball rolling!

What all these e-mails have done is to bring many of us together again, in some cases after years of separation. Often, via these emails, we were introduced to each other as strangers whose only bond was being "from Bisbee." Through this modern miracle of email, we are now friends. We all share a special bond as Bisbeeites, a bond that is hard to explain, but a bond that is certain, a bond that is real, and a bond that is tangible. This bond and the resulting memories have led to this effort on my part to put it all into book form. Much of the book will be fictional. Much of the book will be factual. *All* of the book will be based on these memories.

I am writing this book from the memories of Bisbeeites covering the decades of the 1940's, 1950's and 1960's. When a contributor to the email memory list is mentioned, I will put his or her graduation date by that name. This will aid the reader in determine which decade the respondent attended Bisbee High. I believe that it was during these three decades that this Bisbee bonding was the strongest.

I believe that this Bisbee bond has lost some of its "holding power" for those who lived and grew up in Bisbee during and after the 1970's. I get the feeling that the "modern" Bisbeeites do not share this same bond, this love, this loyalty, if you will, for Bisbee and all that means. I hope that I am wrong. I pray that those who have called Bisbee their "hometown" since the 1970's have the same "feeling" for Bisbee that we "old-timers" have.

I was born in Bisbee in 1933, grew up there, and graduated from Bisbee High School in 1952. I have returned numerous times to Bisbee though I have resided in many other places. At various times I have, as a soldier, teacher, and coach, lived in Tucson, Arizona; Fort Ord, California; Tempe, Arizona; Pulaski, Virginia; Carmel, California; Prescott, Arizona; Flagstaff, Arizona; Sioux Falls, South Dakota; Phoenix Arizona; and presently, Sterling, Kansas. Each of these places holds special memories for me and to this day, I have many friends in most of these places. Even so, Bisbee has always been and always will be "my home-town".

Others who share my feelings for Bisbee are legion. This book will attempt to explain why.

There are people "from Bisbee" everywhere. I have run into folks "from Bisbee" on Ocean Avenue in Carmel, California; in the faculty room at Carmel High School; on the parade ground at Ft. Ord, California; on a trolley in San Francisco, California; in a frozen yogurt shop in Myrtle Beach, South Carolina; in a hotel lobby in Busch Gardens, Florida; at a post-card rack in the crowded Los Angeles Train Depot; on the sidelines at a football game at Ottawa University, Kansas; and of course, many, many times over the years, in Flagstaff, Prescott, Tucson, and Phoenix, Arizona. My wife has commented on occasion, "Nobody lives in Bisbee. They have all moved away." Jim McNulty, long time Bisbee lawyer and Arizona Congressman once stated, "If three people in Arizona get together for a conversation, one of them is from Bisbee."

In World War II when the U.S. Marines stormed the beach at Guam, two Bisbeeites came face to face while dodging Japanese bullets. On a darkened troop ship crossing the Atlantic during World War II, one Bisbeeite recognized the cough of another Bisbeeite. The Bisbee bonding is indeed special.

I cannot count the number of times the Arizona license plate on a car has led to talk about Bisbee. In my travels across this great country, I have seen Arizona license plates frequently. If I have the chance, I always ask, "What part of Arizona are you from?" In most cases, of course, they are not from Bisbee, but when I say, "I am from Bisbee", and then the next question from them is invariably, "Bisbee! Do you know so and so?" Most of the time I can say, "Yes." If I *can't* say, "Yes", then most of the time I *can* say, "No, but I know his/her mom or dad or uncle or cousin, etc." Most recently, on February 21, 2004, while I was drinking coffee at a local restaurant in Lyons, Kansas, I met a man from Phoenix, Arizona. In our conversation I had the opportunity to mention that I was "from Bisbee". He immediately got more animated and told me what a unique place Bisbee is and how much he enjoys his travels through Bisbee. His business takes him through Bisbee several times per year. When I mentioned the possibility about myself writing a book about Bisbee, he made certain I had his mailing address in Phoenix. He wanted to buy a copy. I had not written the book much less printed or published it, and I already had my first sale!

Being "from Bisbee" *is* special.

This book will center on my old friends and their memories; my acquaintances and their memories; my newfound Bisbee friends and their memories; and me and my memories. This is not meant to be an autobiography of Hadley Hicks, but rather a composite of memories that will serve to further cement the bond we Bisbeeites have with each other. There is so much variety, yet so much sameness. My prayer for my Bisbee friends is that this effort will cause you to say *those were good days. We were blessed to have grown up in Bisbee.*

1

1940's

MY MOST POIGNANT MEMORY

Patty was the cutest girl in the 4th grade class of 1944 at St. Patrick's Grade School. I can make that statement positively because I was the maturest girl-evaluator in school. I had been kept out of school a year between my 1st and 2nd grades, and was therefore older. It was pretty obvious to all my schoolmates that I had been around the block a time or two. I knew cute girls when I saw one and Patty was a cute girl!

I knew she thought I was pretty cool too, because of how she tried to ignore me when I would say something mean to her. The only reaction I would get from her was when I would pull her hair or punch her. She would yell, "Leave me alone!" an obvious sign that she was infatuated with me. I was particularly brutal in my conduct towards Patty when we would wait for the bus to take us home at the end of the school day. There was always a group of maybe ten to fifteen kids waiting for the bus, so, being the oldest 4th grader there, it was expected that I should take the lead in the tormenting of the girls and the younger boys. Patty took the brunt of my tormenting because she was the cutest girl in school.

The fun really came when we were on the bus, usually driven by Mr. Wells. Now, Mr. Wells was the grumpiest man in Bisbee…the original Grinch…. he seemed to hate every kid who ever rode his bus. He especially hated me above all the other kids because I was the most mature and coolest of them all. So, obviously I had to let Patty and the other kids see how frequently I could get Mr. Wells to yell at me. I especially had to let Patty see my influence over Mr. Wells, because Patty really liked me. I knew she liked me because she always tried to ignore me and had a way of sticking her cute little nose up in the air whenever I would say something mean to her.

One day, Friday, April 14, 1944, is indelibly etched in my memory. We were on the bus. The tormenting had gone on as usual. Mr. Wells had yelled at me several times as he made the delivery run down Slag Dump Hill letting kids off at their designated stops. And then he stopped to let Patty off, several stops before mine. The buses were the modern kind; they had a front door and a back door. Patty was standing at the back door waiting for it to open and just as she stepped down to get off, she turned and looked directly at me. Our eyes met…and she SMILED!

The pit of my stomach sent a very clear signal to my brain…*she really does like me!*

That moment and that smile are indelibly etched in my memory because that was the last time I ever saw Patty. The following Monday morning, April 17, 1944, Sister Anthony Louise came into our classroom and told us that Patty Bednar would not be coming back to St. Patrick's Grade School. Patty and her dad and mom were all killed in a horrible automobile accident over the weekend. That was my first taste of the reality of life. Most of my classmates cried. I did too.

However, the resiliency of youth is amazing. Life went on. After a week or so, Patty was all but forgotten. Only occasionally over the years did I think about that cute little girl who blessed me with one smile. I have not forgotten.

WARREN. 1930's–1940's

I was born in Bisbee in 1933 in a house just a block away from the Horace Mann Grade School on Roberts Street. Shortly after I was born, my dad, Dr. Hadley H. Hicks, a relatively new dentist in Bisbee, rented a home in Warren on Bisbee Road, the main drag through Warren.

My earliest remembrances of life in Warren were the times after my parents bought Duke Jay's house on East Vista, directly east of the flagpole. It was an ideal place for a young grade school boy to grow up. Out my front door was the Vista Park, the haven of all Warren kids. The Vista Park ran, a half-mile or more, the entire length of Warren. It was the place where youthful fantasies were played out; where Babe Ruth and Lou Gehrig came to life; where Mac McKay, a high school boy who lived a few doors down from me, was always more than willing to play "Flies and Grounders" with us; where Coach Fuzzy Warren and the BHS track team practiced; where we could watch the big kids try to climb the flag pole to sit on the plate half way up. You were not "a man" until you could climb to the plate and sit there for an hour absorbing the accolades of your buddies and a few adoring girls. In all honesty, I never made it even half way to the plate.

Our next door neighbors to the north of us were the McKay family: Mac, "Peachy" and dear, sweet Mrs. Helen McKay. I never saw her angry. She always had such a peace about her. Mrs. McKay did not even get angry with me when I stole a dozen of her homemade tamales. She followed a trail of cornhusks to my house and I was caught red-handed in the process of devouring those delicious tamales. She didn't get angry, but my dad did! I don't remember if there was a "Mr. McKay" living there at the time. If there was, he was gone a lot.

Next door to the McKays lived the Brashear family: Betty, Patsy, and my best buddy at that time, Jack.

The kids in these two families were all quite a bit older than I, Jack being about four years older. Each of them played a prominent and enjoyable role in my early years. "Peachy", five or six years older than I, taught me how to ride a bike and was the first one to my side when I had two devastating and bloody accidents.

HEY, HADDIE! HOW COME YOU ARE WALKING SO FUNNY? HA! HA!

The first of these accidents still brings shivers to me just thinking about it! Here are the gruesome details. Put your kids to bed. Don't read this part to them! Near the tennis courts on the Vista, a block or so away from my house, was a wooden light pole that was a challenge to me. I always wanted to try to climb it and one day when I was alone I tried. I was about 15 feet off the ground when I slipped. Unfortunately, I had just climbed *above* a long, rusty nail and when I slipped, that nail was an obstruction to a clean slide down the pole! That nail sliced into me, *you know where*. And if you don't know where, I will tell you *where* in just a moment.

"Peachy" was playing near by; when she heard me screaming and saw me walking home bow-legged, blood seeping through my jeans; she, too, started screaming for somebody to come help me.

To make a long story short, my mother rushed me to the Copper Queen Hospital where it took the doctors several hours, so I was told, to sew me up. That nail had caught me…. now hold on…. kids in bed??…the nail had caught me at the top of my anus and sliced all the way up through my scrotum, to the tip of my, *you know what!* Really! I have the scar to prove it. My mother was very relieved when Susie, my first child, was born as she was fearful that nail had rendered me sterile.

I had to walk bow-legged for many weeks, much to the delight of my cruel friends. Even Dr. Gans, a neighbor across the Vista, and the one who sewed me up, would greet me with, "Hey, Haddie…how come you are walking so funny?" Ha! Ha! Real funny. I furnished comic relief for the entire community for weeks.

I must mention at this point, that my first and longest lasting nickname was "Haddie"…hated it then and hate it now.

The second accident that "Peachy" was an eyewitness to was also pretty bloody. It wasn't as embarrassing, or as potentially ruinous. My mother drove around the corner of Congdon and onto the East Vista near where I was playing with the neighborhood gang. Being a show-off by birth, I ran after mother's car and grabbed hold of the back bumper. As she accelerated to go the remaining block and a half, unaware that I was running behind her, I slipped but foolishly held onto the bumper. The resulting slide home ripped my jeans off and tore my legs up pretty badly. "Peachy" again came on the scene with her customary screaming. By the time my mother heard her and was able to stop, we were in our driveway and I was stretched out full length, still holding on to the bumper; bleeding and still screaming. Another trip to the hospital was in order, but no stitches this time and no embarrassing after-effects.

THE VISTA PARK WHERE GREATNESS WAS ON DISPLAY

When I think of the Vista Park, I am reminded of a quote written by Lord Wellington almost two centuries ago: "The Battle for Waterloo was won on the playing fields of Eton".

Now, I have no clue who Lord Wellington was, or how Napoleon was whipped at Eaton, but I do know that the Vista Park served as "the playing fields" for many a Warren youth and his future achievements just a block down the street at the Warren Ballpark. Oh, what great athletic feats were on display at the Vista almost daily! If only the Vista Park could talk! It would tell about Doc Blanchard and Glenn Davis, the famous "Mr. Inside and Mr. Outside" of Army football fame, who ran rampant against all opposition. I was usually both "Blanchard" and "Davis" and at various times "we" completely annihilated Notre Dame, Navy, Southern Cal, and whoever. I don't remember "Blanchard" and "Davis" ever losing a game in the Vista Park. Since I lived just a few feet away from the "playing field", I could walk out my front door humming, "On Brave Old Army Team" and within minutes defeat any opponent.

Sometimes, however, Mac McKay was at the park; or, Jerry Smith; or, Johnny Gans; or, Robert Thompson; or, Ken Hunt; or, Ronnie Brooks; or, Bob Browder; or, Bruce Caldwell; or, Duke Milovich; or, Bobby and Judo Vucurevich; or, Tommy Byrd; or, John Wilcox; or, well, any kid who lived in Warren could play in whatever game was going on at the time. Whenever Mac McKay played with us, he was always "Captain" and therefore he told us who we would be. Usually I had to let someone else be "Mr. Inside" or "Mr. Outside". If I was one of the littlest kids there, I had to "be on" some obscure team like Holy Cross, Columbia, or Dartmouth.

When I was alone and could be both "Blanchard" and "Davis", "we" never lost. "We" were great!

A BRIEF STAY AT GREENWAY GRADE SCHOOL

I started first grade at Greenway Grade School in 1939. My father was in the process of building our home on Cole Avenue, just east of the mysterious and mostly deserted Loma Linda Lodge, east of "Sissie" and Judge Thomas', and south of, and caddy corner to, the Allen Apartments. While our home on Cole Avenue was being built, we rented a home on north Arizona Street, directly across the street from Charlene and Joanne Cobb and their family.

Geraldine Sullivan was my first grade teacher. I remember her very well. What a loving and caring lady she was. I remember her as always being impeccably dressed. She usually wore a scarf with a cameo pinned to it. She was "class". We loved her.

Our Principal was Mr. Anthony Nadolski. I guarantee you none of us ever messed with Mr. Nadolski. He was a firm disciplinarian and great guy. He later refereed many high school and college football games. Mr. Nadolski was just a genuinely nice man. He remained our friend for years, long after we left grade school.

I don't remember much about my first grade year, but I remember the following summer very well! It was to be a life changing summer that would take me away from Greenway Grade School for six years.

In the summer of 1940 my parents and I went on a camping trip to The White Mountains in Northeastern Arizona. I remember going to sleep in the tent and waking up from a horrible nightmare. I was getting very, very sick. My parents were so worried that they cut the trip short to get me to a doctor in Holbrook, Arizona. That doctor suggested I go to a hospital in Flagstaff. Immediately! The doctors in Flagstaff believed I had a bad case of pneumonia, and after a couple days of little improvement, they sent me home.

Our family physician, Dr. Rice, agreed that I did have pneumonia. However, when I did not get well all summer, he sent my parents and me to consult with several doctors in Tucson. None of them could diagnose the on-going problem; so out of desperation, Dr. Rice sent me to a children's specialist in Prescott, Arizona. His diagnosis was "TB". *Tuberculosis!* Though the doctors said that it was the non-contagious kind, it had a tremendous impact on my life for the next eight years!

The doctors told my parents that I should stay out of school all that year. What a horrible year the 1940–1941 school year was! I could not play with my buddies. I had to stay pretty much near home. Many of my buddies' parents would not let their kids near me because I had tuberculosis. One particular time was especially hurtful. I was walking with Tommy Byrd when his mother drove up and told Tommy to get in the car, and she said loud enough for me to hear, "You know we have told you not to play with *him.*"

Most of the days were spent inside listening to the radio. My constant companions were *The Lone Ranger; Sgt. Preston of the Mounties and His Faithful Dog, King; The Shadow; The Green Hornet;* and even the cast of, *As The World Turns.*

That entire school year I was pretty much one big, self-contained *pity party.*

INACTIVE AT ST. PAT'S

The doctors had told my parents I should be in a small school where I would be as inactive as possible. St. Patrick's Catholic Grade School was one, they felt, where I would not be as active as I would if I stayed in Greenway.

My mother had grown up on Brophy Street near St. Patrick's and had developed a close relationship with some of the nuns. Though neither mom or dad were Catholic, they agreed that St. Pat's would be the best school for me since its enrollment was quite a bit smaller than Greenway's.

So in Sept. of 1941 I began an adventure with some wonderful teachers and some boys and girls who would become life long friends. I was to be a student at St. Pat's from 1941 to 1946.... five "inactive" years!

ANYONE HERE PLAY DOMINOOOOS?

The nuns and priests did all they could to persuade my parents to let me convert to Catholicism. They were never successful in doing so, even though I became the only non-Catholic altar boy in Bisbee. I could ring that bell with the best of them, though I never did understand the Latin. To me, it always sounded like, "Anyone here play dominooooos?"

I took catechism classes, made many trips around "the Stations of the Cross", and at one time, I had them pretty well memorized. Once, on the urging of Bob Browder, I even got to the altar to take Communion. Bob knew the horrible "sin" it would be if I, a non-Catholic, took Communion. He had talked me into seeing if I couldn't sneak by Father Howard's scrutiny. "Just keep your head down and Father Howard won't know who you are." Bob had said. I got in line, kept my head down, knelt at the altar, and in no uncertain terms was sent back to my pew by Father Howard. He recognized me.

Bob was pretty disappointed. I am sure he wanted to see if God would strike me dead.

SEEDS OF FAITH

I am very grateful to those nuns and priests. They instilled in me a very real and sincere reverence and respect for God, which in later years, at age 41, led to my faith and commitment to Jesus Christ.

BOB BROWDER, SKATING PARTIES, AND OTHER HAZARDOUS THINGS

The doctors who prescribed inactivity for me should have examined the student body of St. Pat's. First of all, Bob Browder was one of the students. He was my buddy, and the most active of all the kids, to put it mildly.

Secondly, St. Pat's had two play grounds, the upper-play ground under the direct supervision of the nun on "play ground duty" and a huge all dirt and rocks play-ground which was down a series of steps and adjacent to the town skating rink. Evidently, the nuns and priests were never told that I was to be inactive.

I enjoyed all the activities; running laps around the lower play ground trying to keep up with Jimmy Hallstead; playing "Pom-Pom Pull-a-Way"; "Red Rover, Red Rover…"; kick ball; and our rendition of soccer, which was not soccer at all, but rather a form of, "grade school mayhem." Every student who ever played on that lower play ground left several layers of skin mixed in with the dirt and rocks.

Barbara Riggs was in my class and I can remember she was the only one that I couldn't out run. I learned very quickly that I couldn't mess with Barbara and get away with it. I think it only took two times teasing her and trying to run away from her, that I found out she could catch me and whip me!

Back to my buddy, Bob Browder. In my view, Bob was "Little Big Man" well before the movie. Bob was one of the smallest kids in school, though at the time, I never considered him as "little". His air and demeanor always exuded confidence and he walked with an, "I can whip your butt anytime…" kind of strut. I didn't want to mess with him either, though I could always out run him. Bob was in the 3rd grade when I enrolled at St. Pat's in the 2nd grade in 1941. He was one of the "big kids". He was a good Catholic. He gave up strawberries and watermelons every year for Lent. We had known each other for a few years since we lived close to each other in Warren.

Bob's dad owned The Warren Electric Store near the bus stop across from the Warren Drug Store. Bob lived in the hub of activity in Warren. He knew everything that was going on in Warren and was the catalyst of much of what was going on. Bob lost his dad sometime in the early '40s and was raised by his mother; a very sweet, tiny lady. Mrs. Browder converted the electric shop into "Browder's Variety Store". And, what a variety shop it was! She carried everything from the latest line of kids' clothing, all the latest kids' toys, to the best candy in town. Mrs. Browder was what one might call, a "soft touch". All a kid had to do was hint about how much he would like to have a sucker or a piece of candy, and it was his! Once Mrs. Browder gave me a boomerang I was admiring. It was one of the three-bladed, folding kind. The kind the nuns wouldn't let you play with on the upper playground. Bob insisted that since his mom had given it to me, that I bring it to school and see whom I could hit with it. He never threw it, but always made me throw it. I had that boomerang maybe two days before Sister Pious confiscated it for her "end of the year auction".

Often, I marveled at Mrs. Browder's generosity. Years later, I commented to my dad about how Mrs. Browder used to give stuff away free. My dad, in his inimitable manner, said, "Free, my eye!".... that was a favorite saying of his, "my eye!" "Free, my eye", he said, "...I would get a bill from her every month for all that candy she gave you!"

Mrs. Browder was still one of the sweetest ladies I ever knew, even though she was a shrewd business-lady.

Next to Bill Plumb, and I'll get to him in a later section, next to Bill Plumb, Bob got me into more trouble, mischief if you will, than any two kids put together. He got me in trouble with Duke Jay for putting a snake in his car. Then he got me in trouble with Andy Endicott because we ran into his barbershop to hide from Duke Jay. He got me in trouble with one of the Hargis twins (never did know which was which) because Bob was encouraging me to show my buddies how to scratch "HH +??" on the Hargis' new car's fender. Dad got a bill for that one, also. Bob even got us put in jail on VJ Day by I.V. Pruett, the Sheriff of Cochise County. All Bob and I had wanted to do was celebrate America's victory over Japan in World War II. We had heard the news on the radio. The war was over! We had defeated Japan! Cars were honking all up and down the street. People outside the Warren Drug were hugging each other. We had to show our patriotism some way. Bob got the idea to climb up on the roof of the service station across the street from the Warren Drug and bang on their tin sign with his baseball bat.

We were banging away celebrating jubilantly, when Sheriff I.V. Pruett, drove up and sternly demanded that we come down immediately. We did and he put us in the back of his patrol car just like common criminals and took us to jail in the courthouse "up town". All the way up, we got a severe lecture from Sheriff Pruett. He told us in no uncertain terms that we would have to spend some time in jail for our infraction. "Damaging property", he said. The whole time Bob had this "don't say a word" look on his face. The wheels were turning. I could just sense the makings of a trial lawyer in Bob. "If this ever goes to court", he was thinking, "...we can beat the rap. In the meantime, we will plead the 5th!" That was stuff all good trial lawyers are made of!

Sheriff Pruett kept us locked up for what seemed like hours, but was probably only ten or fifteen minutes. After another stern lecture when he unlocked the cell door, Sheriff Pruett then put us back in his car and took us home. I believe I detected a slight smile on his face when we got out of the car. I know I detected a very smug look on Bob's face. He seemed to be thinking, "We beat the rep! They had nothing on us!"

SKATING PARTIES...LIVING DANGEROUSLY

Bob was the one who introduced me to the very dangerous past time of roller-skating in Bisbee. Roller-skating in Warren was a piece of cake due to the level sidewalks. However, roller-skating in Bisbee demanded cool nerves, superb skill, a devil-may-care attitude and stupidity. Bob had all these attributes, and more. St. Pat's sponsored Friday night skating parties during the summers. One had to be very adept on skates to even get on the cement at St. Pat's. We're talking serious skating! Friday night skating parties at St. Pat's were not for the faint of heart. I did not even know how to skate. But, Bob was my buddy, and he taught me how. Bob started me off pretty slowly as I remember it. I was a slow learner. Bob first got me "up" in front of the Warren Drug Store. Since most of the kids in Warren hung out at The Warren Drug Store at one time or another during the summer days, I felt the very real pangs of peer pressure as we practiced. In fact, most kids in Warren learned to skate in front of the Warren Drug Store so there were probably several others practicing right along with me. None of them, however, had the taskmaster I did. Bob was a veteran skater. He had long ago mastered the art. He skated right along with me, and gave me the same instructions that Johnny Monahan, one of the big kids, had given him the summer before.

"Haddie, you can't learn to skate sitting on your butt! Get up!"

"How many times do I have to tell you to keep your toes pointing straight ahead!"

"If you fall one more time, I am going to tell Norman Wright to come sit on you!" Norman Wright was a high school kid who *had* sat on me one Halloween Night. He weighed 300 pounds!

After several of Bob's stimulating lessons, I was ready to solo. I made my first trip without Bob by my side by skating around the Warren Drug Store going west, past Duke Milovich's house, and back. Bob declared me ready for the "big adventure"! I was ready to go to a skating party at St. Pat's!

Now, you need to understand that, in the minds of my friends and I, Bob was the most "worldly" kid in Warren. He was a friend of Charlie Ryan, a freshman in high school. Bob thought it was pretty neat to be able to run around with Ryan. Sometimes Bob would even condescend to wave to me whenever Charlie Ryan gave him a ride in his car. That was a funny sight. Bob riding in Ryan's car! Picture "the man behind the fence" on TV. Bob was the "little kid looking over the dash board." Bob got to get in on all the "girl talk" and the "Naco talk" when Charlie was with his high school buddies. In my mind, and I am sure in Bob's mind, he pretty much knew all there was to know about *things. Things* that only "the big kids" understood and could talk about with any degree of credibility. Bob was good about sharing all that talk his other buddies and me. Bob was our resident "expert". He knew *things.*

Finally, Friday night came. I was about to confront my first real venture into the world of "the big kids". I got out of the house by telling my dad and mom I was going over to "Browder's to skate". Bob's reputation was still pretty spotless at this time and they let me go. My parents would often allow me to hang out by the Warren Drug at night. There was a street light by the Warren Drug which kept the area pretty lit at night; unless Bill Plumb had knocked the light out with a rock; which he did with regularity. My parents didn't worry about me going "over to Browder's" at night. Had they known all I knew about Bob, there is no way they would have let me run around with him at night. Bob knew *things.* Charlie Ryan had told him.

That night we hitched a ride to St. Pat's, skated for a couple of hours and then hitched a ride home. I was home in good time and my parents never questioned where I had been. So far, so good. Rather disappointing, really. Nothing too exciting happened.

The next Friday was a little different. Same scenario, only this time Bob showed me how a "big time operator" works. He skated several times *holding hands* with Joyce Andrews and he made me skate *holding hands* with Margie Per-nell It was kind of a strange feeling holding hands with a girl while skating. I had held a girl's hand a time or two playing "Pom-Pom-Pull-Away", but somehow it was different holding hands when skating. I kind of liked it.

When Bob tried to quiz me afterwards how I liked "Pernell", I replied with some vague comment like, "She is ok". It always was strange to me how Bob referred to girls by their last names only. I figured it was just a "big kid's'" thing. Maybe that was what Charlie Ryan did.

Every Friday night that summer Bob and I went skating and when the summer was over, I remember thinking that Bob kind of exaggerated *things*. He never did take a girl home after skating and Charlie Ryan never did pick him up at the skating rink to "take him somewhere".

The next summer I branched out. I went with Bob most Friday nights but often skated with Vincent Ogurek and his friends. I still found time to skate with Margie Pernell. We always held hands and several times when we stopped skating to rest on a bench, we just kind of forgot to let go.

I remember watching "Cuzzie" Trestrail skating with Bernice Uhles. Nobody could skate like "Cuzzie". He just kind of flowed along effortlessly. "Cuzzie" would somehow manage to skate with both arms around Bernice. "Hmmm, I wonder what would happen if I tried that with Margie?" However, the physical deformity I was born with took over. I had no guts! I never got up the nerve to try, and I knew if I ever did, that I'd fall and make a fool of myself, and probably forever damage my reputation with Margie.

We skated together a lot that summer, Margie and I, but I also spent a lot of time with Vincent, Bob and other boys, playing "crack-the-whip". If I fell playing "crack-the-whip" that was ok, because only the daring and brave would dare venture to play that game. Margie said she was too scared to play "crack the whip".

CRACK-THE-WHIP AND SKATING HOME; A KID COULD GET KILLED!

Bob was a hazard when he played "crack-the-whip" because he was fearless and would "crack" us better than any of the other kids could. It seemed as if every time Bob was "the cracker" he could time the "crack" just right and the guy on the end would always manage to fly into a group of girls. Sometimes, we'd argue to see who could be on the "tip" of "the whip". The girls cushioned our fall. That was always fun.

It was also that summer that Bob talked me into skating home! Now, that was real adventure! From the skating rink, down Main Street in Bisbee, through Lowell and home to Warren was at least ten miles. All of the way to Lowell was *down hill.* We did not have brakes on the skates. We did not have a way to slow down. We did not have elbow pads. We did not have kneepads. We did not have helmets. We did not have good sense. Looking back on that, it is amazing to me that no one was killed. Fortunately, there were not too many people walking the sidewalks of Bisbee at nights. When we came to the few intersections between St. Pat's and Lowell, we took it on childish faith that we could zip across without meeting an automobile. We never did. As I recall, there were only four intersections. The first one came on to Main Street from Subway Street, the narrow, and one lane road behind the businesses on Main Street. The second intersection was where Subway Street started between the bank and the hospital. The third was where Brewery Gulch joins Main Street in front of the hospital. The last one was where OK Street met Main Street. Other than that, it was a pretty clear shot all the way to Lowell.

Coming around the corner by Allen's Furniture Store and flying past The Elks' Club was usually when maximum speed was reached; about two hundred miles per hour. On Bob's orders we'd try to time it so that when we reached the steel man-hole cover just before Chase and Angus Grocery Store, we would jump and try to land in the middle of the steel cover. It would make a racket that we knew could be heard all over downtown Bisbee. If the timing was off, you jumped over the cover, thus revealing your poor skating ability. Bob didn't like that at all. He was usually the lead skater and if there were three behind him and he only heard two loud tumultuous rackets, he let it be known that whoever missed the steel cover was pretty much a novice. He might well be kicked off the gang of those who got to skate home with Bob. We tried hard to hit it. If we missed, Bob's chastening had to wait until we reached Lowell and level ground. This was no time to talk or lolly-gag. Our attention had to be focused on staying upright. We still had the long downhill stretch between Bisbee and Lowell. We would soon be approaching the sidewalk down "Slag Dump Hill"; the part of the journey that was only for the fearless. That section of the sidewalk was not in the best of repair. It was uneven, had chunks torn out of it, and was quite dangerous to walk on at night, much less skate on. As dangerous as it was, I don't remember any of us ever falling. We were afraid we'd be left behind and Bob wouldn't wait for anything.

Before we would start down from St. Pat's, Bob would gather us together for our "briefing". We were told to keep our eyes on him the whole way down, as he would signal orders to us by hand. Since he led the way, he would be the first to encounter any danger or unusual hindrances in the way. We had no problem watching Bob because we knew that if he fell and we saw him, we would have more time to avoid what caused him to fall. He never fell that I could remember.

Bob called the sidewalk between the Bisbee Police Station, just beyond the Lyric Theatre, to where Slag Dump Hill begins to level out, "The Quiet Section". This was the part of the trip that Bob did not want us talking. We had to skate quietly so those who lived in the houses which lined both sides of Slag Dump Hill would not be aware we were coming by. If the kids in these houses heard us coming, Bob told us, they would throw things at us as we zoomed by. Bob said that some of them would probably be waiting with water hoses primed. The tougher ones waiting for us would either pelt us with rocks or try to trip us and then beat us up. We must not let them hear us coming. This was not a trip for the faint of heart.

Bob's instructions to us were that he would hold up his hand, the universal signal for "Quiet", when he deemed the danger as imminent. We were to immediately cease talking, which we weren't doing anyway, and we were to watch for Bob's next signal.

As we coasted close to the first house, Bob's up-raised arm was brought down violently. This was the signal to "skate all out". To accelerate!

Bob's strategy always worked. We never once were pelted with rocks, nor hosed down as Bob predicted we might be. I guess Bob was just more experienced than we were. He knew *things*.

The rest of the skate home was usually pretty uneventful and easy. The only up-hill part of the journey was just after we passed Lowell Grade School. We usually just walked up that hill.

On the first trip home, I was worried about skating through Bakerville. Bakerville included *Goat Row* where the *Goat Row Gang* lived. They were mostly *bohunks* and were the meanest kids in Bisbee. They struck fear in the hearts of all of us from Warren! However, Bob assured us that all *bohunks* were in bed at that hour and would not bother us. They never did. Not like they did at Halloween.

MARGIE PERNELL, ONE OF THE "PERKS" OF THE SKATING PARTIES

One evening, on Bob's instigating, I got up the nerve to ask Margie Pernell if I could walk her home from the skating party. Bob gave me moral support. He came with me. Margie and I hit it off pretty well. I was not much of a conversationalist. Margie wasn't either. But, that was ok, because Bob did all the talking. I found out that Margie lived just a few houses up the canyon from The Wooten Apartments where my uncle, Don Fergus and his family lived. I started going with my mom every time she went to visit Uncle Don. Margie and I became good friends. Her mom was a very pretty lady and was always so very nice to me. She always had cookies and milk for us. Margie and I would sit on her porch and eat cookies and milk.

That *romance* did not blossom however, because Margie and her mom moved to New Mexico soon after her father died. I saw Margie only one time after she moved. I was on the football team at the UofA. We went to Las Cruces to play New Mexico State. Margie and her mom came to the game to see me. I was humiliated. I sat on the bench the whole game. I did not get in for even one play. I was totally embarrassed when Margie and her mom came up to say "hello" after the game. *Macho* pride. That was the last time I ever saw my favorite skating partner.

ST. PAT'S ATTACKED BY TERRORISTS

The playgrounds at St. Pat's were never devoid of excitement. And danger…especially in the winter after the first snow falls. It happened every time we had snow. And, we never were prepared. I remember so well, the first time we were attacked. We were playing very peacefully in our upper playground when all of a sudden huge snow balls rained down on us from the hillside to the south of us. Horace Mann Grade School was built on that hill and it looked down on us. It was a coordinated attack. Those Horace Mann bullies led by Don Newsome, Cecil Nelson, "Cuzzie" Trestrail, Chuck Cunningham and a hoard of others had hidden in the brush until we were totally engrossed in innocent play. We were at a decided disadvantage. In the first place, we were given explicate instructions by Father Howard that we were *never* to throw snow balls, not even in self defense. And secondly, have you ever tried to throw a snow ball *uphill?!* They cheated too. Most of their snowballs had been manufactured ahead of time. They were molded around rocks! They were made of solid ice. That was our first taste of WMD; "Weapons of mass dispersion." When they started bombarding us, we *dispersed* quickly!

I stayed at St. Pat's until my 6th grade year, 1945–46, when I went back to Greenway Grade School. I left behind many wonderful friends and many wonderful memories.

GREENWAY GRADE SCHOOL

My return to Greenway gave me my first taste of competitive sports. Jack Miller was our 6th grade teacher and Al Ridgway was our PE teacher. Both these men were coaches and encouraged us to be very competitive in schoolyard play. Every recess was more than just play; it was dog eat dog competition.

We had different teams each day, and we played spirited games of football, softball and basketball. Often the games were 6th grade vs. 7th grade and the winner played the 8th grade. The 8th grade was always loaded. Not only were they older, but they had Alejandro Morales and he was quite a bit older. He had repeated 8th grade numerous times. "Hondro" could kick the ball out of the park, he could run over us, he could pass the ball unerringly, and he did all that with a huge smile on his face. "Hondro" played each game with a degree of joy and enthusiasm that was fun to watch. It was especially fun when he was on our side when we got in the 8th grade.

It was in the 8th grade, when Al formed us into teams, which competed against all the other grade schools in Saturday morning games.

THE *JETS* WERE BORN

One day when Al was assigning us positions, George Bays suggested to Al that we be called The Greenway *Jets*. This was in 1947 when jet engines were just becoming popular on airplanes. George, being one of the more intellectual students, had read about jet engines and thought it would be a suitable name for us. The name stuck. We even painted *JETS* on our uniform t-shirts. Since we each painted our own t-shirts, they were not exactly uniform in script, but we looked very professional. If I remember correctly, we were the only team that had *uniforms*.

Ladies and gentlemen, here is your Greenway *JETS'* starting line up:

At the end positions, Bob McDonald, 6 foot tall, weighing 120 lbs. and George Bays, 5'0 and weighing 91 lbs.

At the tackle positions, Ronnie Brooks, 4 feet 1/2 inches and 67 lbs., and Bruce Caldwell, 4 foot 3 inches tall and weighing 50lbs.

At center, Roy Hudgins, 3 feet 3 inches tall and tipping the scales at 51 lbs.

At guards, Judo Vucurevich, 4 feet tall and weighing 88 lbs. and Donnie Sanders, 3 feet 2 inches, and weight would not register on the scales.

In the backfield, at quarterback, Hadley Hicks, 5 feet 6 inches tall and weighing 130lbs.

At left half is speedy Jim Baker, 5 feet 1 inch and weighing 100 lbs.

At right half is "Lefty" Jim Weld, 4 ft. 5 inches tall, weighing 95lbs.

At full back is chunky Jinx Richards at 4 ft. 4 inches tall and weighing 135 lbs.

Expected to see a lot of action in tonight's game is "Happy" Wolfe who will substitute at all positions. "Happy" is 5 feet tall and weighs a solid 101 lbs.

If he can make it in time, veteran Alejandro Morales, 6 feet and 190 lbs., will add much needed punch to the running game. And if the *Jets* have to punt, Morales will handle those duties as well. However, his wife may have things for him to do around the house.

The *Jets'* peppy and vivacious cheer leading squad is comprised of Kay Reppe, Carol Gentry, Sophie Blagovich, Blanche Baker, Bee Benko, Helen Bergmann, Beverly Buford, Connie Moya, Joanne Cobb, Betty Little, and any other girl who is available. These girls will add much spirit to the game and on Monday will offer an in-depth critique, position by position.

As I have mentioned, we played every Saturday morning against one of the other grade schools. We had our toughest competition from Lowell Grade School; mainly, because they had Ramon Garcia, Lowell's answer to Alejandro Morales. Ramon weighed at least 300 lbs. and could run. He usually drove his car to the games. Others on the Lowell team were Jay Peeler, Harvey Leonard, Bobby "Harpo" Windsor, Javier Jaramillo, Ronnie Moore, Hector Torres, John Henry LaRoe, Howard Holloway, and 5' 3", 100 lb., Bobby "Hooty" Howell. "Hooty" was a threat to contend with because his right arm was always in a cast and he used it as a lethal weapon. We never worried about him catching a pass, but we did have to worry about being clubbed into submission.

Horace Mann was pretty talented, as well. Their "stars" were Fritz Kuehnlenz, Paul Amaro, Ronnie Haynes, Bobby Lopez, Willis Webster, Harold Wright, and John Dabovich.

St. Pat's seldom offered much competition as their only threats were Bill Monahan, a tough Irishman who could inflict pain to all who got in his way, and the only other "regular" on St. Pat's team, J.B. Taylor, a shifty, crafty running back. When we played them, we could always count on them sneaking in a bunch of "ringers", usually cast-offs from Horace Mann.

I have to mention that I was still not *supposed* to be playing competitive sports. The doctors had still not cleared me to play. However, Coach Ridgway just kind of looked the other way when we took the field.

Once, we played against Lowell at half time of one of BHS *Pumas* game. The games were always broadcast locally by KSUN, and my parents, who were not regulars at attending the high school games, would often listen to the games on the radio. I was fearful that they would hear my name on the half time broadcast so being the clever kid I was, I took a tube out of the radio, just in case they would try to listen. I did not get away with it, however, as Johnny Caldwell who manned the PA for the *Puma* games, saw my dad at the next week's Kiwanis meeting. He made some comment to my dad about "Hadley's good game". The jig was up. Dad was pretty upset. No matter how hard I tried to rationalize that the game only lasted 30 minutes, he had a talk with Al Ridgway. Al promised him that he would never allow me to play at half time again. I never did. Al knew that that game was the last one a grade school team would play at half time that season. But, we still played football every Saturday morning in the fall, and somehow my parents never heard about those games.

We played our Saturday games at the Warren Ballpark, and they were always played "two below". No real contact took place. But, the unwritten rule was that the same two teams that played Saturday would meet on Sunday afternoon at the Warren Park for a real game of *tackle!* Those games were violent! The *Jets* had a decided advantage in those games because we lived in Warren and we always had old discarded Puma football equipment to wear. Coach Dicus and Coach Ridgway always made the old stuff available to kids. Most of us had a well-worn leather helmet and some of us even had old shoulder pads. Jim Baker kept my equipment at his house so my parents never saw it lying around our house. I never worried about them finding out about me playing in those games.

Basketball season was another story. Those games were written up in the Bisbee Daily Review, complete with box scores. To get around the possibility that my parents would read my name in the paper, I was always listed as "Donnie Sanders" in the box scores. Donnie was the littlest kid in our class. Once, Mrs. Hennessey, our teacher, commented to Donnie how proud she was to read his name in the paper; so small and yet still playing with "the big boys". Donnie kept our secret and just modestly smiled and mumbled something in response to Mrs. Hennessey's compliment. My parents never did find out about those Saturday morning basketball games.

The summer of 1948 was when I got some great news. At my annual check up in Tucson, the doctor told my parents that tests had verified that I **did not have tuberculosis!!** I did have, what was called, "Valley Fever" a disease which had many of the same symptoms as tuberculosis. HALLELUJAH!! No more being a liar, a sneak, and a deceiver! I could now play sports with impunity.

THE WARREN BALL PARK, HOME OF THE BHS *PUMAS*

My tangible childhood hero's, the Bisbee High School *Pumas,* practiced and played their games in the Warren Ballpark, just a block down the street from "Army Stadium" and "the playing fields" of the Vista Park.

The Warren Ballpark had been "home" for the *Pumas* since the early 1930's. My grandfather, Robert Fergus, or "Big Bobby" as I called him, remembers seeing a game at the Warren Park in the early 1930's between the BHS *Pumas* and The Ft. Grant Boys' Reform School. It seems that during the game one of the Ft. Grant players took a *Puma* kick-off and ran 90 some odd yards for a TD and as he crossed the goal line, he dropped the ball and kept going! The huge gate had been left open. The kid took the opportunity to try an escape. An ever-vigilant sheriff's deputy captured him at the other end of the Vista Park, about a mile away.

In my earliest memories of the Warren Park, it had a tall green fence all the way around the park. The fence was separated in the dead center of the park, immediately behind home plate, by a large adobe grandstand. Both the home team and the visitors had locker rooms underneath the grandstand and both locker rooms had an exit to the field; the visitors to the west of home plate and the home team to the south. On the west corner of the park, way down the right field line, was a large gate to let buses and trucks in. Near by was one of the three ticket windows and this window was only open during the football season. All spectators for football games came in through this large gate. Upon entering the field, the fans went either to the east where the visitors' bleachers were or to the west where the Bisbee bleachers were. All fans came through this gate, both the visiting fans and the Bisbee fans. Not a good idea.

BISBEE vs. DOUGLAS. MORE THAN A GAME

Every other Thanksgiving Day the entire population of Cochise County would flock to the Warren Park for the annual home and home "Turkey Day" battle between the BHS *Pumas* and the hated Douglas *Bulldogs*. The game was played for possession of the coveted "COPPER PICK", which went to the winner of the game.

Big Bobby was a ticket taker and self-appointed bouncer for most of these games. Once, as he remembered it, as the huge crowd of both Bisbee and Douglas fans were crowding in to the park through the common gate, a near riot broke out. Of course the fight was started by some of the reprehensible *Bulldog* fans. They always started the fights. The fight started, as Big Bobby remembers, when some words were exchanged and had to be broken up by the ever-present sheriff's deputies. Big Bobby verified that the Bisbee fans won the fight.

It was the following year that city officials decided that from then on visitors were to enter and exit through the gate behind the visitors' grandstand-dugout on the East End of the park. Wise move.

Ken Hunt, BHS, '51, recalls another near riot which he was a witness to: "Among the many memories of my youth in Bisbee, one that still stands out is of the events during and after a football game in the Warren Park on a sunny autumn afternoon in the late '40's. The game was between the Bisbee High *Pumas* and their archrivals, the Douglas High *Bulldogs*. Emotions, as always, were running high among the citizens of both communities. In the closing seconds of the game, Bisbee had a narrow lead, but Douglas had possession near mid-field, and there was just time for one more play. The Douglas quarterback completed a long pass in the end zone. Douglas seemed to have won the game. But wait, one of the referees had called a penalty against Douglas, and their apparent touchdown was nullified. Douglas ran another play, but this time the Bisbee defense held. The game was over and Bisbee had won. The Douglas partisans thought they had been robbed.

During the game, my neighbor, Jack Gilbert, recognized one of the referees as an old buddy he hadn't seen since college, and Jack decided to renew their acquaintance. Immediately after the game was over, Jack jumped the low fence in front of the Bisbee bleachers and ran out on to the field. He caught up with the referee friend right in front of the Douglas section of the bleachers. The referee recognized Jack and an animated conversation between the two began. Most of the Douglas fans were still in the bleachers and observed this exchange between Jack and the referee. To some of them it confirmed their suspicion that the referees had sided with Bisbee, and they proceeded on to the field in a fighting mood. The Bisbee partisans from the opposite side of the field responded in kind and a general melee ensued. Scattered fistfights broke out and continued for a good many minutes until the sheriff's deputies were able to restore order. The deputies surrounded and protected Jack and the referees from injury, but some of the other participants suffered black eyes, split lips, and other assorted contusions and abrasions. I don't believe any of the injuries were serious. There were, no doubt, several misdemeanor arrests, but no serious charges. Most of the combatants were grown men. Kids my age (probably about 12 years old) were not actively involved. I was, however, an intensely interested bystander."

Obviously, feelings ran deep for both Bisbee and Douglas fans. We grew up with an inbred animosity for Douglas folks. A favorite saying of Coach Waldo Dicus was that "…they are just dogs of a different breed."

The major discussion each Thanksgiving was, of course, who would win *The Game*, but running a close second was, "I wonder how many fights there will be?" Ralph Echave, BHS '48, recalls "I assure you that all Bisbee/Douglas games had fights involving fans. I watched the games from the bleachers before I started BHS. During half time, boys from both schools would gather behind and under the "home" bleachers and slug it out. When the second half started, the fights were turned off, just like on radio, and everyone went back to watching the game."

Ralph played for BHS from 1944 to 1948, then went to the University of Arizona and then the military. Upon return to Bisbee, he was not aware of any fights, but he concludes, "…from 1933 to 1943 there were fights. So long as they stayed under the bleachers, the police did nothing. Once they meandered on the field they were pushed back to under the bleachers by the deputies to finish their fights."

Once in my senior year when we played Douglas at home, I remember during a time out, of seeing a fight in our stands. I never did find out if it was between a Bisbee fan and a Douglas fan, or if it was just a couple Bisbee fans letting off steam.

As a grade school kid, I spent much of my time during these games behind the bleachers where we played our own brand of football. We missed most of the fights that broke out fairly regularly in the stands when one or more of the *Bulldog* fans would come over to our side of the field and instigate trouble.

THE HALF TIME SHOW AND THE DRUM

Our behind-the-bleacher games came to a halt at half time. We would never miss the half time performances of the BHS marching band under the direction of Mr. Arthur Reppe. Those half time performances were always most entertaining. Mr. Reppe had constructed a huge wooden drum that was on wheels and could hold a couple of students inside. It was always fun to see what kind of skit the band had in store for the fans and who or what would come out of the drum. Usually, it involved students dressed up like a "Puma" and a "Bulldog" or the mascot of whoever the opponent was. Here is how Ed "Pappy" Swierc, BHS '57, describes his adventure as participant in a half time show "…. some bright soul in the band decided that it would be funny and clever to have a skit during half time with a little Puma chasing around a great big ol' cowardly person representing our opponents that night.

To do the skit, Dick Dicus (Dick was the littlest kid in school. hh) and I were dressed up in our respective costumes, and then secretly put into the huge fake drum (about 6 feet tall) on big wagon wheels that the high school had lying around somewhere. At half time Dick and I, hidden in the drum, were wheeled out to the middle of the football field, and the stadium lights were momentarily put out. That was the signal for us to pop out of the drum with Dick chasing me. I was dressed as the opponent's mascot, and Little Dickie was dressed as a Little Puma. We were to run around with the chase for a little bit, ending with the little ol' Puma tackling and defeating that big cowardly opponent.

Ok, despite not having rehearsed all this too much, everything went as planned right up to the chase. As I ran from him, I decided to really ham it up and run with my shoulders thrown back, head facing up, and my knee coming up real high and short at every step…like a Keystone Kop scene…apparently running like crazy, but not moving too fast. I guess I made a bad estimation of my speed, 'cause suddenly through the crowd noise, I could hear Dickie way behind me hollering, 'Pappy!! Slow down, I can't catch up with you!!' Oops. I almost had to come to a stop, running in place to let him catch me for the big Puma victory take down. We both had a big laugh about it. It was a night for both to remember. But…to this day I wonder if I could always run faster than I thought, or were Dickie's legs so short I could beat him running on my knees?"

AN HONEST MISTAKE HAD SERIOUS CONSEQUENCES

Mr. Johnny Caldwell, the popular Lowell druggist, was the BHS public address announcer for all home games. Once, at half time of a heated Bisbee-Douglas battle, Johnny made a slip of the tongue that proved to have serious consequences.

As Mr. Arthur Reppe and the Bisbee High marching band were proudly lined up under the south goal posts, Caldwell announced over the loud speaker, "Ladies and gentlemen, presenting the *Douglas High School Marching Band.*" You could have heard a pin drop. Caldwell tried to regain his composure and uttered something like, *"I mean, the Bisbee High School Marching Band."*

However, the insult had been registered. Mr. Reppe angrily walked to the middle of the field, turned, faced the press box, thrust his right arm towards Mr. Caldwell, and displayed, for all to see, the universal sign of disapproval.

Needless to say, that had the town buzzing for several weeks. The good news, though, is that Mr. Caldwell and Mr. Reppe remained good friends.

PRO BASEBALL AT THE WARREN BALL PARK

According to David Skinner, a reporter for the Bisbee Observer, the Warren Ballpark may be the oldest baseball park in the country. Skinner reports that recent research indicates that the first pitch was thrown at the Warren Ballpark on Sunday, June 27, 1909. Up until this recent research was revealed, a Ballpark in Birmingham, Ala., which was first used in 1910, was considered the oldest.

The Warren Ball Park at various times during the 1930's to the early 1950's housed a number of professional baseball teams, the earliest being The Bisbee Bee's an independent professional team, which was in the Class C Arizona-Mexico league.

Mr. Skinner wrote an excellent two-part article on the history of the Warren Park's association with professional baseball. Ron Sanders, BHS '55 sent me the articles and I found them most interesting. Here are just a few excerpts from Mr. Skinner's research:

"Bisbee began its long association with organized ball in 1928 with the creation of the Arizona State League. From then until 1955, whenever there was a league to play in, be it the State League, the Arizona-Texas League, the Southwest International League, Warren Ball Park hosted a minor league team, sharing the franchise with Douglas the last nine years."

Mr. Skinner continues "The teams were variously known as the Bees, the Cherubs, (the *what? hh*), the Javelinas, (I'll tell you how that name came about in a minute, hh) the Yankees, the Copper Kings. The Bisbee-Douglas squads played half of their home games at Copper King Stadium in Douglas."

Ok, back to the *Javelinas.* That year, must have been 1948 or so when I was in 8th grade, they had a contest to name the professional team for that summer. I entered the contest using the name my granddad, had suggested, "Javelinas". And I WON! The banner headline on the sport page of The Bisbee Daily Review read, "*14 YEAR OLD HADLEY HICKS WINS BASEBALL NAME CONTEST.*" Just beneath the headline was a large picture of Mel Steiner, the general manager of the team, and me. Mel Steiner in later years was a major league umpire, and I was a major league "wanna be".

The article really played up the appropriateness of the name, *Javelinas*. It told how J.C. Agajanian of San Pedro, California, the owner of the team, was very pleased with the name. The article went into great detail to explain the derivative and meaning of the word. It explained that, "javelina, or peccary, is a New World representative of the *pig* family." It told how the "...javelina is most courageous and pugnacious, and they are found throughout Cochise County....for the person unfamiliar with Spanish derivatives, the *j* in javelina is pronounced *h*....". And on and on. It was a long article. It must have been written on a "slow news" day!

The selection committee was praised for their hard work in selecting the name out of over 150 names submitted. The committee was comprised of both of the mayors of Bisbee and Douglas, H.T. Price of Bisbee, Everett Jones of Douglas. Ed Plumb, president of The Bisbee Chamber of Commerce was on the committee, as were a number of other citizens of both communities.

My award for this brilliant name was two free passes to all home games. BIG DEAL! I snuck into all the games, anyway. I can't remember for sure, but I believe I gave the passes to my uncles to use.

For several weeks after the article appeared, everyone I ran into congratulated me. I was the local hero. But, here is the "kicker". The team was *horrible!!* I wish I could find out what their record was that summer. I know they finished last in the league. And, guess who took the brunt of all the jokes and derisive comments about the team. Yep, you guessed it...THE GUY WHO NAMED THEM THE *JAVELINAS*......remember that javelinas are a member of the *pig* family! It didn't take much originality to come up with such comments as, "Hay, Haddie, how did The *Pigs* do last night?", or, "Hay, Haddie, you sure named them right...The *Pigs*...ha! ha!", etc., etc.

The Bisbee Daily Review even started referring to them as "*The Pigs*". They were *bad*. It was a miserable summer for me. I went to, maybe, four games all total.

Mr. Skinner continues in his article by mentioning some familiar names of ball players to Bisbee baseball fans "Over the years, many Bisbee players took advantage of the spacious outfield at the Warren Ballpark, with its outrageous 444-foot gap in left-center field, to win league titles and set single season records in various statistical categories. Bisbee native, Clarence Maddern, a future big leaguer, had the most runs-batted-in for 1941, and several home run leaders padded their totals with inside-the-park shots. The 1930 and 1931 batting champs, Tony Arntista and Johnny Keane, hit .430 and .408 respectively, not only the highest averages in Arizona State/Arizona-Texas League history, but the highest in all of the minor leagues for those years. Keane managed the St. Louis Cardinals and the New York Yankees, winning a World Series with the Cards in 1964 and then being hired away by the losing Yanks."

Mr. Skinner really jiggled my memory bank when he wrote "In 1947, Warren Ball Park saw more than baseball action on the field when two Yankee farmhands started what became a classic feud. The rivalry began when Billy Martin, later famous as a Yankee player and manager, sought revenge against catcher Clint Courtney of the Bisbee-Douglas Yankees. Martin, playing for the independent Phoenix Senators, was trying to even the score after Courtney had spiked the Phoenix manager (Arkie Biggs, maybe? hh). Fist fights, more spikings and just plain brawling continued throughout the season in Bisbee and Phoenix. Altercations between the two lasted into the 1950's when both men played for separate major league teams."

What a great summer that was! I remember it well.

Billy Martin was arguably the most popular/hated player in the league. The guy was a reincarnation of Ty Cobb. He didn't know the meaning of "take it easy", "slow down". Everything he did on the field was "all out", "full bore ahead". He was "Mr. Hustle" long before Pete Rose came along.

Clint Courtney was made out of the same mold. He was your classic catcher; short, stocky, thick thighs and calves, and a "hose" for an arm. He hit for power and could run as well as any of them. And he knew how a catcher should block the plate. Any runner sliding into home plate saw only shoulders, elbows, knees, the left hand and glove and the right hand, with or without the ball, coming at the runner full force. He was tough! His nickname when he reached the major leagues was most appropriate, *Scrap Iron.*

As Mr. Skinner wrote, the two of them had an on-going battle all season. The Warren Ballpark was packed when Bisbee played Phoenix. Bisbee fans always loved a good fight!

Of course, Courtney was the darling of the Bisbee fans and Martin was the object of all their curses, taunts and razzing. Martin was not helped at all by his most distinguishing physical feature; his *long, prominent nose!* He was referred to by Bisbee fans as *The Bugle.* I can still hear my uncle, Don Fergus, who was a die-hard baseball fan, yelling, "Hay, Martin, why don't you blow your *bugle?!"...or...* "Hay, Martin, you'd see the ball if you could get that *bugle* out of the way!"

They were fun to watch. But, I am not so sure that all the battles were between enemies. Between competitors for sure, but, I don't believe they had any animosity toward each other off the field. Here is why I say that. One of my big thrills:

Most of the kids in Warren who went to the ball games would kind of hang out at The Toot'n Tellem after the games and wait for the players to show up for an after game snack. We loved to hang around their booths and listen to them as they re-hashed that night's ball game. Most of the players were very friendly to us.

One night while waiting for the players to show up at The Toot'n Tellem, Jim Baker, Jinx Richards and I, and others, I am sure, got a startling surprise. Our hero, Clint Courtney came in with...*gasp!*...Billy, *The Bugle*, Martin! We couldn't believe it! The two bitter combatants were actually going to sit in the same booth and eat together! Needless to say, we hung around in anxious anticipation. It was pretty disappointing at first. No fights. No arguing. I am not sure what we expected, but what we got were two very friendly guys. They were both gregarious and pleasant, just your everyday eighteen or nineteen year old kids having fun playing pro baseball and soaking up the adulation's of younger kids.

After they ate and drank a couple of pops, one of them asked Charlene Cunningham, the waitress, if he could have a dish of ice cream. Charlene informed him that they were all out of ice cream. They then asked us where they could get some ice cream at that time of night. We had heard that Douglas had a store that stayed open all night and we mentioned that to our two heroes.

Courtney said, "We'll take you to Douglas and buy you some ice cream, if you show us where to get it." Of course we said, "No thank you, our parents told us to come right home after the game. Sorry, Mr. Courtney and Mr. Martin, as much as we'd like to, we just can't disobey our parents." WRONG! We jumped at the chance! We said we would be most glad to have the honor of showing "you two gentlemen" where to get some ice cream. You talk about three excited kids!

Courtney had a car parked near by and the three of us, Baker, Jinx and me, piled in the rumble seat. What a thrill! All the way to Douglas, we excitedly talked about getting to school on Monday. "Just wait until we tell Lefty, and Bays, and Kay Jean, and Bee, and Bev, and Bruce, and on and on...about going to Douglas with Courtney and Billy Martin!" Man, would we be big shots! Would we be envied! Would we be *important!*

Ok, here is what happened. We got to Douglas and went to the store on G Avenue. Courtney parked the car, gave us some money, told us to, "...go in and buy as much ice cream as you can and don't forget to get spoons." We floated into the store, probably just dying to tell the guy who waited on us that we were buddies of Courtney and Martin and they wanted some ice cream. As I remember, we got a large tub of ice cream and five wooden spoons. We paid, left the store and, guess what....? Those bums had driven off and left us! We couldn't believe it. We waited around for several minutes believing that sooner or later they would come back for us. Maybe they had just gone to get gas. Then one of us suggested that maybe they had gone to Agua Prieta, "across the line", to.... well...to do what they do "across the line". At that point we realized that if we wanted to get home before daybreak we had better start thumbing! They weren't going to be coming back for us any time soon. Our heroes had feet of clay. They were bums. They were liars. They were deceivers. They were cruel. We hated them. What hurt most of all was that we could no longer brag to the entire school that we were buddies with Courtney and Martin. We took a vow that we would never tell anyone what happened.

We started thumbing. We did have a lot of ice cream to eat, though. All that ices cream and no way home. I did tell my mother what had happened because she had called the sheriff's office about midnight when I hadn't come home. I am not so sure she believed me.

A number of years later, I went to a spring training game in Tucson. I recognized a familiar short, squatty catcher down in the bullpen. It was none other than Clint Courtney. I went down and got up to the fence, almost on top of him. When he wasn't busy warming up a pitcher, I said, "Hay, Courtney, do you remember that time in Bisbee when you and Martin took three kids to Douglas and left them?" He kind of got a blank look on his face for a few moments; then he broke into a smile and said, "Were you one of those kids?" We had a good laugh about it. But you know what? He never did say he was sorry. Nor, did he tell me where they went that night! I can only guess.

PRO-BASEBALL, A COMMUNITY ENDEAVOR

Baseball, professional or amateur, has always been in the lifeblood of Bisbee. Be it "pick up" games in Jiggerville, which "Pappy" Swierc will describe later, or, in the Vista Park, or, wherever, baseball ruled the day for much of the year in Bisbee.

It all began in the summer of 1909. A very enjoyable little book titled, *Warren Ballpark and its first game,* by Margaret and Gary Dillard, which was sent to me by Ron Sanders, BHS, '55, goes into full detail about the beginnings of baseball in the community. There was much political wrangling, it seems, over who would get how much of the profits of the games. According to the Dillards "There is little doubt that the Warren Co., a subsidiary of the C&A, had an interest in the community's progress and happiness, and that certainly was important in the decision to make the new town site of Warren as accommodating to residents as possible. That's one reason the company would have invested $3,600 (that's 1909 dollars) in building a new park."

The Dillards go on to write about another reason the Warren Ball Park was built "......The trolley system was built to convey miners from their abodes to the mines; with a trolley miners could live further from where they worked. That made the development of Warren—where there was little mining—possible.

"If you have such a trolley, however why not create other reasons for its use as well? Quality shopping in Warren, for example, could bring people from around the district to the area; every shopping trip meant a fare for the Warren-Bisbee Railway. Another way to build ridership was **a baseball park.**"(emphasis mine, hh)

So, the Warren Park was constructed to bring money via riders on the trolley to the coffers of The Warren Co. Any time money is the bottom line, wrangling is bound to follow.

Again quoting the Dillards "A couple of months before the planned Fourth of July opening of the new ball park, there was some concern that the park wouldn't be finished, despite assurances from Louis Powell, president of the Warren Co., that it would be......

There was also some confusion about a team....it was likely there would be a park, but there was uncertainty about whether there would be a team."

Where would the players come from? Obviously, to put together a first class team that would draw fans on a consistent basis (paying fans!), there had to be a quality team. The article tells about the conflicts between the streetcar company, the Warren Co. and other invested persons. Where would the players come from? How would they be paid? Where would they live? Who would manage the team? And, the *biggie,* **how would the profits be divided?**

It seems that, as the Dillards said, "...it is impossible to get together a winning team without the cooperation of the big companies, which have heretofore declined to put any of the ball players to work."

To make a complicated issue simple, "When the first game was played...the Warren Co. took 30% of the receipts,...the 'understanding'...though nothing was in writing…was that the park owner was going to take half the profits, after expenses, at the end of the year.

If this issue wasn't settled, it may put the kibosh on baseball for this district just as the season is beginning."

However, "Despite wrangling and uncertainty, the game did go on."

The headline in the *Miner* on June, 25, 1909 read, "El Paso Games Open Baseball Season". The rest, as they say, is **history**! And what a history it has been!

For a quick and enjoyable read, I recommend this interesting book by the Dillards.

The Bisbee team, The *Warriors*, won that series of games with The El Paso *Browns* but lost the next series to the Douglas team. And, yes, fans, there was a **fight** between players and spectators which had to be broken up by local officials. Thus, the precedent was set; it has been an unwritten rule ever since that Bisbee vs. Douglas has to have its mandatory fight.

Pro baseball at the Warren Park flourished over the years, and my earliest memories were of The Bisbee *Bees*. Junie Hamrick Schaub, BHS '65 recalls some of the names of the 1938 Bees which were in an autograph book belonging to Junie's mom, Shirley McGuire Hamrick, BHS '47. I remember some of the names:

Charles Maglia, manager of the '38 Bees

Roy Myers, 1st base

Roy Potter, catcher

Al Plummer, 3rd base

and one of my favorite people, **Angel Salas**, catcher.

Deputy Frank Ash also signed his name in the book. Mr. Ash was involved in a confrontation at one of the Bees' games, which had very serious and traumatic consequences. My uncle, Don Fergus, was witness to the incident and it went something like this as best I could remember Uncle Don relating it to me:

During one of the games, a melee broke out on the field, and in the heat of it, Deputy Ash, for what ever reason, took a baseball bat to one of the combatants and hit him in the head. Evidentially, it was a pretty ferocious blow and the player was injured quite severely. I was in front of my house on the Vista and witnessed Deputy Ash driving away from the park. He stopped in front of my house, got out of his car, and vomited. He was obviously pretty shook up over the incident. I seem to recall that Mr. Ash suffered serious consequences. Demotion, law suit, what ever, I don't know for sure. But, I do know he must have really clobbered the guy.

THE ARIZONA-TEXAS LEAGUE

Hugh Keyes, one of my favorite Bisbee people, wrote the following in the February 26, 1952, *Cochise County Servicemen's Roundup* "The Bisbee-Douglas Copper Kings will be back in action this summer and back in the popular Arizona-Texas League; that is, the Copper Kings will be in action if baseball fans in Bisbee and Douglas will come through with donations to the tune of a neat $22,000. Directors of the club explain that it will take that much money to get the team ready for play. If it is collected, it will be the largest amount ever contributed toward baseball or any other one sport in this district. Since the Brooklyn Dodgers stopped their working agreement with B-D, the entire amount will fall squarely on the shoulders of the local organization."

The money was collected and The Copper Kings took the field that summer.

The Warren Ballpark is a vast reservoir of memories for generations of Bisbee youngsters going all the way back to the early 1900's. It is a place many of us almost hold sacred. Les Fenderson, BHS graduate told me he took his young son, Fred, to the Warren Ball Park in the late 1970's to show him where "Dad used to play baseball." Upon arriving at the gate, Les realized all the cars parked outside the park were not there for a baseball game; they had come to a *rock concert!* Les said he wanted to cry.

Dale Hancock, BHS '57 makes this statement: "I do not know how anyone who had lived in Bisbee and had experienced the Warren Ballpark could ever walk in again and not have flash backs like those in the movie *Field of Dreams*". For Dale, the flash backs bring special pangs of nostalgia. Dale's dad, B Hancock, was a member of one of the early 1940's Bisbee "Bees" team. Dale became a team mascot who was often allowed to sit in the dugout with the players. Once, Dale even got to make a long road trip with the team riding in the bus with them to Nogales. One of the players told Dale that the only way one could eat ice cream without getting a headache was to sprinkle black pepper on it. Dale did as instructed and no headache! He did that for several more years before finally realizing that the player was probably pulling his leg. Remember, Dale was a Lowell Grade School product at that time so was not likely the sharpest knife in the drawer. Thankfully, when Dale reached Bisbee High he was able to catch up to the rest of his peers.

B Hancock was a true baseball fan even after his playing days were over. Dale remembers going to all BHS Puma games, home or away, with his dad. A very close bond between father and son was developed mainly through B.'s love for baseball. This love for all sports was passed on to Dale. B died of a heart attack at the young age of forty-two while working under ground in the mines. B. died prematurely, but not before a wonderful legacy generated by the Warren Ballpark was passed down from father to son.

Pete Vucurevich BHS, '47 has many such flash backs as well. Pete remembers a very speedy centerfielder for the Copper Kings named Frank Lucchesi who later managed the Kansas City Royals. Lucchesi was a great impersonator of the minstrel singer, Al Jolson. Once, between games of a double header (remember when they used to have double headers?), Lucchesi came out to home plate with his face painted black and sang a medley of Negro minstrel songs, including the one that brought the house down, "Mammy, how I love you, how I love you, my dear ole Mammy." Besides being a great baseball player, he was an accomplished entertainer.

Pete remembers Charlie Metro, a popular manager for the Copper Kings, and the man who may have invented the batting-tee. If he didn't invent it, he was the first one to introduce it to Bisbee. Metro delighted having a local youngster, like Ted Sorich come on to the field and demonstrate hitting a few balls off the tee.

Bisbee native, Jim "Boom-Boom" Bynon was one of Pete's favorite memories. "Boom-Boom" once hit 36 home runs for the Bisbee club. Bynon played right field and had a terrifically strong arm. A favorite trick of his was to charge a solidly hit ground ball and pretend to have it go through his legs. He would turn around, having the ball hidden in his glove the whole time, take a few quick steps as though to chase after the ball, and then suddenly wheel and fire the ball to second base. He would often catch the base runner thinking he had second base for sure on the "error", only to find Bynon's strong, accurate throw waiting at second for the surprised runner.

SID COHEN, A LEGEND.

The name, *Sid Cohen,* is synonymous with baseball in Bisbee and the entire Southwest. He is responsible for the resurgence of Bisbee-Douglas baseball. Again, Hugh Keyes:

"Signing of the veteran baseball man (Sid Cohen, hh) was one of the finest breaks the Kings have had in a long time. Not only is he one of the smartest managers in the business....but, Cohen will be able to sign Mexican players to strengthen the Kings who do not have a hook-up with a major league team to provide players.

Cohen is no newcomer to baseball in these parts. He started his baseball career here in Bisbee in 1928 as a first baseman, and he has often expressed his love for the Bisbee district and the enjoyment he receives from helping Bisbee and Douglas have pro. ball."

Hugh Keyes continues, "Cohen went up to the Washington Senators as a pitcher at the close of the season in 1934. That year, the immortal Babe Ruth hit his last American League home run off of one of Cohen's pitches.

In 1936 Cohen whiffed the great New York Yankee first baseman, Lou Gehrig, six times out of nine at-bats against him."

Cohen bounced around the major leagues with several clubs until he went down to the Pacific Coast League in 1946. In 1947, he managed the El Paso Texans and took them to a championship in 1949. In 1950, he managed the Juarez Indios and led them to the crown.

Sid Cohen was loved and respected every where he went. He was a charismatic personality. His antics on the field and his confrontations with umpires are legendary. Hugh gave written testimony to this fact "Sid, a showman from the word go, gives the fans their money's worth both in baseball and color. His frantic, explosive arguments with the men in blue are as enjoyable as his crafty managing."

I witnessed first hand one of Cohen's "frantic, explosive arguments" with an umpire at the Copper King field in Douglas. He did not like a call the home plate umpire made against his Copper Kings and he let the umpire know in no uncertain terms that he did not like the call. When Sid argued with an umpire, he always made a mad dash for home plate and would get face to face with the umpire. That's what he did the night I observed him. After several minutes of jawing, the umpire told Sid to get back to the dugout. Of course, the fans loved it and were all loudly encouraging Sid to, "Let the bum have it."

An inning or so later, another "bad" call and again Sid sprinted out to home plate and again got face to face with the umpire. Sid's mouth was going a mile a minute! The umpire took Sid's abuse for a few minutes and then took his mask off and told Sid that if he came out of the dugout to argue one more time, he'd be out of the game. The umpire's hand gestures told it all.

Sid obediently walked back to his 3rd base dugout. He was pretty subdued for an inning or so. But that didn't last long. Another bad call and everyone in the stands could hear Sid's loud scream of, **"What?! That pitch was a mile outside!"** At which point he came sprinting out of the dugout headed straight towards the umpire. We all knew this was *it*. Sid was going to be booted out of the game. The umpire, seeing Sid flying towards him, took his mask off and we knew that umpire meant business! Sid was a "goner".

To everyone's amazement, Sid sprinted right past the umpire and headed straight to a water-fountain near the 1st base dugout. He got a drink, turned around and again sprinted past the bewildered umpire, right back to his dugout. He took his place on the dugout steps without another word to the umpire. The game continued. The fans loved it.

Sammy Moore, BHS '56 recalls seeing Sid pitch in one game where he displayed his version of the seldom used *blooper pitch* "I remember one game where Bisbee was getting clobbered and I guess he had used all his pitchers so he went in to pitch. I guess you would call it pitching. When he threw it, he arched the ball about 20 feet high, hoping it would come down across the plate. The ball must have been going all of 10 miles per. hour when it crossed the plate. The fans loved it." The umpire and the batter hated it.

In my opinion, baseball needs more "Sid Cohens" today!

BEATING THE SHAGGERS AT THEIR OWN GAME

The management of the home team always hired high school boys to act as *ball shaggers*. To land one of these prestigious positions was considered by the high schoolers to be just about the best summer job anyone could land. Not only did the team pay for a good night's shagging, but the shaggers got to see most of every game free. Every summer only four boys were chosen to be shaggers. Those four were usually four of the toughest kids in Bisbee and on a good summer the shaggers were strengthened by one of The Goat Row Gang. The Goat Row Gang *were* the toughest kids in the Bisbee area. And, the shaggers had to be tough and fast. Their job was to get every foul ball hit out of the park at each game. To retrieve a foul ball usually meant out-running a number of younger kids who were waiting outside the park near the Toot'n Tellem, and left and right down Ruppe Ave. Usually the shaggers won the race as they could bully their way to the ball by verbally intimidating the younger kids.

Very few kids ever messed with the *shaggers*. One summer I remember that Norman Wright was a shagger. Norman Wright weighed 300lbs. and if he caught you trying to steal one of the foul balls, he would sit on you. He sat on me one Halloween night. However, the shaggers met their match in "The Hicks Gang". I will let Ted Sorich, BHS '55 tell the story lest you think I am bragging:

"Yours truly, (affectionately known as *Teddy, Lefty, or Hunkie,* depending on who is doin' the talkin'…Shanty Hogan, Angel Salas, Sr., or Al Ridgway) has a story to tell. As many of you remember, the Sorich's lived no more than a 5-wood (putting it in perspective for all you golf nuts) east of Warren Stadium, on Clauson Street. Since baseballs were a major part of each team's budget and sometimes hard to come by, the General Manager (someone like Mel Steiner comes to mind), would hire "ball shaggers" to go into the streets and fields which surrounded Warren Stadium, to retrieve all the "foul balls" which went over the fence during the course of a nine inning game. The problem was the Hicks Gang was on the prowl, controlling the territory from lower Vista to Mamie Bugen's Toot'n Tellum (which I understand was later owned by Charlene Cunningham's family). The shaggers on first base side of the stadium had no chance to successfully retrieve a foul ball, which entered this territory, once the Hicks Gang went into action! Speedy Hadley Hicks was generally the first one to the ball. He had a pretty good arm and his job was to relay the ball up the street to Jinx Richards who was stationed somewhere in the vicinity of the Warren Bowling Alley. Jinx had a fairly weak arm, and he would proceed to relay the ball on several bounces to Lefty Weld up somewhere by the Warren Drug Store. Lefty was a lefty and Hadley didn't want him throwing the ball to anyone, so his job was to run up Congdon Avenue and hide in Bruce Caldwell's yard until the 'All Clear' was given, usually by shouts from the Gang of, 'Here comes another one.'

Hiding in the bushes, next to George Hershey's house, observing all of this exciting action taking place, on a game by game basis, was a seven year old boy named Teddy (too broke and too honest to sneak into the stadium, hohoho, to watch the ball games) taking mental notes on 'How to become a worthy successor to the Hicks Gang', once they decided that they had more than enough baseballs to last the rest of their young adult lives! While the Hicks Gang had to rely on 3-4 people to get the job done, Teddy became a 'gang of one', due to the proximity of his home in relation to the Warren Stadium (remember the 5 wood). But, first things first. I quickly recognized that retrieving any foul ball that went over the fence on the first base side of the stadium was an absolute lost cause. Why? Because Les Fenderson and Jack Gilbert decided bilaterally that the lower Vista was now their territory! Those ratfinks!

But, there was still the 3rd base side of the stadium available, or so I thought. But, as Lee Corso would say, 'Not so fast my friend". Lurking in the drainage ditch that ran parallel to Douglas Road was none other than Earl Bradshaw, Tommy Vercellino, and Leroy Lucero! Triple ratfinks!

The territory that was now available for 'harvesting baseballs' had shrunk by 2/3rds!! Not to worry. I soon realized that most foul balls that left the stadium, actually, came directly over the center of the stadium, which was right up my alley figuratively speaking, and now, My Territory!

I would hide behind bushes, out in the field next to Hershey's, coiled like a rattlesnake ready to strike, just waiting for a 'center cut' ball to leave the stadium. Once it did, it was all over but the shoutin'. No chance for the shaggers, no chance for those ratfinks. I was on my way up Clawson Street (hallelujah!) and in my house before you could say, 'The Hicks Gang'.

PS. I even had the nerve to go back to the stadium after the games were over to have ball players autograph 'my baseballs' as they were walking to their cars!! Yes!!!'

BISBEE HIGH'S CONTRIBUTION TO PRO BASEBALL

My uncle, Forbes Fergus, was a fireman in San Diego for many years. He was a huge baseball fan, and his hero was a BHS graduate named Clarence "Clary" Maddern. Clary played for The Los Angeles Angels in the Pacific Coast League. Clary was with the Chicago Cubs in the "bigs" for a couple years before he went down to the PCL. Forbes was a regular face in the crowd of many of the games when Clary was playing in San Diego. Often he attended the games courtesy of Clary. They were good friends. They were both *from Bisbee*. Forbes mentioned Clary often and what a great baseball player he was. Clary was the earliest memory I have of a Bisbee High graduate who made it "big" as a baseball player. Clary's younger brother, Don Maddern, also played pro. baseball after graduating from BHS in '47. Pete Vucurevich BHS, '47 is going to tell you something about the BHS team of '47 in the next section, but let me just say now that that team contributed four players to the pros.! I doubt if any other BHS team can make that claim.

BISBEE HIGH'S FIRST STATE BASEBALL CHAMPIONSHIP

Pete Vucurevich, BHS '47 was, in my opinion, the finest pitcher and possibly the best all around baseball player to ever wear the Red and Gray of BHS. Besides being an over powering pitcher, he once blasted three home runs in one game. Pete, immediately out of high school and just weeks after he led the Pumas to the 1947 Class B State Championship, was signed by The New York Yankees.

The Pumas of '47 were arguably the best baseball team ever to represent Bisbee High. Besides Pete, the Waldo Dicus coached Pumas had several other outstanding players on that team. The Yankees signed Sam Kitterman, Bob Holland, and Don Maddern, as well as Vucurevich, in '47. Others I remember from that great team were Bennie Hamrick, "Mousie' Echave, Fred Hague, Gilbert Ruiz, Freddie Terrin and Ross Thompson. Pete has some interesting insights into that championship season "….It was only the second year that BHS had a baseball team since before WW II. Our baseball field was being renovated and we practiced at the old Bisbee airport while preparing for the season. Talk about bad hops. Maybe that is why we played so well during the season!"

Pete goes on "We beat Amphitheater High at the Warren ball park 5-0 to earn the right to play Marana at the UofA field. We then beat Marana to advance to the championship game against Tempe High. (A note, Ross Thompson was filling in for Bob Holland as our catcher. Bob had broken his wrist a short time before. Ross did a fantastic job for us throughout the final three games.) Sam Kitterman pitched the game against Marana and beat them. I pitched the championship game against Tempe and beat them 2-1 on a three hitter. Although regular high school games were 7 innings, the championship game was 9 innings."

I read one article from a Tempe newspaper that gave a glowing report of, "The Dicus Men". The article said that the *Pumas* could play with any team in the state, including most of the bigger schools, and that, "The Pumas rode the strong right arm of Pistol Pete Vucurevich to the title…." It also told how Ross Thompson gunned out several base runners attempting to steal second. Ross was more than an adequate replacement for the injured Bob Holland.

Pete apologized for not remembering the score of the Marina game, but said his sister kept the records he has and only kept records of the games he pitched in! That's what you call sibling loyalty!

Pete relates an oddity that occurred in 1950 in Charleston, South Carolina. Pete had just completed spring training and was getting ready to head for an assignment in Binghamton, New York, with the Yankees' farm club. As Pete was leaving the restaurant where he had eaten breakfast, he ran into his former BHS teammate, Don Maddern! Don was headed for Hagerstown, Maryland, also for his assignment in the Yankees' farm system "Talk about a small world!" Pete commented, "Two buddies meeting by accident over two thousand miles from home!"

It's like I said in the foreword to this book, "There are people *from Bisbee* everywhere."

SHADES OF JOHNNYMACKBROWN

The mention of Ross Thompson made me recall with much fear the time I thought he was going to kill me!

Ross's younger brother, Robert Thompson, and I were good buddies and would often play in the copper water ditch. More specifically, we would play under the bridge over the copper water ditch on B Avenue just west of the Warren Ballpark. We played *under* the bridge because we didn't want any adults to see us and tell our parents. Our parents were pretty unreasonable when it came to us playing anywhere near the copper water ditch. We'd get dirty they said.

It was one day shortly after we'd seen a JohnnyMackBrown cowboy movie at the Lyric. His name was *JohnnyMackBrown*. Roy Rogers was "Roy"; Hopalong Cassidy was "Hoppy"; Gene Autry was "Gene"; JohnnyMackBrown was "JohnnyMackBrown". In that movie JohnnyMackBrown shot the hat off one of the villains. I thought that was a pretty cool thing to do. Robert was wearing a straw Mexican sombrero. We both had our BB guns, which was another big "no, no" in our parents' minds. I asked Robert to stand real still while I tried to shoot the sombrero off his head just like JohnnyMackBrown had done in the movie. Robert, out of fear for his life, stood statue still. I pumped several bb's into that sombrero, but nothing happened. The sombrero didn't even wiggle. After several more shots, I gave it up. We went on and played for a while and then went home.

Later that evening, I heard a loud banging on my front door. I answered it and was greeted by a livid Ross Thompson. He grabbed me by the neck and started shaking me. "You little s.o.b.!!! We just took Robert to the hospital and they had to dig three bb's out of his head!". To this day it is beyond me why Robert stood so still and didn't cry out when I hit him with the first bb. He never uttered a word. He just stood there and let me go on trying to shoot that dumb sombrero off his head. My dad, however, said several words when he heard about it. I got a good licking.

JohnnyMackBrown got me in trouble one other time, also. My only real fist fight! George Blagovich and I got in a wild, free-swinging fistfight outside the Warren Park. George had insulted my family; he had said something derogatory about America; he had belittled everything I held sacred and dear. Really, I don't remember what actually started the fight. Probably something like, "Roy is tougher than JohnnyMackBrown." Whatever it was, I had JohnnyMackBrown on my mind as George and I fought. In all his movies, JohnnyMackBrown got into fistfights and often with several bad guys at one time. What he did was *duck* the blows thrown by the bad guys. I don't remember his ever getting hit by one of the bad guys' fists. He would *always duck*. So, I went into this fistfight with the same mind-set. I would simply *duck* every time George tried to hit me. Well, George must have been thinking the same thing. After all, he went to the movies, too. I should have figured that possibility in my pre-fight planning! The fight began. Every time I would swing at George, he would duck. That in itself wouldn't have been so bad had we not been standing close to, and parallel to, the green, wooden fence that was around the whole park. You see, George was standing facing east and I was facing west. The fence was on my left. I am right handed. All this was in George's favor. I would swing, he would duck. My fist would *smash* into the fence. *He* would swing. I would duck. His swing smashed into air. This continued on, and on, for maybe five minutes when I realized my strategy was not working. I waved the white flag. My right fist was pretty well bloodied. Mine was the only blood shed it that fight. My first and last fist fight. *Diplomacy* became my by-word from that day forward.

BILL PLUMB WAS NOT NORMAL

How does one describe Bill Plumb? Even though he was in high school while I was still in grade school, he was my buddy for several years. We were neighbors when I lived on Cole Ave. Bill and his family lived on Oliver Circle. Mr. and Mrs. Plumb were very nice, pleasant people. Bill's sister, Mary Kay, was a cute little blond about four or five years younger than I was. She seemed *normal* to me. Mr. and Mrs. Plumb seemed *normal*. Bill was *not normal*. That is the only way I can describe him. Not *normal*. Yet, he was a bright kid, a friendly kid, a good looking, blond kid, but, take my word for it, Bill Plumb *was not normal!*

Let me explain. First of all, he was obsessed with killing *Japanese*. Not your everyday living, breathing Japanese; but rather the make-believe *Japanese* that Bill conjured up every time Ernest Gabrilson, Bob Goar and I played with him.

Secondly, Bill loved the United States Marines, especially the Marines who defended Wake Island against the Japanese in WW II. When we played, we always played "Wake Island". Two guesses who got to be "The Marines" and only one guess who got to, no, who were *forced* to be "The Japanese"? You guessed right. Bill was always the "Marines" and we were always the "Japanese".

"Wake Island" was played in "Sherwood Forest" which was a large section of land behind the mysterious Loma Linda Lodge. "Wake Island" was covered with boulders, large mesquite trees, and tall, dry, grass. Bill always gave the "Japanese" explicit instructions on how the game was to be played on any particular day. It usually centered around the "Japanese" unsuccessfully trying to sneak up on the "Marines". It always turned into a prolonged game of hide and seek. We would play the game for hours, which always culminated with the "Marines" soundly defeating the sneaky "Japanese". We knew the game was over when Bill would march off to the top of the hill singing, "From the Halls of Montezuma…"

One particular "battle" was the coup de grace, the battle to end all battles, and **end it, it did!** When the police told my parents what had happened, I was never allowed to play with Bill again. In fact, I believe he was forced to join the military soon after this battle. It could have had very serious consequences. It *did* have serious consequences. Bill was told he had to either go to jail or join the service. He joined the service.

Here is how that final battle of "Wake Island" was fought. The "Japanese" were told to go to their usual hiding place behind a large boulder and were told to wait until the "Marines" had adequately hidden. After several minutes the "Japanese" were to deploy and sneak up on the well-fortified "Marines". Suddenly, before we could deploy, we heard *"pow-ping"* and felt a shower of rock fragments. Again, *"pow-ping"*, and more fragments. It didn't take too much intelligence to know that the "Japanese" were being shot at by *real bullets!* Needless to say, the "Japanese" *did not* deploy. We cowered down as low as we could behind that boulder. We even shouted, "Bill, stop shooting!" As far as we were concerned the "Marines" had won; we surrendered! However, the battle lasted several more minutes. The shots ended as suddenly as they had begun. But, there was no way we were getting out from behind that boulder until we knew for sure the "Marines" had run out of ammunition. As we lay there waiting, we suddenly smelled…. *"SMOKE"*! We were being burned out of hiding! We heard the flames getting closer and that's when we made a run for it. As we ran, we saw Bill running up the hill well ahead of us. He was getting out of there too, as he knew the fire would soon be out of control. I noticed that Bill was carrying a familiar looking rifle. He must have had it hidden in "Marine Headquarters". Little did I know how familiar that rifle was until a day later.

I was scared to death. I ran into the house and screamed to my mother that Bill Plumb had set the whole field on fire. She would have thought I was nuts if I had told her that "the Marines" had set it on fire. She believed me because by then she could see the flames and smoke about fifty yards from our house. Someone had already called the fire department, and they soon had the fire out before too much damage was done.

My parents grilled me until I told them the whole story, including the live ammunition the "Marines" had used. This did not set well with my parents. I am not sure what all transpired next, but I do know that the next day around suppertime a knock came at our door. I remember I was sitting at the dinner table when my dad answered the door. He ushered Sheriff I.V. Pruett and a very sheepish-looking Bill Plumb into the dining room. Sheriff Pruett was carrying a familiar looking rifle. I immediately recognized it as the Japanese training rifle that my uncle, Dad's brother, had sent Dad as a souvenir from the war. It was a .22 caliber rifle that shot *real* bullets! The "light" went on!

I remembered that several months before our last battle, I had showed the souvenir rifle to Bill and had thought nothing of it. I should have known better because, as I said, Bill Plumb was not *normal*. At some time when we were not home, Bill had come into our house and taken the rifle from the closet. Being a bright kid, he figured out that the rifle took .22 caliber bullets. The next battle for "Wake Island" would have a degree of reality!

Did you catch the irony of that story? The "Marines" used a stolen Japanese rifle to pin down the "Japanese"

Bill confessed to stealing the rifle and setting the field on fire, and no doubt he confessed to numerous other transgressions the authorities had wondered about over the years. As I mentioned, Bill was given the choice of jail or the military. He chose the military, and I always wondered if he joined the Marines. He was a good one!

Besides not being normal, Bill Plumb was also a pyromaniac. He would set fire to empty lots and then watch the fire department put the fire out. As an example, the night my mother went to the hospital to give birth to my sister, Cathy, Bill ignited the empty lot across from our house to "celebrate" Cathy's birth. Bill then went home, called the fire department, got in his pajamas, got a comic book, rumpled up his hair, and walked the half block to the front of our house. From there he watched as the fire department extinguished the fire.

Then there was the time Bill and I were in his garage that had a window over-looking the Callison family's house on Oliver Circle, below the Plumb's house. Bill was looking out the window with a look of anticipation on his face. He would look at the Callison house, then at the empty lot between his house and the Callison house, and then he'd look back to the Callison house. What he was doing, he finally told me, was calculating the number of steps he'd have to take from his back gate, through the empty, *grassy* lot, to the street and back to his gate. Being the innocent, young grade school kid that I was, I had no clue what he was up to. But, I knew what ever it was, it would be exciting because Bill was not normal.

After Bill had it all figured out, he put on a large topcoat and felt hat. He pulled the felt hat down over his head, pulled the collar of the coat up, and made me walk close to his *right* side. Bill had a box of wooden matches in his *right* coat pocket. Bill was *left*-handed and he struck the matches with his left hand while his right hand held the matchbox and the striking edge. As we walked rather slowly through the empty lot, I was partially shielding his right hand, which was holding the matchbox that Bill was using to ignite the matches that he held in his left hand. We walked like that all the way through the empty lot (approximately thirty-three steps one way, Bill had informed me) Bill furtively dropping lighted matches with every other step. We reached the road, turned around, and walked back the way we had come. Again, Bill was dropping lighted matches with every other step. I noticed that some of the grass was beginning to ignite. By the time we reached his garage and looked out the window, we could see that a pretty good fire was blazing. I believe it was Bill who called the fire department, but I wasn't sure because I got out of there quick! I ran home, but I didn't tell my mother about this adventure for a number of reasons. Mainly, because I was afraid she would never let me play with him again. He was not *normal,* but he was exciting to be around.

I never did know what Bill had against the Callisons. Bill Callison was my age and he and I had a lot of fun together. Bob Callison was older, but was nice. Gordon Callison was even littler than I was. Gordon, too, seemed normal. The whole family seemed fairly normal to me. But, there was something about them that rubbed Bill Plumb the wrong way. Or, maybe it was just because they were *there.*

On a number of occasions Bill would get eggs or tomatoes and throw them at the Callison's house. I was there a couple of those times, and Bill always made me lay down behind a low wall the Plumb's had in their back yard. He would throw whatever he had been able to get out of the refrigerator that day and then quickly drop down behind the wall. After a few minutes he would peek over the wall to observe the damage and accuracy of his throw. That was *not normal.*

I always believed Bill could have made a great left-handed pitcher. He was the most accurate left-handed thrower I ever saw. One of his favorite past times, besides setting fires, was to walk around Warren at night with a pocket full of rocks and break out streetlights. In those days they did not put protective covers over the lights. All the streetlights for two blocks around our neighborhood were systematically being broken. Bill would start at one end of a neighborhood and work his way around in a circle until he got back to the starting point. Sometimes it took him weeks to make the circle as he only broke one or two a night. By that time the first light to be broken had been replaced, Bill would start all over. That too, was not *normal.*

And, you talk about accuracy! I remember one night we were walking down the alley behind our old house on the E. Vista (Elaine Jays' old house) and Bill noticed a number of lighted windows on the third floor of the Wolslagel's service station building on Arizona Street. Those rooms were rented apartments. There must have been four or five windows in a row at the top of the three-story building. Bill picked up a rock and said, "Which window?" Ernest Gabrilson said, "Second from the left." Bill let go and sure enough, second from the left…*crash!* That was really not *normal.*

Pete Vucurevich BHS '47 shares this "Bill Plumb" story:

"We were in 7th grade at Greenway with Anthony Nadolski as principal. This incident happened in Ms. Helen Hunter's English class. Billy was cutting up and was seated near the door that went into the hall. The principal's office was straight across the hall. Ms. Hunter walked up to Billy, and he stood up. She told him to behave and to sit down. He refused to sit. She told him again and he refused again. The third time she asked him to sit, Billy let go with a roundhouse left and hit her on the side of her cheek. She staggered toward the floor but caught herself on an empty seat ahead of Billy's and sat in it. Almost instantaneously, a long arm (seemed about ten feet) reached through the door and had Billy by the neck. I swear, his feet came up off the floor. It was Nadolski. Billy was suspended for a month, and Ms. Hunter took just about that long to get rid of her black eye and swollen cheek."

Pete concluded with this assessment of Bill Plumb:

"No doubt Billy caused some problems, but I believe he was a good person at heart. He seemed to have a chip on his shoulder with regard to authority and at times he paid for it. I never remember him giving any of his class mates trouble."

I have to agree with Pete's assessment. Bill Plumb was a good guy. He was happy-go-lucky and always had a smile on his face. He was most respectful to my parents. My mother was amazed when I would tell her, in later years, about my exploits with Bill Plumb. "He was such a sweet boy." she would say. Yes, he was. But he was not *normal.*

I have to admit the last time I saw Bill Plumb, he looked pretty normal. I must have been a junior or senior in high school, and I was driving through Lowell. I had not seen Bill for probably seven or eight years. I recognized him walking up the street and he had a beautiful, well-dressed young lady with him. Now that, to me, appeared to be normal. I was so busy eye-balling the beautiful lady, that I did not notice the car in front of me stop. *Crash!* It was just a minor "fender-bender", but it got Bill's attention. He recognized me driving, got a big grin on his face, and said, "Hi, Haddie, what were you looking at?"

SHERWOOD FOREST AND THE MYSTERIOUS LOMA LINDA LODGE

Bobby Goar and I used to have very intense rubber-gun fights in "Sherwood Forest". Bobby would always win those fights as his rubber bands could fly farther and carry more sting than mine. His rubber guns were more technically advanced. The barrels of his guns always seemed to be longer in length or something. Maybe the inner tubes he cut his ammunition out of were fresher than mine. I don't know. But he always won. Of course we had these rubber-gun fights in other places besides "Sherwood Forest", but somehow the fights were more competitive in the dark shadows of the "Forest". It should be explained that "Sherwood Forest" was not really a *forest* in the true sense of the word. It was rather an acre or so of thick mesquite bushes. I suppose that whoever was the first one to play there had played "Robin Hood" and the name stuck. There was also a small inhabited house just on the west edges of "Sherwood Forest". Even though my house on Cole Avenue was just over the hill from "Sherwood Forest", (about 200 yards as "Bill Plumb flies"), I never did know who the mysterious people were who lived there. We always tried to stay hidden from them. That was not hard to do. Bob and I had learned well how to hide. We had "the Marines" to teach us all the tricks.

This house was on the most easterly section of the very mysterious and vacant **Loma Linda Lodge.** Possibly the people in this house were the caretakers for the Loma Linda. If they were, they were pitiful caretakers. We could break into the Loma Linda at will and often did. It was a very scary experience to break into the Loma Linda, even in broad day light because it always *looked like* someone lived there. We thought it might be haunted. The rooms were always clean. The cabinets had sheets, blankets, etc. in them. And, once, I remember that the refrigerator in the kitchen had a couple cold Cokes in it. Now, that was scary! We would tiptoe from room to room expecting at any moment to be confronted by *someone*. Worse, we expected to find a dead *body* in one of the beds! Never did though.

As I write this I am trying to remember just *how* we broke in. I can't really remember for sure, but it seems to me that there was a door on the west side that we could force open. Or maybe we crawled in through a window. I don't know.

Bruce Caldwell, BHS '52, reminded me of the time he and I ditched school from Greenway when we were in about the 7th grade. We hid in the vast back yard at the Loma Linda until noon. Bruce recalls that when he and I went back to school that afternoon, that we had not even been missed. That was pretty humbling, to not even be missed! The back yard of the Loma Linda served as the hideout from Mr. Nadolski for many a Greenway Grade schooler over the years. If Mr. Nadolski caught us ditching, we were in big trouble. He did not need any truant officers to help him. But, to my knowledge, he never searched the Loma Linda's back yard.

That back yard of the Loma Linda was very impressive. It was all in terraces, which were ivy covered. I recall a few fruit trees scattered throughout the back, but they must not have been very fruitful as we never raided them for their fruit.

It is still a mystery to me. Who took care of the place? Who mowed the lawns? Who dusted and cleaned the inside? I don't recall ever seeing anyone there. At least when I was in grade school, I never saw anyone. Years later, I remember people lived there, but don't know who. I was above breaking into places then.

The Loma Linda had a very large front yard that was the dead-end of the eastern edge of the Vista. Cole Street ran in front of the Loma Linda. This large front yard had a very tall flagpole, which was just about the same size as the flagpole in the Vista Park. The flagpole was 25 yards or so from the front porch of the Loma Linda. The southern edge of the front yard was lined with very tall oleander bushes. Attached to the flagpole was a long cable used to hoist the flag up (though I never remember seeing any flag flying from it) which, when unhooked from the bottom end of the flagpole, would reach to the front porch of the Loma Linda. It was great fun to get this cable stretched to the porch, then stand on the porch's ledge, and swing in a circle around the pole. If we attained a little momentum as we pushed off, we would get pretty good altitude in our swing; at least ten-twelve feet off the ground. If we did not grip the cable high enough to shorten the length of our swing, we would sometimes crash into the oleanders on the south side. Those oleanders would scratch us up pretty good if we weren't careful.

The Loma Linda had two circular driveways on the north and south sides. These circular drives were secluded in very dense oleander bushes. As a kid, I would often see cars at various times at night drive into the circular drive on the south side closest to my house. The car headlights would go out and an hour or so later the car would be gone. I could never figure that out until I got in the 6th grade. Then I understood.

HALLOWEEN. TRYING TO AVOID THE GOAT ROW GANG, AND NORMAN WRIGHT

Halloween was always a time when we could be ornery and semi-destructive legally. The phrase, "Trick or Treat" carried some clout to it! They gave us a "treat" or else! Hudgin's Warren Grocery Store did a booming business selling bars of soap the week before Halloween. We weren't prepared for a serious evening of "tricking" unless we had a bar of soap in our pocket. Some of the more experienced older kids would load up on short nails and electrical tape. They could somehow rig up the doorbells so that whoever answered the door couldn't turn them off very easily. I never did learn that "trick". The old "fresh manure in a paper sack trick" was tried many times each year, usually by "first timers". I never heard of anybody falling for it. The flaming paper sack was just kicked into the front yard.

The real excitement each Halloween was trying to avoid **The Goat Row Gang!** I can only recall a few of them, but they had a **bad** reputation in Warren. The few I remember and feared most were Danny and Pete Vucurevich, Bosco Verbica, Mike, Roy and Jack Lazovich, and Al and Mike Marusich. It was rumored that one year, The Goat Row Gang had snuck up on about ten Warren kids, surrounded them and demanded all their loot. After they had confiscated all the candy, nuts and oranges, they then proceeded to *de-pants* all of them. They tied their pants together and ran them up the flagpole. We never could verify that rumor because the victims vowed secrecy. To be de-pantsed by The Goat Row Gang was the biggest humiliation one could endure. The kids I ran around with on Halloween always made sure we were wearing underwear just in case.

I will never forget the first Halloween I was allowed to go out on my own. I was about six years old and not yet very brave. At least not brave enough to venture much beyond the Warren Drug Store area, up and down Arizona Street. I remember being with John Gans, and was coming back from a Halloween party at the Community Church. As we got closer to the Warren Drug Store, we saw a group of about seven older kids. From a distance the group looked like they were standing by a bus of some sort. When we got closer, I recognized that the "bus" was none other than *Norman Wright*. Besides being **big**, about 400 lbs., Norman was *mean!* He was especially mean to kids that he caught on Halloween night. That night he caught me. He didn't catch John Gans because John had run the minute he saw that "the bus" wasn't a bus. There wasn't much fanfare to it at all. He just caught me and **sat on me!** No rhyme or reason; he just caught me and sat on me. He didn't laugh at me; he didn't belittle me; he didn't mock me; he just **sat on me!** All his buddies seemed used to it as they continued talking and laughing about things. They did not at all seem concerned that right in front of their eyes, Norman Wright was killing a little kid! After about eight hours someone said, "Let's go, Norm." He got off me and just left. Just like that. He just got up and left. He did not say one word to me the entire ten hours he sat on me. I have never forgotten that first Halloween. More specifically, I have never forgotten Norman Wright.

As I got older, in about the 6th or 7th grade, Halloween became more fun. We were still fearful of the Goat Row Gang, (Norman Wright had disappeared from the scene), but we were always successful in avoiding them. Our big thing at

Halloween was stealing pomegranates and harassing Les Fenderson, Ted Sorich, Bruce McDoniel, Sammy Moore, and all the other little kids who were starting to venture out on Halloween.

They say that "*forbidden fruit*" is the sweetest. In my view, my uncle, Dr. Robert Fergus had the sweetest and most forbidden fruit in all Warren. His back yard on the Vista was just loaded with delicious pomegranate trees. My mother, Dr. Fergus' sister, had told me in no uncertain terms that I was never to get caught stealing from those trees. She never told me *not to steal* from them, but just not to get *caught*. That made the forbidden fruit just that much sweeter. Mother would have been totally humiliated if I was ever caught stealing from her brother. More specifically, she would have been totally humiliated in the eyes of Uncle Bob's wife, Aunt Rosemary! Mother and Aunt Rosemary had this ridiculous rivalry between them. They both had this thing about trying to outdo each other in buying clothes. It had something to do with the fact that both my dad and Uncle Bob were dentists. Which one made the most money seemed to be a concern of my mother's. Aunt Rosemary would tell mother that she got her clothes from Goldwater's. Mother got most of her clothes from J.C. Penny. If mother ever wore a new dress over to Aunt Rosemary's, mother would cut out the *J.C. Penny* tag and sew in a *Goldwater's* tag. It was this fear of being humiliated by Aunt Rosemary that caused mother not to want her "sweet, perfect, little Haddie" to ever be caught stealing pomegranates from Aunt Rosemary's back yard. So, I never got caught. It was easy to do. My strategy was perfect. Jinx Richards would ring Uncle Bob's front door. While Jinx was keeping Uncle Bob busy filling his sack with candy, Jim Baker and I would climb over the back fence and steal as many pomegranates as we could carry. We never went through the back gate as we were afraid it would squeak. It worked every time. We never even woke up my bratty little cousins, Gayle and Marty Lou Fergus!

Next door to Uncle Bob on the south was the Folsom Moore home. It had a big back yard with a tennis court. It was a very pretentious home. I could never figure out why they had a tennis court. The city tennis courts were just out their front door on the Vista. I always thought a swimming pool would have been more useful. But, they did have good pomegranates as well as a fig tree or two. That made for good picking. We never got caught there, either.

We never messed with the house to the north of Uncle Bob's. That house belonged to Mr. and Mrs. Ben Kelly. They had some very tempting fruit trees that we studied long and hard each Halloween. The Kelly's also had three kids. Edie Kelly was a very sweet high school girl. We weren't afraid of her at all. *But,* the deciding factor that kept us out of their yard, was the Kelly boys! Roy Kelly was a big kid who had played football for the University of Arizona and John Kelly was a star football player for the BHS *Pumas*. We gave their home a wide berth.

GREENWAY GRADE SCHOOL "FIELD TRIPS"

I loved it when I was finally in the 7th and 8th grades and our class could go to the Lowell Grade School Auditorium to watch special events which were put on for the entire district. I don't ever remember riding in busses to go the three miles to get to the Lowell Auditorium. Greenway Grade School kids were always just a "cut above" the other grade school kids. Besides being brighter, we were tougher. We usually walked the entire distance both ways. I don't remember if a teacher walked with us or not. One probably did.

We went to various high school plays, high school musicals, the yearly high school Vespers service each Christmas (this was before the ACLU got all up-tight about the mention of Jesus and God) and often touring performing groups. What I really loved was when a magician would come to entertain us. Once we even had the famous **Blackstone, the Magician**. He was able to somehow make an elephant disappear off the stage. I remember wondering if maybe he could make Norman Wright disappear. Watching him do all his tricks got me all excited. I determined then that I was going to become a *magician*. I got a catalogue from *Douglas Magic Land* in Dallas, Texas. Before all was said and done, by the time I got to be a sophomore in high school, I had purchased a bunch of magic paraphernalia. I put on some high quality, professional magic shows. I entertained most of my friends at one time or another. Bob Gore even remembers watching some of my magic shows in my living room. In his email telling me he remembers watching them, he did not say if he enjoyed them or not. I thought I was pretty good. I did not charge admission.

The Lowell Auditorium was where we held our eighth grade graduation. What excited me most about eighth grade graduation was that *Diane Carver* came back for it!!

Diane had been my friend ever since I came back to Greenway Grade School from St. Pat's. She and her family moved to Mesa at the beginning of our eighth grade year and I really missed her as did all of Diane's classmates. She was one of the few girls I knew who had a "boy's" sense of humor. I don't mean she told dirty jokes; she didn't. But, what I mean is, when she kidded with you she kidded by hitting and punching you. Diane was a tall, beautiful blond, and I did not mind being hit or punched by her at all. I was saddened that she did not go to high school with us. But, she did come back to share in our eighth grade graduation and the party after. I even danced with her a time or two that night. Diane was another "romance" that did not blossom because of her move out of Bisbee. We did correspond over the years and one weekend I rode the Greyhound bus to Mesa to go to a Mesa High School dance with her. I loved her parents. What fun people. I stayed at her house after the dance and slept on a hide-away bed. Diane's mother was embarrassed when she pulled out the bed to put sheets on. A bunch of mouse droppings fell on the floor. Diane just laughed.

NIGGER PATTY

It is repulsive for me to even write that word. However, that is what I knew her as all the time I was growing up. She was simply referred to as, "Niger Patty". Today that word, *the n word*, is demeaning to the highest degree. Society has made it that way. In pioneer days, in the 1700's and 1800's, "Niger" was a term of endearment. Mountain men and pioneers often used the word to identify one another as a companion. I do not know the origin of the word, nor do I know how the word fell into disfavor with the black people. But, what I do know is that when I was growing up in Warren, the word "Nigger" meant a black person, nothing more, nothing less. The same as "Mexican" or "bohunk". A Mexican was a person whose family members came from Mexico. A bohunk was a person whose family members came from Yugoslavia. A nigger was a person whose family members came from Africa; they were black. Nothing more, nothing less.

For as far back in my youth as I can remember, my mother always referred to her as "Nigger Patty". I can tell you with certainty that my mother was not prejudiced. She did not say *nigger* in a belittling tone at all. That was just her name, "Nigger" Patty. A case can be made I suppose, that my mother and others who referred to her as "Nigger" were not sensitive to her feelings. I don't know. I was never aware that the term caused her any discomfort until I was out of high school. When I got out of the comfortable confines of Bisbee and became familiar with many more black people, I was made aware that there was much prejudice against them as well as other minorities. I was never aware of prejudice growing up in Bisbee. I have to admit, however, that I *was* prejudiced against Norman Wright.

Hereafter, because of the high level of discomfort when the word "nigger" is used, I will refer to her as "Miss Patty". Those who knew her better than most, called her "Miss Patty". She was an institution in Bisbee while I was growing up in the '40s. Besides being the only black lady in town, or at least, the most visible one, Miss Patty was also the most *unique* in her style of dress. It appeared as though she never changed her dresses, but instead just put another one on over the one she had on. She had a "layered look" which was rather distinguishing in that she stood out in a crowd, so to speak. Miss Patty lived "up the canyon" just off Tombstone Canyon. Her dwelling place was easily visible from the street. Her humble abode was indeed *humble*. The shack she lived in was made out of boards, tin, tar paper, and cardboard. She had chickens in her yard, which I suppose she kept for eggs and an occasional meal. What is interesting, to me, is that her neighbors were all living in nice homes. Miss Patty seemed to be "squatting" on private property. I could never figure that out.

Dolly Adams, BHS,'52, had a beautiful relationship with Miss Patty:

"We got to be great talkers. Every time I saw her, I stopped and talked to her. Sometimes our conversations went on for over an hour. She rarely complained about anything or talked about anything that went on in Bisbee. She would launch into tales of her life as a young woman living on a plantation and being the maid for a young woman. She described the lavish parties, balls, usually. She helped the young woman get laced into her corsets, did her hair and make-up, and then described in detail the elegant ball gowns 'her' young woman wore, and what everyone else wore. Then she would tell me what had occurred at the ball, who was there, the menu, etc. It all sounded like something out of 'Gone with the Wind'. I never was 100% convinced that everything she told about really happened, but she included such detail, I always wondered if someone living like she did in Bisbee could have made all of it up without having experienced it first hand.

I tried to talk to her about her family, but she would immediately change the subject. I tried to talk to her about her 'house', but she changed the subject. I talked to her about the few chickens that were pecking about in her yard, asking her if they laid eggs for her, and anything else I could think of, but Miss Patty usually did the story telling.

Whenever my family baked, I took a little package of whatever it was down to her. If she wasn't in her yard, I stuck it through the gate where she would be sure to see it. She always liked that and then would launch into a description of the mouth-watering pastries they had on the plantation. All the servants got to have anything that was left over; they never served leftovers to the master's family. So she claimed to be quite a connoisseur of all the fine food the master's family had.

One time when I came with something I'd baked, she came to the gate holding an egg one of her chickens laid as if it were the finest jewel. She wanted me to have it and use it to bake something special. I argued for a bit that I didn't need it, but when I saw tears in her eyes, I realized that she wanted to give me something, too. So I took the egg home and worked like a beaver to find a recipe I had never tried before but sounded quite special. It was a poignant moment to take her the little pie I had made with her egg. She actually equated me with the chef on the plantation!

We had quite a special friendship for many years. It was a sad day when I came back to Bisbee one time and mentioned walking down to see her and found out that she had died. So many unanswered questions......"

Miss Patty was an oddity to most Bisbee youth. Her short, plump stature draped in black drew the stares of all the kids who watched her as she made her daily rounds of the grocery stores and restaurants filling her ever present pail with scraps of food. Mothers would speak to her as she passed by and would have to "shush' their children when they would ask their embarrassing questions within ear shot of Miss Patty. Miss Patty would just smile and say something nice to the children. She was never a frightening presence to the kids, just a mysterious one.

Ralph Echave, BHS '48, recalls seeing her often and she once playfully pulled on his ear after he had called her, "Nigger Patty". He remembers years later when he returned from Korea and he met Miss Patty in front of *GEM CLEANING WORKS, which* was owned by Ralph's father. Miss Patty seemed genuinely glad to see Ralph and she spoke with him for an hour or so. She told him stories of her youth and the rich family she worked for. She told him she was in their employ for years until they died. Evidentially they left her large sums of money, though she did not tell him that. Ralph recalls that when Miss Patty died, the police found over $30,000 in cash in her shack along with dozens of uncashed checks from a bank back east. Ralph concluded, "She was a splendid person and I never heard her say one bad word about anyone even when they called her 'Nigger Patty'. By the way, she was well read and quoted poetry. I loved her."

Pat Jay, BHS '54 has this memory of Miss Patty: "I will never forget Patti as she walked up and down the canyon wrapped in layers and layers of black, carrying a metal pail. Rumor said that she lived in a structure like a chicken coop and when she died a lot of money was found buried there."

Sammy Moore, BHS '56 remembers Bisbee kids dressing up like Miss Patty on Halloween nights. He recalls his parents painting his face with burnt cork as he went out on his trick or treat rounds. It was a thrill for him when his parents drove by her shack and in his childish curiosity he looked hard to see if he could see her. She was indeed an oddity.

My favorite Miss Patty story involved Mr. Wells, the grouchy bus driver. Miss Patty took the bus down the canyon every morning to downtown Bisbee where she would make her rounds doing what ever it was she did. Then in the afternoon she would get on the bus and ride back up the canyon to her shack. Often, Mr. Wells was her bus driver. Mr. Wells made Miss Patty ride in the back of the bus. That was just the way it was. Mr. Wells made his disdain for Miss Patty pretty obvious.

One day, my grandfather, Big Bobby, was waiting at the bus stop next to the post office. There were four or five others waiting with him, and when the bus stopped, four or five more got off. Miss Patty was the last one to get off. All those who were getting on and most of those who got off, plus those still on the bus, witnessed a piece of Miss Patty's humor. As she stepped down to got off, she paused, turned around and loudly said, "Oh, Mista Wells, I 'bout fogot to tell you…when you wuz up visit'n me las' evening, you done went off an plum fogot yo' hat."

As Dolly Adams has said, "…so many questions." What brought her to Bisbee? Did any of the adults reach out to her? Did any of them befriend her? How did she spend her Christmases? Did she have a family? Did she have children? Did any child call her "Grandma?" Did she have anyone to love? Miss Patty, in all probability died alone. All alone, except for her memories of the rich family who loved her so many years before. So many questions, indeed.

MY FIRST EXPERIENCE WITH COND0MS

(I'll bet that got your attention)

First of all, there were no such things as "condoms" when I was a kid. They were *rubbers* or *TROJANS*. That's all. Just *rubbers* or *TROJANS*. I suppose that I first became aware of the term *rubbers* from Bob Browder because he knew "things". He was a friend of Charlie Ryan, and Charlie really knew "things". Though I did not understand all the complexities of the uses for them, or the reasons for them, I did understand that "big kids" *always* had one in their wallet. "Just in case." Jim "Lefty" Weld and I were talking one day and we decided that since we were soon to be freshmen in Bisbee High, we needed to have a rubber in our wallet…just in case. We were in a quandary, however, because the only place we knew where to buy rubbers was at the Warren Drug Store. Bob Browder had told us that is where the "big kids" got theirs. But, the people who worked at the Warren Drug Store knew us, and we didn't want our parents to know we were carrying a rubber in our wallet. Bob had told me that my parents would really get mad if they knew I had a rubber.

The problem was solved one day when "Lefty" told me his brother, Herbie, was working at the service station in Warren on Congdon Avenue. I was surprised to learn that service stations sold rubbers. (Maybe that was what they meant by "full service".) Herbie had told "Lefty" that he could *steal* a couple of rubbers for us! We'd be in business now! And, just in time, because that weekend "Lefty" and I had a *date* with two girls on Saturday evening. Bob had told us that whenever we had a *date* we needed a rubber in our wallet, *just in case*. Now, understand that we weren't quite sure what all was involved in the *just in case* part. But, if the "big kids", and Bob Browder, said we needed a rubber in our wallet when we had a *date*, we knew we'd better have a rubber in our wallet, *just in case*. Herbie got us each a rubber. We put them in our wallets. Just in case. The moment I put mine in my wallet, the wallet immediately felt heavier. I kept my wallet in my right pocket. I felt like I was *listing* to the right.

Understand also, that 8th graders' *dates* were pretty loosely structured. Our *date* for that Saturday was arranged when we heard these two girls talking. (I will not mention the names of the girls because it may cause a misconception on the part of the readers of this book. These girls had no clue that we had rubbers in our wallets and they had no clue as to the significance of *just in case*.) The girls were talking about one of them spending the night at the other's house on Saturday evening. We overheard them talking. We couldn't help overhearing as they were almost face to face with "Lefty" and me. If we didn't know better, we'd have thought they were talking so we would hear and respond. We responded. We said we would come up to see them. They were not at all *coy* about this possibility and said, "Ok". We had a date!

On the walk to the girl's house that night, the first thing I noticed was that "Lefty" was *listing* a bit to his right, also. "Lefty" and I had a pretty deep conversation about what *tactics* we should use. Our conversation probably went something like this:

"Lefty":   Did you bring yours?

Hadley: Yep…did you?

"Lefty":   Yep.

Long pause......

Hadley:	Should we tell the girls we have them?
"Lefty":	I don't know. What do you think?
Hadley:	Don't know. Wish I would have asked Browder. He knows about these "things".

Long pause...

"Lefty":	How will we know when we should use them?
Hadley:	Browder just said we would know.

Long pause...

"Lefty":	I unrolled mine this morning.
Hadley:	How come?
"Lefty":	I just wanted to see if it is long enough.
Hadley:	Is it?
"Lefty":	It is probably too long. I think I should have told Herbie to get us "smalls".

Long pause...

Hadley:	I'm not going to mess with mine tonight! I'm gonna wait until I talk to Browder.
"Lefty":	Good idea.

Two long, collective sighs of relief...

When we got to the girl's house, we were invited in. We sat around and talked for awhile, ate some cake and ice cream, and then went outside. We walked around, talked and even held hands. "Lefty" and I felt pretty smug. We knew something the girls didn't. We were kind of prepared, just in case.

2

1950'S

SUMMER, 1948

The summer before my freshman year in high school was a great summer! I played my first season of real baseball under the tutelage of a Bisbee legend, Angel Salas. I was on the L.A. Engle Post No. 13 American Legion team, and we got to travel all over Southern Arizona playing games. We played American Legion teams in Douglas, Nogales, Tucson, and Globe-Miami. We played quite a few games against the Naco town team. Angel knew the manager of the Naco team and since they were only a few miles away, we played them often. I will never forget the first game we played against them. It was our first game of the summer; it was played in the Warren Ballpark. It was played at night under the bright lights, and **people came to watch!** You cannot imagine how scared I was. I had no idea what to expect. I don't believe any of us on the team knew what to expect. Angel had not told us much about the Naco team; just that we were going to play "Naco". What he didn't tell us was that they were a bunch of grown men! They weren't kids. They had been playing baseball for years and for most of us, we were playing baseball for the first time. We did not have Little League baseball to prepare us. Most of the Naco players did not speak English. They were very intense. They did not laugh or joke around. They were all business. It was more than a baseball game to them. It was *war!*

They clobbered us that first game. The Naco team had a pitcher they all called *"Submarino"*, which Angel told us meant, *submarine.* The guy threw underarm. The ball came at the batter from down around the pitcher's shoe tops. I had never seen anything like that in all the practices we had had.

My first at-bat was a most *forgettable* experience. I have not forgotten it! Hugh Keyes was the public address announcer. I was not at all prepared to hear my name blasted out so loudly. And, with all those people there; including many of my friends; "Now batting for Bisbee, *HADLEY HICKS.*" I just wanted to crawl

55

in a hole somewhere. How embarrassing! And, what a horrible name! That was the first time I was ever conscious of my name. I could not imagine how anyone could ever name a kid "Hadley". My dad was stuck with it and I was too. I managed to sneak into the batters' box, hopefully invisible. I knew, however, that people could see me because I heard my mother yell "Come on, Honey!" How embarrassing! Then there was *the first pitch* I ever saw in real live competition. I had no idea what to expect. *Submarino* not only threw the ball under-arm, but he threw it *fast!* And, he threw that first pitch at my head! My reflexes took over! The ball was coming fast, and it was coming at my head. I ducked as quickly as I could and bailed out of the batters' box. As I ducked, I turned my head away from the ball and in doing so, I was looking right at the catcher as he caught the ball. He had a grin on his face. The umpire said, "Strrrrike one". I had just witnessed my first *curve ball!* I saw hundreds more over the years of playing baseball. The results were usually pretty much the same. How embarrassing!

I don't remember any other pitch, either in that first at-bat or in subsequent at-bats. I know I did not swing at a pitch all night. My mother told me so when I got home. But, I made sure that I swung a bunch of times in the on-deck circle. I looked pretty good swinging in the on-deck circle.

In spite of the embarrassment of that first game, the other games that summer were fun. What I enjoyed most was the association with Angel Salas and my teammates.

I found out, to my amazement, that there were nice kids who went to other grade schools. Greenway was not the only grade school with likeable kids. On the Legion team that summer were a few of my Greenway buddies as well as guys whom I had known from a distance and some I had never seen before. My Greenway buddies on the team were Jinx Richards, Bob Vucurevich, Bud Taylor, Wayne Wolslagel, and Leon Benivediz. Joe Hillman lived in Cananea, Mexico but stayed with relatives in Warren during the summer. He was probably the oldest kid on the team. He was 6' 2" tall and our best pitcher. We lost him in mid-season as he went into the military. George Ducich took Joe's place as our #1 pitcher. George had a strong arm and I always suspected he had been one of the Horace Mann terrorists. I never confronted him about it because he was a junior in high school and frankly, I was afraid of him. I had good reason to fear him as I will explain later. Charlie Leftault and Tony Silva were on the team, and those two guys and I would become very close friends in high school. Ed Shaffer, Leo Pavlovich, Henry Kendricks, Ron Haynes, Benny Parra, Lou Prince, and a Tucson native, Larry Hart were the remainder of the team. Angel had Jack "The Rock" Miller, and Billy Murray as part time assistant coaches.

Larry Hart went to Amphitheater High School in Tucson but lived with his mother in Bisbee during the summers. Larry was a very good baseball player and had much more experience than most of us. He led our team in hitting and was a tremendous hustler. Unfortunately, when we played in the district Legion tournament to qualify for advancement to the state tournament, we were shocked to find out that Larry would be ineligible. He was not a resident of Bisbee. Angel had to tell Larry he was ineligible just before our team picture was taken. I have the picture in my scrapbook, and you can tell Larry had been crying. He was a real competitor and had become very close to all of us. We hated to lose him.

We opened the district tournament at home in the friendly confines of Warren Ballpark against the very strong Tucson Legion team. Hugh Keyes reported in the Bisbee Daily Review that that game drew one hundred thirty paying fans, more than most of the Bisbee-Douglas *Javelinas* games. The Tucson team had been running roughshod over opponents all summer, including a sound thrashing of us just several weeks earlier. They were loaded. The Tucson line-up included Bennie Rincon, Ron Nicely, Hal Preston, Ed Marques, Jim Starkey, Eddie Gentry, and a young pitcher named Don Bacon. With one exception, these guys would lead Tucson High School to several state championships and later they would star for the University of Arizona. The one exception was arguably the best player of the bunch, Don Bacon. Bacon was a big strong kid who could throw bb's! He was considered a *can't miss* future professional. When he wasn't pitching, Bacon played the outfield. He was a power hitter. Sadly, he was killed in an automobile accident a year later.

Angel Salas had boldly predicted in the Bisbee Daily Review that "his young kids" would win the tournament. We had been improving with each game. We were gaining confidence. In his quiet, low key way, Angel was a great motivator. We went into our first game of the tournament really believing we could beat Tucson. We didn't. They beat us 4-3 in a very hard fought and well-played game. Hugh Keyes reported in The Bisbee Daily Review that the game was a much better game than any the *Javelinas* had played that summer! It was a heart breaker to lose. The score was knotted 3-3 until the 8th inning when Tucson pushed across the winning run. George Ducich pitched a great game and led us in hitting with two key hits. Jim Starkey, Tucson's ace, limited us to three hits. Don Bacon who was playing right field drove in the winning Tucson run. The Tucson team went on to win the district tournament and eventually won the state tournament.

Watching the game that night were several representatives of the Anaheim California Invitational Baseball Tournament. They were so impressed with the Bisbee Legion team's hustle and never-say-quit attitude that they extended an invitation to Angel Salas to bring his team to Anaheim to play in their seventy-three team tournament. What a thrill that would have been to play in a tournament in Anaheim, California with other teams from across the United States. We could not participate as the insurance coverage the Legion Post had on us would not cover our out-of-state trip. We were very disappointed.

FINALLY, A WHITE MOUNTAIN CAMPING TRIP

My parents had been promising me a camping trip to the White Mountains ever since my first grade year when the last camping trip had been cut short due to my illness. When the Legion baseball season was over, dad and mom packed the car and loaded Jinx and me in the back seat and we took off for beautiful Luna Lake in the White Mountains. I had talked dad and mom into letting me take Jinx since he and I were good buddies. We had a blast! Dad taught Jinx and me how to fish and clean what we caught. We did not *camp* in the true sense of the word because we rented a cabin complete with electricity and running water. But we were in the mountains on the shores of Luna Lake. We stayed a week, and Jinx and I got to know every foot of the lake's shoreline. We even got to know some of the other campers and one young couple was especially nice to us. Once, when Jinx and I were talking to them, they asked us to stay for hot dogs. They were true campers. They were in a tent and cooked over a campfire. We found out they were on their honeymoon. I thought that would be a neat way to spend a honeymoon. It appeared very romantic.

Jinx and I messed around quite a bit that week. When we weren't fishing we were exploring all the many trails that meandered through the woods. We spent a lot of time around the camp grocery store. I bought my first pocketknife there and immediately got caught carving my initials in the store's front porch railing. Since there were many other initials already carved there, I did not get in too much trouble. Jinx and I both carved our names and initials in trees and other wooden objects all that week. Lee Bodenhamer, a Bisbee lawyer, told me several years later that he and his family stayed in the same cabin we had stayed in and he saw "Hadley Hicks" carved in a semi-circle around the inside of the toilet seat in the cabin. Every time he would see me for years after, he would say, "Haaadley Hicks" while his arm made a semi-circular motion.

On the way home, Jinx and I realized that in just a few days we would be in **high school.** That was kind of scary. Jinx wasn't sure he was going out for football because the guys were so big. He told me I probably shouldn't go out either. He said my legs were not big enough. I did have skinny legs. Coach Waldo Dicus and Al Ridgway had both talked to my dad about letting me play football before they knew I did not have TB. After I got the clean bill of health from the Tucson doctors, it was a "done deal". I would be going out for football.

What occupied most of our conversation on the way back home from the White Mountains was not football. It was not even about all the new girls we were going to meet. What concerned us the most was the dreaded *FRESHMEN INITIATION!!*

BISBEE HIGH SCHOOL, AT LONG LAST

We had heard rumors for years about what we could expect our first day when we got to be freshmen. We had heard firsthand stories about freshmen getting de-pantsed and then having their pants strung up the flagpole. We had been advised to make sure we had on underwear the first day of school. Our principal, Mr. Wilcox, had sent letters to all parents of incoming freshmen and advised them to make sure the boys wore old clothes and a plain white tee shirt. His letter did not advise regarding underwear as pantsing was not under the guise of legitimate initiation. Only what happened inside the school building was authorized by Mr. Wilcox. It was what happened *outside* that had me worried. My friend, Myrle Luna, BHS '50 had been a patient of my dad's for a few years and had a solution for me, possibly. Since Myrle and I were going to be teammates on the football team that year (Myrle was going to be a junior), he said he would try to help me avoid being de-pants. He couldn't help me once we got inside, but maybe he could be of assistance outside. Most of the new freshmen would be met by some upper-classmen as they walked on to the school premises. Some were even met at the several bus stops in downtown Bisbee and escorted to school. It was very difficult to avoid an upper-classman. I was planning to ride most days with my dad since his office was in down town Bisbee. I would be let off on Subway Street where my dad parked behind his office. However, that was very risky on the first day. Several upper-classmen would be sure to be waiting as that was near the main downtown bus stop. Dad would not be of any help because his philosophy was, "You are in high school now. You have to learn how to take it!" What Myrle told me to do was to have dad let me off in Lowell near Junction and Erie streets and he would pick me up there. I would then lie down in the back seat of his car and ride to school hidden from view. Myrle made me promise not to tell any of my buddies what he was doing as he was afraid he would get in trouble with the seniors. So that is what we did. And, I got away with it! I stayed hidden in the back seat of his car even after he parked it in the sparsely occupied parking lot. Only five or six students drove cars to school and counting the teachers' cars there were fewer than fifteen cars in the entire parking lot. Myrle had parked as close to the school building as possible and he told me to stay down until I heard the bell ring. When I heard it, I was to get out of his car as fast as possible and run down the ramp to the auto shop area. Myrle said that only Mr. Dickey, the auto shop teacher, would be there before class and he wouldn't tell on me. That is what I did, and I got to my homeroom with my pants on. Some of my buddies were not so lucky. Jinx, Jim Baker, Ron Brooks, and "Happy" Wolfe were de-pantsed and a few others whom I did not know at the time. Mr. Roy Coon, our school custodian was on hand to help the semi-naked freshmen get their pants down from the flagpole. I was worried about lunch hour, but the worst thing we had to do was try to catch egg-yolks in our mouths as the eggs were cracked open from a second story window. After that first day, I knew that the worst was over. I didn't have to worry about any other initiation until May when the annual Lettermen's Club picnic was held. I had heard about it, but it was so far away that I didn't give it much thought. Besides there was no guarantee that I would even earn a varsity letter.

BISBEE HIGH FOOTBALL, 1948

What impressed me the most about my first days at practice was how **big** they were! They were huge, and Norman Wright was not even on the team. Some of the biggest ones were Bill Deen who later played several years at the UofA, George McGregor, Don DeFord, Dave Andrews, and Cecil Nelson, to name just a few. All these guys were over six feet tall and weighed two hundred lbs. or better. A couple of times during those first few days, I caught myself thinking that maybe Jinx was right. Maybe my legs were too small for "big time" football. This was not Greenway Grade School any longer. This was Bisbee *Puma* football and they were big!

I soon learned a lesson I never forgot. It was a lesson on *team unity*. *They* soon became *we!* All those upper-classmen made all of us "rookies" feel very much a part of the team! Over my four years of football at BHS I learned why there were no "prima donnas" on the team. Coach Dicus would not allow it! He insisted that we all treat each other with respect and dignity. The lowest freshman was made to feel that he was a valuable asset to the team. Coach Dicus was a very special man and was a huge influence on the lives of many a BHS student.

I was so blessed to have been a part of such a great bunch of guys my first year at BHS. Neil Phillips comes to mind immediately. Through a series of mishaps, which I will delineate later, I became the starting quarterback after the third game and in all honesty, I felt much pressure. Neil would always be there to give me encouragement. I had to wear thick rubber-framed glasses because I had very poor eyesight and Neil would kid me and call me "Barney Google". He would sing, "There is old Barney Google with the goo, goo, googly eyes." Neil broke a lot of tension at practices and in the games with his sense of humor. Joe Quintenares, no doubt one of the toughest defensive backs to ever wear the Red and Gray, had a way of smiling at me and without a word, let me know that all was "ok". Jimmy Hallsted, who was our quarterback and leader until he broke his ankle in the second game, was always there to give me encouragement. Not only did he encourage me, but he was a huge morale booster to the team at every practice. He never missed a practice after his injury. He stood on crutches in each huddle and told me what play to call and how to run it. He became an unofficial assistant coach. I remember Jerry Ballard and Doug Hall being there with encouraging words when needed. No one on the team ever, to my knowledge, bemoaned the fact that a skinny freshman had to step in and play quarterback. I got nothing but encouragement. I have neglected to mention the encouragement the coaches gave me. Besides Coach Dicus, Al Ridgway, Fuzzy Warren and Jack "The Rock" Miller were in my corner at every turn.

It was only by default that I became the starting quarterback. Jimmy Hallsted was our starter until he broke his ankle; second string quarterback Tony Silva was also hurt in one of our early practices. That left me as the only available quarter back. In spite of all the injuries we did fairly well. We won some and we lost some. However, with the upcoming Turkey Day Game against Douglas, things didn't look too good for us. Douglas was undefeated and had soundly beaten some of the bigger schools in Arizona and even whipped Texas powerhouse, Bowie High of El Paso. The game was to be played on the *Bulldogs* home turf where DHS had not lost in **3 years!** This was to be my first taste of what is was like to play in *the Big Game!*

BISBEE-25 DOUGLAS-0

This game ranks up there with the all-time great upsets in Bisbee High football history. It ranks right up there with the *Puma's* stunning, come from behind win over Douglas in 1961.

Gib Dawson led the Douglas *Bulldogs* this year and was one of Arizona's all time great running backs. After graduating from DHS, Dawson went to the University of Texas and became an all-American his senior year. He even had a brief fling with the pros.

However, on November 26, 1948, Gib Dawson was reduced to an ordinary mortal, gaining a total of 1 yard rushing before he was forced out of the game on a jarring tackle by Bill "Tex" Howard in the second quarter. Bill Howard was the meanest, toughest high school player imaginable. He didn't just "tackle" Dawson, he "buried" him! The *Pumas* were not to be denied. Jim Hallsted had recovered from his broken ankle and had been moved to halfback. He replaced Red Hopson who had been injured a few weeks before. Jim, behind the blocking of the powerful Puma line, shredded the Douglas line at will, gaining over 100 yards. Jerry Ballard, Joe Q. and, Doug Hall also had a number of fine runs. The game was a "no contest" right from the first quarter when Jerry Ballard blocked a Dawson punt in the Douglas end zone. The *Pumas* were called for roughing the punter on the play, but the *Pumas'* aggression and desire sent a loud message to Douglas that we had come to the game hungry! Douglas never saw the light of day and to rub salt in their wounds, Coach Dicus put the injured Red Hopson in with the clock ticking off the final seconds and the *Pumas* leading 18-0. The ball was on the Douglas 7-yard line. Hopson got the call, showed his speed and scored standing up. Final score, BHS-25, DHS-0.

The win was especially sweet for Coach Fuzzy Warren. Fuzzy had coached and taught at Douglas High School quite a few years before. We never knew why he was fired, but we knew he carried much bitterness over the whole incident. Douglas High's loss of Fuzzy was definitely Bisbee High's gain! As our fans left the Douglas parking lot, the noise was deafening. Cars honking, bells clanging, Bisbee fans counting off the score and right in the middle of all the celebration was the *Puma* team bus driven by an exuberant Fuzzy Warren. Fuzzy was leaning on the bus's horn. He was laughing and crying at the same time. He was singing "Onward Bisbee" at the top of his very hoarse voice. He had his window open and every time we passed some disgruntled Douglas fans, Fuzzy would stick his head out the window and yell, **"Hey! Which one was Dawson?"** What a sweet win!! We lived with it for a long time.

The entire school was still flying high on Monday. We had a special pep rally and our beautiful majorette, Bernice Chunn led the band is several loud renditions of *Onward Bisbee* and *Cheer, Cheer for old Bisbee High.* We had speeches from Coach Dicus, our principal, Mr. C.W. Wilcox, and the superintendent of schools, Mr. Chet Hall. Mr. Hall was my football teammate, Doug Hall's dad. That Friday, we had a very much anticipated pep assembly; the Douglas High School *Bulldog's* three team captains, all-stater Gib Dawson, quarterback John Stewart, and lineman David Rabago, came to the assembly along with their coach, Otis Coffee. They presented us with the "Copper Pick". Douglas had won the 1947 game and, therefore, the "Copper Pick" had been in Douglas' trophy case ever since. The "Copper Pick" was at last back where **it belonged!** I was impressed with the brief speeches that were given by the DHS contingent. Coach Coffee complimented Coach Dicus and the *Pumas* for playing such an inspired game, and Gib Dawson, in his very low-key manner, told us we were the better team that day (duhh!). The *Puma* captains, Bill Deen, Jimmy Hallsted and Joe Q. accepted the "Copper Pick" on behalf of the entire school. I am proud to say that the Bisbee High student body showed a lot of class at the assembly. We were most polite hosts and did not "boo" or "hiss" the Douglas group. Coach Dicus always insisted that the Bisbee High students exhibit good sportsmanship. We even gave Gib Dawson a very loud and sincere reception when Jim Hallsted, our student body president, introduced him. He was a great football player, we respected him very much, and we were certainly glad that he was graduating.

MOTHER

It was early in my freshman year that I became very conscious of the fact that my mother was an alcoholic. It was not coincidentally that at the same time I became very much aware of my peers. I had made many new friends on the football team and in the halls of BHS. My peers became more and more important to me. I wanted so very much to be accepted and well liked. I tried very hard to please my peers. I loved my mother and father and so wanted to share my new friends with them. Often I would get a ride home with one of my football teammates after practice, and I wanted to invite him in for a Coke. But, I didn't dare. I was scared to death that when I walked in the house I would find mother either passed out on the floor, or at a high level of intoxication. Mother spent most days drinking with some of her many friends and I never knew until I walked in the house just what condition she would be in.

This was the fear I faced after that memorable upset of Douglas on Thanksgiving Day in 1948. Mother was so excited after the game that at our family Thanksgiving dinner she announced that she was going to have the entire team and coaches over to our house for a taco dinner. Mother was a terrific cook of Mexican food. Her specialty was tacos and she loved nothing better than preparing a huge batch of them. Both of Mother's arms bore ugly scars from the splattered grease that she had accumulated over the years from cooking tacos. It took mother most of an afternoon to prepare and cook all the tacos, and it was not at all uncommon for her to down a couple six-packs of Coors in the process.

When Mother was drunk, or "tight" as Dad called it, she became melancholy and would cry at the slightest provocation. Mother was always a very loving person and when she had been drinking, she became much more demonstrative and would hug everyone in sight. That, of course, added to my discomfort and embarrassment. Her speech was slurred and her balance very unsteady. She was a typical *happy drunk.*

The team taco dinner was planned for the Friday evening after the Douglas game and before basketball games began. I was a nervous wreck all that day. I could not concentrate in class, and I was moody and surly around my friends. I did not want to have the whole team and coaches over that evening for fear that Mother would embarrass me and everyone would know she was a drunk. I feared the worse when I got home from school. And my fears were realized! Mother was drunk. I went into my bedroom and cried. I just knew the evening would be horrible and that all my buddies would laugh at her drunkenness.

However, I did not fully realize the compassion and understanding of Coach Waldo Dicus and his wonderful wife, Fran. They were the first ones to get there that night; probably a half-hour before the starting time. Fran immediately went into the kitchen to help Mother with the final preparations. When the team and other coaches started arriving, Coach Dicus, in his unique manner, took charge of everything. He assigned a player or two to carry in the tub of iced sodas. Coaches' Fuzzy Warren and Al Ridgway served the tacos. Mrs. Wilma Warren and Mrs. Jane Ridgway got Mother to come in the living room and sit down where she was treated like a queen. Mother was in her glory. She laughed, talked, and cried. All my buddies seemed not at all bothered by the fact that she was obviously drunk. They were too busy eating tacos and having a good time. The logistics of the entire evening went completely over my head. All I knew was that I was not embarrassed and that my buddies had a good time. It was not until years later that I realized what had happened. Every year for four years, at the end of every season, Mother cooked a huge taco dinner. I was a nervous wreck at every one of them. And at every one of them, my coaches and their wives saw to it that everything went smoothly. Did they know just how worried, frightened, and embarrassed I was? I don't know if they understood my concerns or not. But, I do know they were there for me when I needed comfort and assurance.

You might be wondering where my father was; just how he fit in to this picture. In public Dad was very quiet. For the most part he just kind of blended in with all the others and was a pleasant conversationalist. He knew not to try to help Mother as she would tell him in no uncertain terms to leave her alone and to get out of the way. Mother was not a *happy drunk* around Dad. Dad and Mother did not get along. Many more times than I can count, I cried myself to sleep over their knock down fights after one of Mother's days of drinking with her friends.

"NACO, NO MAS"

Naco, no mas for many of us was the first Mexican phrase we learned. I first heard that phrase spoken when I was a little kid and was in the back seat of the family vehicle. When we stopped at the Naco, Sonora inspection station to cross over into Mexico, the driver of the vehicle, usually my mother or one of my uncles, would roll down the window and simply say to the on-duty inspector, "Naco, no mas". We would get a bored look in return, accompanied by a rote, "Muy bien. Buenos dias", and a lethargic wave of the inspector's arm. We could then proceed into Naco, Sonora, Mexico, the favorite vacation spot of a significant number of Bisbee folks. Translated loosely, and as understood by the uniformed inspectors, the term "Naco, no mas", if spoken by an adult during the hours of 10:00 am until 5:00 p.m. meant, "We are going shopping in your quaint little village and we will significantly add to your economy." The inspectors would simply nod and say, "Muy bien. Buenos dias", and wave the car through. "Naco, no mas." spoken anytime, by anybody, after 5:00 p.m., was understood to mean, "We are going into Naco to spend some gringo money. We will buy some curios, some liquor, and maybe visit a bar and whore house or two. If you leave us alone, we will only make some noise, but will not cause trouble. If we do cause trouble, we understand that we will spend the night in your cockroach infested jail and will be released in the morning for a small fee."

Wally Quayle, BHS '53 was an exception to the above scenario. Any time Wally went through, day or night, he was greeted by the inspector with, "Hey, Wally. Que' dices? Como esta'?" It was rumored at the time that Wally had been granted the only valid credit card Naco Mayor, Al Rochin BHS '53 had ever issued. Naco loved Wally and Wally loved Naco. As he said, "Where else could you go and dance to a ten member band, eat frijoles and tacos with meat and potatoes? Where else could you get mariachis to sing at your table and encourage you to sing along with them…all this and still come home with change in your pocket!?" It is said that Wally was never in jail over night. His credit card was good under any circumstance.

Paul "Casper the Ghost" Renner, BHS '56 relates a typical evening on the town in Naco:

"As a rule, we had a crowd, Ron Sanders, Ted Sorich, Ken Allen, George Hershey and others. We thought we were all pretty bad, and after a brew or two, we could take on the world. One night we were walking down the street going to 'Chacho's' and pretty much forcing everyone off the sidewalk, 'cause as I said, we were bad! Well, we saw a bunch of Mexican kids about our age coming up the sidewalk towards us. We more or less forced them off the sidewalk, and we said in passing, 'Yah, us gringos are going to 'Chacho's' to get barracho and we'll see you later!' We were *bad!*

About midnight, here they came! Twenty of them! We thought, 'Oh, oh, here it comes!' They had no more walked in looking for us, than right behind them walked in twenty miners from Bisbee who had come down for a nightcap after the P.M. shift. What a sight for bleary eyes! They sure saved our sorry rear ends!"

Dale Hancock, BHS '57 knew a lot about Naco second-hand. He was never personally involved, he says. He heard stories of high-class establishments such as the "The White House" (*Casa Blanca*) where the *girls* wore formals. He was told that the real danger in going to Naco was that one might run into a friend of your dad's who would tell on you. Dale's only venture to Naco, he says, occurred after the last basketball game in 1957 against Casa Grande at Casa Grande. When the team got home in the wee hours of the morning, most of them and whatever girls they could round up at that time of morning, all piled into cars and headed for Naco. The boys wanted to properly introduce Dale to the nightlife of Naco and **all** that entailed. They went to *The Casa Blanca*, ordered drinks and looked around to see if any of the "young ladies" were available. The management of this fine establishment had learned over the years that they should always operate on a "pay in advance" philosophy. When Dale's buddies were told to pay up, they knew they would have to postpone Dale's initiation. The whole group could only come up with about 50 cents. They were unceremoniously escorted to the door; they left with their honor and Dale's innocence, still intact.

Ron Sanders, BHS '56 has a most honest appraisal of his memory of Naco. Ron even remembers the screeching of peacocks at night near the Calaboose (jail). He can name the whorehouses, though his account does not include the layout of the interior of any of them. He recalls the Casa Blanca, The Blue Moon (*Luna Azul*), The Crystal, The Rainbow, and the previously mentioned *Chachos*, which had a brief period of notoriety, from 1955–1958. Ron had a pretty good memory, but Jimmy Elkins, BHS '57 holds the modern record of naming all **six** of the whorehouses in alphabetical order, along with their licensing dates and owners' names.

Tom Vercellino, BHS '55 remembers a BHS student named Marcos Siqueros who was from "across the line". Marcos' mother was the owner of The White House. He was a living testimony to the value of gringo money to the economy of Naco. Marcos always dressed very classy and drove new white Studebakers to school.

The Joe Louis Club was another of the whore houses Tom remembers others talking about. His understanding of it is that it was located east past the Naco Bull Ring.

Elaine (Jay) Corcoran, BHS '51 gleefully remembers several of her trips to Naco. "A group of us, boys and girls, would pile in a car and go to Naco to harass the girls at the Blue Moon and other such establishments (BHS coeds were too refined and cultured to call them "whores" and "whore houses". hh). As we neared the targeted establishment, we girls would lie down on the floor of the car where we couldn't be seen. When we pulled up in front, the boys would whistle and call the girls over to the car. They came eagerly. When they saw us on the floor in the back, they got furious and said something in Spanish that probably was not, "Have a nice evening." We were all giggling as we sped off."

Wanda (Talley) Owens, BHS '52 was much more progressive and bold in her dealings with the whores in Naco: "Frankie Ann (Holland) Windsor and I would tuck our hair under ball caps and drive up to the front of the White House or the Blue Moon. We mostly wanted to check out the cars to see who was there and what was what. I guess you could say we were nosey. Yep! Most definitely, we *were* nosey. After approaching the car, the 'worker bees' made some dreadful suggestions to us. Some, I believe, were physically impossible. We put the pedal to the metal and shot out of there, scared but giggling hysterically. Whose cars did we see? Well, you might ask, but we're not telling."

Pat Jay, BHS '54, Elaine's sister, adds her two bits worth to this intellectually stimulating discussion of the nightlife of Naco. She remembers Marcos Sequires being well dressed, but to Pat's recollection, Marcos drove large white *Caddies*, not Studebakers. According to her, Marcos got married and was never seen at BHS after that.

Pat remembers Alfred Rochin's mom owning a "lovely curio shop and outside there was a large patio that at night was transformed into a brightly lit dance floor where all of us could dance and get a shot of Tequila for fifteen cents." Wally Quayle, BHS '53 is also tucked way back in Pat's memory bank. Pat tells of the time in her "sheltered life" when she rode in Wally's car traveling one hundred miles an hour down Purdy's Lane on their way to Naco. Seems Wally was in a hurry to get to Naco before midnight when his credit card expired.

My own personal experience in Naco while I was in high school was very mild compared to some of these aforementioned ones. One evening when Charlie Leftault BHS, '50, Louise Hendricks BHS '51, Mary Louise Stensrud BHS '51, and I were double dating we built up enough courage to "cross the line". We risked having Coach Waldo Dicus hear that we had gone to Naco. Charlie was as fearful of Coach Dicus as I was. We drove past several of the whorehouses and found out that the whores who were gathered in front all yelled the same thing at us as we drove past. We never could determine what it was they said. It sounded something like, "tufeeftyplz." There was definitely a language barrier.

"WHO WAS STUCK?"

I am not sure how the Arizona Education Department funded the public schools during the 1950's, but if Bisbee High School was paid on its *average daily attendance* (ADA), Wallace's Pool Hall caused BHS to lose money! On any given school day a third of the Bisbee High male population could be found gathered around the green felt pool/snooker tables at Wallace's. It was indeed "the mecca of traditional pool halls and a Bisbee tradition." as Dale Hancock, BHS '57 has said.

Year after year, the ritual was the same. The winner at any table would loudly bang his pool cue on the floor, which was the signal for Mr. Terrin, the *racker,* to shuffle over to the table and demand, "Who was stuck?" The loser would then pay for the game and Mr. Terrin would collect the twenty five-cent game fee and rack the balls for the next game. Mr. Terrin was a very stern man who suffered from cerebral palsy. He was all business. The loser paid immediately or else Mr. Terrin would bang the triangular rack on the table without saying another word. Most boys who went through Bisbee High School were "stuck" at one time or another. All of us got "stuck" that is, except for **Richie Maddern** BHS, '51. Richie was the resident *shark.* He "hustled" more victims than *Paul Newman.* Richie **never** lost. Richie spent every assigned study hall period at Wallace's. It is one of the mysteries in the history of Bisbee High; just how did Richie manage to get down the hill to Wallace's, play a game of "8-Ball", and get back up the hill in time for his next class?

Unlike Paul Newman, Richie did not have his own personalized pool cue. He used whichever cue was available at any given time; short, long, straight, crooked, tip on or off, it did not matter to Richie. He could "run the table" at will. Once, it is reported, he challenged "the house" and beat all takers while playing *left handed.* The first and only time I ever played Richie I was suckered into betting a dime. Richie let me break (and I thought he was being nice to me!) and then I sat down. Richie ran the table. I got "stuck". I was smart enough to realize that I was nowhere close to his skill and I never played him again. I couldn't afford to. Richie always played for money.

Richie had lost an eye in a child hood accident, and I do believe that aided him in his unerring sighting in the line between the cue ball and the target ball. Having only one eye to sight in with was a definite asset.

Richie's dominance of the pool halls in southern Arizona was legendary. A close second to Richie in pool expertise was "Cuzzie" Trestrail, BHS '51. The two of them would venture at times to the pool halls in Tombstone, Douglas, Benson and Willcox. They were a great team! Often they would come home from one of their outside ventures with $40.00–$50.00 in change…*each!* Once while visiting The Willcox Pool and Billiards Emporium on a Saturday afternoon, Richie and "Cuzzie" were involved in a two out of three match. It seems that a self-proclaimed pool shark from El Paso traveling through Wilcox on his way to Tucson commented that he never saw an Arizona shark that a Texas shark couldn't beat. Richie and Cuzzie had been watching him for an hour or so, and he had beaten everyone he had played. He was good. But, he was not a *killer.* Often when he had an opponent down, the Texan would try a trick shot or a more difficult shot than was needed. He did not "go for the jugular." The Texan was a softy, a "nice" guy who would tend to take it easy on his opponent. Richie winked at "Cuzzie" and slightly nodded his head. "Cuzzie" knew the sign. He walked over to the Texan and said rather softly, "Sir, my buddy and I would like to take you on. Two out of three. If you are tired we'll come back in an hour or so. Give you a chance to rest up." The Texan took the bait. "Why, friend, I am just getting warmed up! Which one of you do I wup first?" Here is where "Cuzzie" really laid it on. He said very quietly, "Sir, my friend only has one eye as you can see. That causes him great difficulty in sighting in and focusing as you can imagine. So, if you wouldn't mind, you play him first. But, since he is handicapped, would you let him call the game and *let him break.*" The Texan couldn't believe what he heard! The player who breaks is often at a disadvantage since the second shooter would have the well-dispersed balls to play. He gladly agreed to the terms. Richie called "rotation" and prepared to break. The Texan was licking his chops, just waiting his chance to possibly run the table. Rotation is the simplest game of pool for a good player to run the table. Being a big spender from El Paso, he put a dollar bill in the side pocket. Richie feigned reluctance at such high stakes. But, finally he put a dollar bill in the opposite pocket. Then, taking an unusually long time to line up his shot for the break, Richie appeared uncertain and not at all confident. The Texan was smiling. Most of the crowd, which had gathered, had seen the two Bisbee sharks before. They, too, smiled. Richie shot. It appeared as though he mis-hit the cue ball. The ball was barely moving towards the one-ball at the apex of the triangle of balls. It had a weird spin on it. The cue-ball barely nudged the one-ball and spun slowly down and around to the back of the pack. The Texan was left with an impossible shot. In order to hit the one ball, he had to try to bank the cue ball off the back cushion, down to the front cushion, and up to the one-ball. He banked the shot and being a good pool player, he did hit the one-ball. The force with which he had to shoot the ball scattered the rest of the balls. In so doing, the Texan left Richie with an open shot at the one-ball. Richie pocketed the one-ball and left himself in good position to pocket the two-ball……and the three-ball…and the four-ball…and the five-ball, etc, etc, etc. Game over. Richie pocketed the two dollars and said, "Your turn, 'Cuzzie'." Since Richie won, "Cuzzie" got to call the game and the Texan had to break. "Cuzzie" called "rotation". The Texan broke and did not pocket a ball. "Cuzzie" did. The Texan did give "Cuzzie" a better game than he gave Richie. With sweat on his brow, he managed to make two balls. "Cuzzie" made all the rest.

Another day, another pocket full of change, plus two dollars each from the nice Texan.

COURAGE ON WHEELS. HUGH KEYES

In 1935, 13 year old Hugh Keyes was playing in a pickup baseball game in the Warren Ballpark. It was to be the last game Hugh ever played. The high fly ball Hugh chased was to be the last play he would ever actively be involved in. As Hugh ran after the ball, he slipped on the wet grass and as he fell, the ball hit him solidly in the jaw and his head hit the ground with a sickening *thud*. It was obvious to all that witnessed the accident that Hugh was badly hurt. He lay on the outfield grass unconscious. Blood was oozing from his nostrils and ears. Hugh was rushed to the Copper Queen Hospital where he was discovered to have a serious concussion and a broken jaw. Hugh spent many weeks in the hospital in critical condition and even after being dismissed it was obvious that he was not recovering as quickly as he should have. Five weeks after Hugh's accident he was diagnosed with the dreaded disease **polio!** The doctors believed that somehow Hugh's accident had brought on the disease. Hugh would never walk again. He would never realize his dream of becoming a professional baseball player. However, Hugh had a courageous heart. He would achieve much, much *more* than what he ever dreamed!

This is how Hugh described those early months after his accident: "When I first contacted polio, no one knew what was wrong with me. They all just stood by the bed and shook their heads. When the doctors finally decided I had polio, and they didn't know it was polio until I was paralyzed, they gave me up for dead. But, I fooled the hell out of them and lived!" And live he did! Hugh Keyes lived life to the fullest for thirty-two very meaningful, productive and fun-filled years. However, it was not always with a smile on his face and a heart full of love for his fellow man. Early on, Hugh was bitter. Like so many that are faced with life's seemingly unconquerable challenges, Hugh wanted to give up. He suffered from bouts with depression and self-pity. It was an unnamed coach who gave Hugh the impetus to make the most of a bad situation. Here is how Hugh tells of that incident: "I was watching the American Legion baseball team work out right after I got out of the hospital and I was feeling remorseful because I knew that I would never play again. I was feeling sorry for myself, when the coach came up and shoved the scorebook into my hands and told me to keep the score. I tried to complain and tell him I couldn't. Instead of feeling sorry for me, he said, 'What are you going to do, just sit in that wheelchair all your life?' and after a few innings, I realized that I was having almost as much fun keeping the score as I once had playing.

"I never felt sorry for myself after that, and by being scorekeeper it gave me an active part in the game and I love it."

Hugh went on to Bisbee High School and the love and concern of his buddies and the dedicated teachers he encountered saw to it that his life in the wheelchair was not the handicap it could have been. Hugh's Spanish teacher, Ester Louise Smith was one of his biggest sources of strength. She was a stern and demanding teacher. She did not give Hugh the satisfaction of letting him take the easy way out. She demanded excellence from him just as she did from all her students. Miss Smith had this to say about Hugh: "He will always be to me an example of what can be done in spite of a great physical handicap. His record should make those of us without such disadvantages stop to evaluate our achievements."

Another dedicated BHS teacher, Irene Shepherd, was there for Hugh when he needed encouragement. "Hugh was in my algebra class that met just before the noon hour," Miss Shepherd said. "He generally spent lunch period in my room, ate his lunch there, talked with other students, or sometimes worked on his lessons. We often talked of his plans for college and for life. He was very interested in everything at school, his special interest, even then, being athletics. I think his years at BHS were busy and happy ones." It was those busy and happy years at Bisbee High, which fortified in Hugh's heart the desire to achieve excellence. Miss Shepherd had many intense talks with Hugh about his future. She encouraged him to pursue his dream of becoming a journalist. She encouraged him to continue his involvement in athletics via the path of writing. Hugh graduated from BHS and enrolled in The University of Arizona. His toughest challenge was before him.

The school administration at The University of Arizona tried to persuade him against going to the school because of the lack of facilities for a wheelchair. However, what the administration did not understand was Hugh's heart and the hearts of his many buddies. They did not understand "the Bisbee bond" that was cemented during his days at Bisbee High School. Lou Pavlovich, a 1941 graduate of Bisbee High and perhaps Hugh's closest friend, had also enrolled at The UofA. I had the good fortune of riding with Lou from Tucson to attend Hugh's funeral in Bisbee in May of 1954. Lou shed much light on Hugh's early years at The UofA. "I know from first hand knowledge, that it was a terrific struggle for Hugh to make the grade at the university. The casualty rate at the UofA was high enough, considering studies alone. Hoping to go through the school in a wheel chair was tougher, yet.

"Early in his freshman year, Hugh was naturally disheartened. He was lonely, homesick, and worried about making good. He was on the verge of going back home. But a group of his Bisbee friends realized this, and knowing Hugh's intense pride and aggressiveness, used a bit of psychology. They called it a 'challenge' for Hugh, and in so many words, put a chip on Hugh's shoulder. Hugh Keyes, who never ran from a challenge in his life, suddenly forgot about quitting school, and he went on to graduate." In his sophomore year at the UofA, Hugh was enrolled in a geology class that made a field trip to Colossal Cave just outside Tucson. The professor tried to talk Hugh out of making the trip. It would be too demanding for one in a wheelchair, Hugh was told. The professor had misjudged Hugh's courage and heart. He misjudged the Bisbee bond that was evidenced by some of Hugh's Bisbee buddies who went with him that day to Colossal Cave. Hugh became the first invalid in a wheelchair to negotiate the dark recesses of Colossal Cave. Hugh was aided at every turn by Lou Pavlovich, Max Spilsbury, and his other Bisbee buddies.

Lou told me one humorous story that epitomizes Hugh's *warrior's heart.* One evening after a fraternity party where Hugh and Lou had consumed a few adult beverages, they ended up in a Tucson park where the party was to continue. As often happens in these settings, an argument broke out which ended up with a fight between rival fraternities. Though Hugh was confined to his wheelchair, he nevertheless participated in the fight as best as he could. Lou says that all through the fight, Hugh kept yelling, "Knock 'em down, Lou, and I'll roll over them!"

Lou continues his testimony of Hugh's desire. "This is just one example of the attitude that pushed Hugh into the higher strata of greatness. If he wanted something, he squared his jaw and with sheer perseverance achieved his goal. Because a man like this was so good, so vital, for the community, his loss will be tremendous. Hugh was a great man."

Hugh's contribution to the community of Bisbee and Bisbee High School in particular would be hard to measure in just words alone. His involvement in the community would take many pages to describe. His involvement in the life of many Bisbee High students *cannot* be adequately written about. His constant companions were the many BHS students he befriended. Each of them could write volumes about their love for Hugh. More importantly, they could each write volumes about the impact Hugh made on their lives.

Margaret "Sissy" Thomas who owned the Warren Bowling Lanes, one of Hugh's favorite "hang outs", remembers Hugh fondly. She wrote the following at the time of his death: "The atmosphere of jollity, good fellowship and close friendliness that Hugh Keyes brought to the Warren Bowling Lanes has gone forever. I don't believe any other individual can ever replace him. He never missed a day coming to the lanes, where friends of every walk of life would soon surround him, eating, talking, and having a good time. It was a privilege to have known Hugh and a lasting honor to have been his friend. This community has suffered a great loss. I have lost a beloved friend."

I first got to know Hugh on an intimate basis in the summer of 1948 when I played American Legion baseball. Hugh was at every game and most practices. Often after a game or practice it was a common sight to see a group of us kids wheeling Hugh up the sidewalk to the bowling alley. We would sit around a table and talk with him for hours. He was such a joy to be around. He talked baseball with us and offered many words of encouragement. More often than not, he bought the sodas.

The kids who were old enough to drive had the privilege of driving Hugh to out of town games. Once in my junior year, Hugh had "Hooty" Howell, Bill Wagner, and me drive him to Tucson to see The New York Yankees play an exhibition game against The Cleveland Indians. It was one of my most memorable experiences. I got to see my hero, Joe DiMaggio, play. What excitement! All the way to Tucson we talked about getting to see DiMaggio play. Hugh even told me I could take a picture of DiMaggio with his camera. Hugh had his "press pass", and we were sitting in the press section very close to the field. You can't possibly feel my discouragement when the starting lineup for the Yankees was announced and DiMaggio was not starting. It was to be DiMaggio's last season, though we did not know it at the time. As the game progressed, DiMaggio sat on the bench. I could see him, but I wanted to take a picture of him batting. Finally, in one of the later innings, DiMaggio came to the on-deck circle. He was going to pinch-hit! Hugh gave me his camera and I got down as close to the field as possible. When DiMaggio was introduced as the batter, the crowd gave him a standing ovation. I was ecstatic! I would finally be able to take a picture of my hero swinging the bat. I had the camera focused on him, ready to click it the moment he swung. However, that chicken pitcher threw DiMaggio three straight balls. He was going to walk him! I figured I was not going to see him swing, so I took one picture of him standing at home plate and was going to get a picture the next pitch no matter what. With the count 3-0 the pitcher delivered the pitch. DiMaggio **swung** and hit the ball out of the park! **Home run!** And, I have that picture in my scrapbook! It was a classic Joe DiMaggio swing. The number 5 he made famous is clearly seen on his back as he followed through with his swing. Every time I look at that picture I think of that special boyhood memory and the great guy who took me to the game!

One other event took place in the game that was not fully appreciated until years later. The guy who substituted for DiMaggio in center field misjudged a fly ball and it hit him square in the face. He was knocked to the ground and was *immediately* surrounded by teammates and trainers from the Yankee dugout. The substitute had to be removed from the game. I remember thinking that that guy would never make it in the major leagues. Imagine, a big league outfielder misjudging a fly ball that even *I* could have caught! Years later, I read an account of that substitute in that game and how embarrassed he was to misjudge that ball. That rookie who replaced Joe DiMaggio in that game, the guy I thought would never make it to the big leagues was Mickey Mantle!

Mike Marusich was a long time friend of Hugh's and he summed up my feelings about Hugh pretty well. Mike wrote: "I believe Hugh's greatest virtue was his friendship. This outstanding quality overshadowed his strength of character and his fabulous accomplishments. There was no time during our relationship that Hugh' friendship wavered. With this quality alone, Hugh lived a full and significant life."

When Hugh died in May of 1954 the shock of his death reverberated though out Arizona. A commemorative eight page, full sized edition of the newspaper Hugh published for years was printed eulogizing Hugh. People from all walks of life from all over Arizona wrote glowing accounts of Hugh's many accomplishments and their love for him. It serves as a testimonial to Hugh's *warrior heart.* I wept as I read some of the sincere words written about him by people across Arizona, including one from the Governor of Arizona, Howard Pyle.

I could delineate in great detail the many ways Hugh served Bisbee. Suffice it to say, I doubt if any one person did more for the kids of Bisbee over several decades than did Hugh Keyes. He organized the first Pony League baseball program for kids too young for American Legion. He was instrumental in keeping the American Legion baseball program going year after year. He was supervisor of the Recreation Center activities. He started, wrote for, and published several newspapers, which were delivered to our Bisbee service men stationed around the world. Hugh was a motivating factor in keeping professional baseball in Bisbee for many years. His nightly radio broadcasts over KSUN were a regular feature that were always focused on Bisbee High sporting events and often included interviews with many of the local kids. Bisbee kids were *his* kids.

No one was ever more loved and revered in Bisbee than was Hugh Keyes. He was an *institution.*

CRUEL AND UNUSUAL.
THE LETTERMENS' PICNIC

The highlight of every year for the Bisbee High male population, as well as for those females with a sadistic bent, was the Lettermen's Picnic! The day new lettermen were initiated into the prestigious Lettermen's Club! It wasn't so much the picnic itself that was so anticipated, but rather it was the blood, which was spilled in the halls of BHS prior to the picnic that got everyone so fired up. Several weeks before the event one could sense a distinct change in the mood which permeated the usually happy, joyful, noisy hallways. A much more somber environment was evident. It was easy to pick out the boys who had earned their first varsity letter that year. Their countenances became very forlorn, fearful and downright paranoid. The *old* lettermen walked around with evil smiles on their faces. Some even slobbered; it could be seen dribbling out the corners of their mouths. It was rumored that Jim Hallsted, the president of The Lettermen Club, held secret meetings at midnight all that week to plan new diabolical initiation procedures and to perfect their paddles. All the old lettermen had paddles. Some they proudly made themselves and some of the more barbaric paddles were handed down from generation to generation. Dried blood could still be seen on these. The females loved initiation day. They were not allowed to attend the picnic. That was only for men. The female lust for blood could only be satisfied in the halls of BHS that day. It was in the hallways that the most bizarre and ingenious behavior could be seen; so the females came to school early. They didn't want to miss any of it.

I have previously mentioned my fear of George Ducich. My fear was well founded. The guy was downright cruel. All the old lettermen took pride in their paddles. Ducich's paddle had nails pounded in it. The sharp points glistened on one side. It was said he polished the tips. Several quarter-sized holes were drilled intermittently through the paddle. This allowed for a swifter and more forceful blow. Of course, Ducich was not allowed to use the side of the paddle with the nails protruding. They were only for show. Believe me when I say, that when Ducich told a new letterman to "grab your ankles" those nails had a very demoralizing affect! We never knew when he might *forget* and use the wrong side.

George Ducich had taken a special interest in me ever since we played American Legion baseball together that summer. Whenever he had the chance, George would whisper, "Hicks, I hope you letter in *something* this year." I became his special project. The night before the picnic, I had several phone calls. When I answered, all I heard was heavy *breathing*. He never identified himself, but I knew who it was.

Ok, I hope you are ready for this. Here is what Ducich cooked up just for *me*. Old timers at BHS said they had never seen *that* done before. George met me in the parking lot in front of BHS and escorted me into the school. Several times as we walked in, I had to grab my ankles. He generously shared me with other old lettermen and let them swat me. He got in his blows as well. But, his magnificent, unique display of cruelty was saved for lunch period when he wouldn't be pressed for time. He told me that I would be spending my lunch period with him and that I probably wouldn't have much time to eat. I could hardly wait. In the meantime, my buttocks were becoming a mass of welts. I couldn't understand why some teacher didn't put a stop to all the mayhem, which was taking place in the halls between classes. They pretty much kept to their rooms most of the day. Coach Dicus and BHS principal, Mr. C.W. Wilcox would make an appearance every now and then just to make sure no one was hanging from the second floor railing. Much to my disappointment and the disappointment of all the new lettermen, lunch period was not cancelled. And true to his word, Ducich met me as I left Miss Shreve's freshman English class. He took me to the boys' bathroom and told me to pull my pants down. I fully expected a few swats on my bare butt. But, somehow I knew down deep that what George had in mind was something much more ingenious, much more perverse, than just a few more swats. Sadly, I was correct. George took out a long piece of string, about five feet in length. He told me to take my underwear down, and then unbelievably, he tied that string to the only available appendage on that part of my torso. What was this idiot up to? I soon found out. He then strung the string up between my shirt and my chest and out the neck. To that end of the string, he tied a pencil. I then was told to pull my pants back up. With the pencil dangling down the front of my shirt, we went out in the hall. He gave me a blank piece of paper. He made me stand by a locker and when a girl would walk by, I had to ask her for her *autograph!* Some of the girls would gently hold on to the pencil and scribble their name, while others who were in hurry would grab it, put the paper high up on the locker and sign their name. They must have thought I was out of my mind, climbing that locker like I did. Thankfully, I only had to ask for an autograph six or seven times before the string slipped off. By then the bell had rung, and Ducich did not have time to reattach it. Was *that* cruel and unusual, or what?!

The picnic was rather anti-climatic. We went to the San Pedro River and had a great steak fry. We still got paddled a few times by the old lettermen that had not developed bursitis in their elbows. George Ducich was too preoccupied accepting plaudits from the old timers to fool around with me anymore. His *very cruel and unusual* sense of humor had earned him much admiration from his peers. He did throw me in the river once, just to let me know he was still around. All in all, we had a great time at the picnic. I, for one, could hardly wait until next year. I would be one of the *old lettermen!* I was already beginning to drool.

BHS *PUMAS* ENHANCE AMERICA'S MILITARY MIGHT

In the summer of 1950, America's mighty military power was strengthened considerably when seven valiant and patriotic Bisbee High School students joined The U.S. Army's Organized Reserve Corps (the O.R.C.). When Charles "Red" Bradshaw, Bob Browder, Ruben Leon, Jim "Lefty" Weld, Tony Silva, Jack Hershey and I signed on the dotted line, Communists all over the world shuddered! We were on our way to Ft. Ord, California to take basic training with The U.S. Army!. America's national security was in good hands.

Actually, we had been persuaded to join the O.R.C.'s summer program to get in shape for football. My uncle, Dr. Robert Fergus, was a major in the Army Reserve Corps. Uncle Bob and my dad had convinced me that a summer of grueling training in the O.R.C. program would greatly enhance my physical conditioning. I was able to talk the other six into joining with me. We would be required to spend the summer taking basic training and then for the next two years we would have to attend monthly meetings, plus a week of training in the summers at Ft. Huachuca. The pay was good and we were told the experience would be a "maturing" process in addition to the physical growth we would receive. We were excited kids when we boarded the train at Bisbee Junction. It would be a fun summer for us! Or, so we hoped.

The train stopped in Tucson and Phoenix as well as at various stops in California. At each stop other high school age boys got on the train with us. By the time we arrived at Ft. Ord, in northern California, our group had grown to over a hundred. We were to spend the next eight weeks with these guys going through some of the most rigorous and demanding "fun" we had not counted on. Our dreams of fun for the summer were shattered the moment we arrived at Ft. Ord. We departed the train in the early morning and were greeted by a typical wet, foggy, and cold Ft. Ord, California morning. We were scattered all over the platform at the "reception center". And what a motley looking group! We stood by our luggage anxiously awaiting what was to come next. The first military command we heard was a thunderous shout of, **"DROP!"** I remember thinking, "Drop?" Again, the shout, **"DROP!"** Again, we looked around quizzically. It was then that we noticed a mean looking *Neanderthal* in an Army uniform standing in the foggy darkness. He explained his command in not so gentile terms: **"You lousy civilian s.o.b.'s, when I say 'DROP' this is what I expect you to do!"** He then immediately *dropped* to the wet cement platform and did fifty military push-ups! All we could do was gawk. But, when he again commanded **"DROP"**, believe me, we **"DROPPED"**! My first close up view of the wet platform was not a pretty one. I noticed, and felt, that we had dropped to a cigarette-butt and phlegm covered surface. It wasn't pretty. I kept thinking, "I want my mommy." What came next was pretty humbling. We were marched to a barbershop and our heads were completely shaved. My long time Warren barber, Mr. Andy Endicott, would not have approved.

The first week of basic training was a blur of activity. We were assigned to Company I of the 8TH Infantry. We were housed in nondescript wooden barracks. Every morning we were awakened at 4:30 and our first duty before breakfast was to "police the area". This meant we had to pick up any debris on the grounds, including hundreds of cigarette butts, which were usually wet and gooey. We were issued our "GI" uniforms, which of course did not fit. We learned how to line up in straight lines. We learned how to march in a military manner. We learned what kind of "chow" we would be required to eat. We were issued our M1 rifles. We began to memorize our individual serial numbers, which I remember to this day: "Sir, US 19379259, Sir". We were confronted at least a thousand times that first week with, "What is your serial number, soldier?" At least, we were now addressed as "soldier" instead of "s.o.b." Every time we were asked to reply to a question we had to begin and end our reply with, "Sir".

We met and "soldiered" with a bunch of guys we would get to know most intimately over the next eight weeks. There were quite a few black kids from Phoenix and Los Angeles. This was our first experience associating with blacks, and at first, we were apprehensive about how to react to them. I don't remember their names, but most of them had nick names: "Coconut Willie", "Sexy" and "Blade" were three that I do remember. "Coconut Willie" got that name because, as we were told, he had lived in Hawaii for most of his early years. "Sexy" was a tall, slender guy who was our company's guidon (company flag) carrier. When he marched, he had a very distinctive strut and a "sexy" swing of his hips. "Blade" was a mean looking guy who was said to always carry a "blade" (knife) and who was known to use it freely when angered. They were all pretty good guys, but pretty much didn't hang out with any of the white guys. Maybe if *we* had made more of an effort, but that was just the way it was.

After that first week, we kind of settled into military life. We were starting to feel fairly comfortable and confident that we could handle most of what we would have to endure for the duration of our basic training. Our confidence and comfort came to a screeching halt on the Sunday of our first week. We were awakened to a very somber mood among the R.A. (Regular Army) personnel who were assigned to our company. Something very serious had occurred. We were told that the **KOREAN WAR** had started!! The North Korean communists had invaded South Korea! America was allied with South Korea! A full military alert was in place. And the seven young soldiers from Bisbee High School were right in the middle of it! Our training was about to become much more intense. It now became a matter of life and death.

As our company stood at attention that morning on the company street, I remember the eerie silence that surrounded all of us. Our company commander spoke to us and explained the gravity of the situation. Among other things, he told us what we could expect to occur immediately. We were at war. Our training would reflect that fact. He told us in no uncertain terms that what we learned could make the difference in whether we "came back from Korea" or not! Wait a minute! Time out! Whatta ya mean, "come *back* from Korea."? We were only high school kids! We wanted to go back to Bisbee High and play football. Wait until Coach Dicus heard about this! He would put a stop to this nonsense! Unfortunately, Coach Dicus, with all his authority at dear old Bisbee High, had no "pull" with the United States Army. We seriously believed that we would be fighting Korean commies instead of running laps for Coach Dicus.

That afternoon as the seven of us sat dejectedly on our footlockers, we didn't have a lot to say. We were a bunch of scared high school kids. We wanted our mommies! Corporal Hammergreen was our R.A. squad leader and a good guy. He came in and tried to boost our morale. He told us that the U.S. Army was the best-trained and most technically advanced fighting machine in the world. He told us the war would be over before we could be trained and sent to Korea. His encouragement didn't do much good. We still wanted our mommies. It was decided that I should call my Uncle Bob. After all, this whole ridiculous thing was his idea. He was a major and surely he could get us out of here. I called Uncle Bob and he had been expecting my call. He told me we legally could not be sent to Korea. We were too young. We all felt a little better when I told the others what Uncle Bob had said. We felt better, that is, until the next morning when once again we were spoken to by our commanding officer. He was livid! He said that "some cowardly, c.s. recruit" had tried to "bug out" by calling his reserve unit's commander (Uncle Bob) and asking to be sent home. He gave us a five-minute tirade about patriotism, fighting for America, and not letting our comrades in arms down. He ended by saying, "Every swinging # % ^ ## here is going to Korea!" Uncle Bob had called him and told him of our fear of being sent to Korea. Evidently, Uncle Bob had asked him to take it easy on us. Not a good move. Our training only intensified. We saw R.A.s being shipped out on a daily basis. I will never forget the day our squad leader, Corporal Hammergreen was shipped out. We saw him packing his duffel bag and asked him what was going on. He told us he had gotten his orders to go to Korea. He said "good by" to all of us, wished us good luck, and then proudly walked up the company street, duffel bag slung over his arm. I was saddened to see him go. I have often wondered if Corporal Hammergreen came back from Korea. He was a good guy.

We took our training beside young R.A.s who knew they were on their way to Korea. We still were not convinced that we would not be going as well. We were undergoing the same intense combat training. We had a first hand glimpse of Army life in time of war. As the days and weeks wore on, we all soon took on the same intensity and seriousness as the R.A.s did. Each morning after policing the area, making out beds, and eating breakfast, we were loaded into busses and taken to the Ft. Ord firing range. Here we had long lectures about the use and value of the various weapons we could expect to use in Korea. Besides learning to fire them, we were taught everything there was to know about the M1 rifle and the carbine. We could take them apart and put them back together blindfolded. We spent hours cleaning and oiling the weapons. I was proud of my fellow soldiers from Bisbee. We each qualified as "Expert" in firing the M1 rifle. We fired from the hundred-yard range, the two-hundred-yard range and the three-hundred-yard range. On the command, "Lock and load. Commence firing" we would load a round in the chamber of the rifle and fire at the square, stationary targets down range. After we each had fired our full complement of bullets from the hundred-yard range, we were given the command, **"Police up the brass and move to the two hundred-yard range!"** Which meant, pick up the spent bullet-casings and walk back one hundred yards to the next firing station. This command was given at each distance. We heard it over and over almost every morning for our entire time at Ft. Ord. One weekend, the seven of us went to a movie on base. It was a murder mystery. The heroine of the film in a very dramatic and tense scene, shot one of the villains. She cried, "Oh my, oh my. What should I do now?" At which point, Jack Hershey, in a true military manner, yelled out, **"Police up the brass and move to the two hundred yard range."** That broke the tension.

One morning we had a break in the routine. We went to the *hand grenade range* instead of the firing range. That was an experience. We had all watched John Wayne throwing grenades at the enemy with unerring accuracy. We soon found out it was not as easy as "The Duke" made it out to be! We had to sit through a long lecture on the nomenclature of a hand grenade, how to throw one properly, and what safety precautions to take when we actually threw live ones; which we did that afternoon. We had seen several live ones thrown down range while we were being instructed so we eagerly waited our turn. The procedure was fairly simple. The hand grenade was fitted with a handle, which had to be depressed before the pin on the top of grenade was pulled. When the pin was pulled, the grenade was activated. The grenade could be held indefinitely as long as the handle was depressed. The handle was automatically flipped off when the grenade was thrown. It took three seconds for the grenade to explode once the handle was released. The grenade range was comprised of a series of deep pits with a platform to stand on in each pit. Each pit had a deep, narrow trench dug around its bottom. There was an instructor in each pit as well as a box of hand grenades. We were each given one dummy grenade to throw to "get the feel" of it. We found out rather quickly that you did not throw the grenade like a baseball. Or like John Wayne did. The thrower had to throw with a stiff arm motion since the grenade weighed almost a pound. It was with much trepidation that I gingerly took the live grenade that the instructor handed me. We got our instructions over a loud speaker from a sergeant in a tower. It was crucial that we each threw on command simultaneously. I held my grenade against my chest as I was instructed. On the command, "Pull pin", I pulled the pin. The grenade was now activated. The pounding of my heart almost bounced the grenade out of my hand. The next command came: "Prepare to throw" and it was at this time that some serious accidents were known to have happened. As the thrower extended his arm back he had to make certain he had a good grasp of the grenade. It was while in this position a nervous recruit could conceivably drop his live grenade. Should that occur, the instructor was trained to yell, "*LIVE GRENADE!*" and at the same time he would kick the live grenade into the deep trench at the bottom of his pit. After he did this, the instructor had maybe a second and a half to leap over the lip of the pit to safety. Hopefully, the nervous recruit was already out of the pit covering his head. If either one of them was slow in reacting, death or at least serious injury was certain. Others who heard, "*LIVE GRENADE!*" were trained to instantly duck into their pit. It was not wise to look around to see which pit had the live grenade in it. We each had two live grenades to throw. If all of us threw simultaneously, the ten explosions would sound like one huge one. We threw our first grenades without any causalities. As I was preparing to throw my second live grenade, we heard the dreaded words, "*LIVE GRENADE!*" My instructor and I immediately ducked. We waited for what seemed like an hour before the "all clear" was given. Nothing had happened. No explosion was heard. It seems that an instructor in one of the pits had noticed a loose handle in the bottom of his grenade box. Thinking his recruit had maybe pulled the pin to activate the grenade, he yelled and he and his recruit jumped out of the pit. Nothing happened. Upon investigation they found that somehow an extra handle had gotten into the grenade box. They were both embarrassed, but that was better than being dead.

After our fourth week of training, we were given weekend passes to nearby Monterey on the beautiful Monterey Peninsula. We had eagerly looked forward to this weekend. We could at long last get away from Army life and get a taste of civilian life again. More importantly, we could find some good restaurants and eat palatable food! We wouldn't have to put up with "s.o.s." (s--- on a shingle) which we had just about every breakfast along with our powdered scrambled eggs. S.o.s. in polite circles was known as chipped beef on a piece of toast. We grew to hate it and to this day, I won't eat it.

Monterey is a beautiful sea side town adjacent to the quaint little town of Carmel. We visited both towns that first weekend off base. We walked the streets of Carmel marveling at the many expensive shops that not many military people could afford to seriously consider. We walked down Ocean Avenue to the world-renowned Carmel Beach. It is one of the few places in the world where the sand is white. Most of the cigarette-butt receptacles in movie theatres get their sand from Carmel Beach. Since we had been away from "civilization" for over four weeks and since we were red blooded Bisbee boys, we naturally missed being in the company of girls. Therefore, it is only natural that we spent time admiring the scenery of Carmel Beach. The Carmel girls were used to the stares and crude remarks of military men. They wouldn't give us the time of day. Not even when Bob Browder and Jack Hershey, the truly bold ones of the bunch, tried their famous "Bisbee moves" on them. What worked to varying degrees of success in Bisbee, did not work in Carmel, California. "Red" Bradshaw and Ruben Leon were the shy, backward type and would just stand in the background and blush whenever we talked to the girls. Tony Silva, "Lefty" Weld and I stood by ready to assist Bob and Jack should something materialize. Nothing ever did. We spent most of the first day in Carmel. Late in the afternoon, we took a bus down the hill to Monterey. We soon found an altogether different environment in Monterey. The main street was lined with tacky "soldier traps"; gift shops to cater to any and all tastes. Bars were plentiful. We noticed numerous semi-attractive women walking up and down the streets and sitting in the bars. Bob Browder informed us that in all probability they were whores. Upon hearing this, "Red" Bradshaw and Ruben Leon wanted to go back to the base. They didn't know how to get back without us so they toughed it out. At one point in our exploration of downtown Monterey, "Lefty" and I found ourselves lagging behind by about a half of a block. We had been "window shopping", just kind of strolling along enjoying the sights and new smells coming off of Monterey's Fisherman's Wharf. Suddenly, seemingly out of nowhere, came a very melodic and sultry, "Hi, soldier boys." I am sure you realize that "Lefty" and I were pretty experienced in the ways of, well, in the ways of "things". Bob Browder had been our friend for a long time and he knew "things". Bob was a friend of Charlie Ryan and Charlie really knew "things". We felt that we could handle most any situation that might come up. "Lefty" and I had been taught by our parents to always be polite to strangers. So, when we heard that angelic voice, we immediately stopped and sought out its source. Lo and behold, sitting at a sidewalk table outside a bar that we were just passing were two very pretty young ladies. They were smiling at us very coyly. Both of them were pretty cute. One was a blond and one was a brunette. The brunette was sitting next to the sidewalk closest to us. She very sweetly said, "Would you like to join us?" Things were getting serious. I looked for our buddies down the sidewalk, but they were too far away to holler to. I really felt the pressure was on *me*. You remember that I was older than most of my buddies since I had been kept out of school a year. I was therefore more mature than "Lefty". I had to take charge of this situation. So I said, "Well, for just a minute. But, we can't stay too far behind our buddies up the street." Without saying a word, the brunette pulled out a chair for me and the blond did the same for "Lefty". "Lefty" and I were sitting side by side with the girls beside each of us. The blond one spoke first. "Now you soldier boys just sit here awhile and relax. We'll have a few drinks and if it gets too late for you to get back to base before the gates close, we have plenty of room at our apartment. You would be welcome to stay with us." I noticed that as she said this she had put her hand on "Lefty's" arm. "Lefty" was just sitting there with his mouth open. Just about that time, the waiter came up and asked us what we'd like to drink. As he was taking the girls' order, "Lefty" leaned over to me and whispered, "Do you still have *yours*?" I whispered back, "No, mine rotted a year ago when I got my wallet wet at the Lettermen's Picnic. Do you have *yours*?" "Lefty" replied, "Nope. I never could get it rolled back up right." By this time, the waiter was waiting for us to give him our drink order. I ordered a *Nesbitt Orange* and Lefty ordered a *Dad's Root Beer*. Now, the two girls and the waiter all had *their* mouths open. I couldn't figure out why. Everyone in Bisbee likes *Nesbitt Orange* and *Dad's Root Beer*. Maybe these brands hadn't gotten to California, yet.

I have to admit that I was pretty relieved to see our Bisbee buddies walking back towards us. When they saw us sitting with two pretty girls, Bob Browder and Jack Hershey gave us the *thumbs up* and smiled at us proudly. "Red" Bradshaw and Ruben Leon just stared at us with *their* mouths open. Without stopping to talk with us, Browder just said as they walked by, "We'll meet you two back here in about two hours. We'll go find us a place to stay tonight." "Lefty" blurted out, "Don't leave! We'll come with you!" I noticed that the blond now had her arm around "Lefty". She obviously had taken a liking to him. By this time, Bob Browder had led the guys on down the sidewalk. Bob was a good guy. He didn't want to crimp our style. Suddenly, Ruben Leon turned and ran back to me shaking his finger in my face. "I am going to tell Coach Dicus!" he warned. "He won't like this at all." With that, he walked away with a disgusted look on his face.

"Who is Coach Dicus and what business is it of his what you do?" asked the brunette. "He is our football coach", I explained. "He always warned us he would kick us off the team if we messed with the whores in Naco. He would probably feel the same about whores here in California." I didn't mean to hurt their feelings, but I guess I did. They just got up and left. Didn't even say goodbye or anything. They just left. As "Lefty" and I were mulling over all that had happened, the waiter came up with my *Nesbitt Orange*, "Lefty's" *Dad's Root Beer* and the girls' margaritas. He said, "Who was stuck?" Obviously, "Lefty" and I were. We paid.

Two more things I want to tell you about our weekend in Monterey. When "Lefty" and I caught up with the other guys, we all decided we were hungry so we started looking for something to eat. Ruben Leon looked very relieved that "Lefty" and I had gotten rid of the girls. He gave me a hug and said, "I knew you wouldn't let us down." He had a tear in his eye. Ruben was the emotional type. We saw a restaurant that was advertising the new food fad, *pizza pie*. We had heard of it in Bisbee but none of the restaurants there sold it. Not even Kitterman's or Ted Saffaravich at *The White House* in Lowell. We had heard that pizza pie had been imported from Italy. We decided to try some. We sat down on stools at a long counter and looked over the menu. We didn't understand most of the flavors. We had never heard of *pepperoni, Italian sausage, anchovies,* or some of the others on the menu. I did understand what *hamburger* was so that is what I ordered. A hamburger pizza pie. I felt I couldn't go wrong with that. I don't remember what most of the other guys ordered, but I do remember what Ruben Leon ordered. He looked over the menu and when the waiter asked him what he wanted, Ruben said kind of at a loss, "I don't see it on the menu, but my favorite is *cherry.*" The waiter paused with his pencil poised. He glared at Ruben. "What are you soldier, some kind of wise guy?" Ruben replied, "No sir, I am not being a wise guy. My favorite pie is cherry. That's all. I would just like a cherry *piece a* pie. If you don't have it, just give me one of what "Red" ordered." Because Bob

Browder knew "things", he explained to Ruben that pizza *pies* were round cookie-like things with tomato sauce and cheese spread over it. What ever it was he got, Ruben liked it. We all did.

After we ate, we decided we would start looking for a place to sleep. It was a beautiful warm Saturday night so we decided that we'd find a park some place and sleep on the ground. After all, we were soldiers and we had had plenty of experience the past four weeks. Besides, by sleeping on the ground we could save some money for our last day in Monterey before we went back to base. We wandered around the many side streets looking for a deserted park-like area. Once we got off the main drag of Monterey, it got harder to see exactly where we were. We had left the bright lights behind. Finally, we found what seemed to be an ideal place to *sack out* for the night. Tony Silva had found a newspaper somewhere and we split it up among the six of us. We used it to lie on as the ground was damp. It was not cold, but we all slept fully dressed.

It was a good thing we were fully dressed because first of all about 4:00am the fog rolled in and it was cold! Secondly, we were awakened about 6:00am by a very upset elderly lady. I could see in the daylight that we had been sleeping almost on her front steps. "You soldiers get out of my yard! I did not give your permission to sleep in my front yard! Go on, get out. Or, I'll call the police!" As we were getting up, Bob Browder tried to explain that we meant no harm. He apologized to her, but she was pretty irritated. She got real irritated when she saw that we had been sleeping on her newspaper. As we staggered off wiping the grass and dew off our uniforms and the sleep out of our eyes, I heard her mumbling something about, "....damn soldiers....should not be allowed to sell liquor to children....glad I had the door locked......" We probably ruined her Sunday.

"Going on *bivouac*" is one of those military experiences you either love or hate! Our first bivouac was a fun experience for all of us except for "Lefty" Weld. "Lefty" had an experience he says he still has nightmares about.

When a soldier goes on bivouac, he packs all his equipment in his backpack, ties on his sleeping bag, and goes for a "hike in the woods". Literally. Only he goes with his entire company. And he doesn't come back for a week. He eats in the woods; he sleeps in the woods; he shaves and goes to the bathroom in the woods. We were all looking forward to our first bivouac.

One morning we were loaded into trucks at 4:00 and were taken way out into the "boonies". We estimated that we were about fifty miles away from Ft. Ord when we finally stopped. We were told to disembark from the trucks, assemble in formation, and stand "at ease" until we got orders to "move out". When the order came, we lined up in columns and began to march down a dusty, dirt road.

It seemed we marched for hours. We took a break every half hour or so at which time we could smoke if we were smokers (which none of the Bisbee guys were. Coach Dicus might have heard about it), or do what ever it was we had to do. After marching for hours, we stopped for lunch. We were surprised to see a "mess tent" set up in a field with a hot lunch prepared for us. "The U.S. Army travels on its stomach" is a truism. We had fully expected to have to endure "C Rations", but we were told that this lunch and the evening dinner would be served from this "mess tent". They were to be the last two *good* meals we would have for a week.

That afternoon, we attended lectures on "combat survival". The lectures were held in a large field with bleachers set up in four sections with each section about two hundred yards apart. Our company was divided into four platoons with each platoon designated to begin the lectures in one of the sets of bleachers. We were sternly reminded by our Company Commander to pay close attention at each lecture because how well we learned might be the difference between coming back from Korea, or staying over there as "fertilizer for a rice paddy". We took it all very seriously. We listened intently. Each of the four lecture sessions was an hour in length, which was a long time to sit up straight and not doze off. To make sure we were attentive, an R.A. cadre (trainer) would walk around behind the bleachers carrying a long stick. If he saw one of us not paying attention or stating to nod off, he would whack the guilty party on the "steel pot" he was wearing on his head. When we were hit like that, the reverberation was like thunder rattling around in our head! It would definitely wake us up!

After each lecture, we would have an hour of hands-on application of the content of the lecture. The two I remember the most clearly were the "hand to hand combat" lecture and the "gas attack" lecture. The hand to hand combat sessions were fun. We were taught how to attach our bayonets to our M1 rifles and how to fight at close quarters with an enemy. We walked through in slow motion in the first stages of this training using our M1 rifles. Our bayonets were attached but were in their sheaths. After we had practiced for a half-hour or so with our M1's, we were told the fun part was about to begin. They started us off with long poles with a "boxing glove" like thing attached to one end. These poles took the place of our M1 rifle. The butt end of the rifle was simulated by the "boxing glove" end of the long pole. We were taught how to deliver a blow to the enemy's head with the butt of the rifle while deflecting his bayonet thrust. We were paired off with a partner who was the "enemy". We went at it, *mano e mano*. And we went at it full bore! The guy I was paired with was not the most agile or aggressive. My early *JohnnyMackBrown* training came in handy. I was able to *duck* many of his blows and was not handicapped by a green wooden fence beside us. I have to admit that I got in more blows to his head than he did to mine. I only remember one grazing blow to my head and several to my shoulder, none of which hurt.

After the "hand to hand" session, we went to the "gas attack" session. We had all been issued gas masks and wore them in a container on our belt for easy and speedy access. Again, we sat in bleachers for an hour where we learned about the various kinds of gases the commies often used in combat and the dangers of each. We learned how to quickly put our masks on. The real key to getting a gas mask on correctly is to put it over your face snugly and then lift up one corner of the mask and **blow** out any gas that may have accumulated inside as we took the mask out of the container. Remember the R.A. cadre who walked around whacking us on the head if we dozed off? Well, at this lecture we had the same thing to contend with only with a very sneaky twist. After we had been instructed for a time, the cadre behind the bleachers nonchalantly dropped a live *tear gas grenade* under us. As the gas rose up to us, he yelled, "**GAS!!**" At which point a bunch of startled soldiers had to quickly apply all the information we had just been given. Most of us did not get our masks on in time and those who did, forgot to *blow* out some gas that had gotten into the mask. That tear gas is wicked stuff! It was not easy to wash out of our eyes.

The last thing we did at this station was to go into the "gas chamber" where we sat on benches waiting for the gas to be blown in the room. When we saw it coming we had to put our masks on correctly. This was not bad and it showed us the reliability of the gas mask we were issued.

That night after dinner we had a night lecture session where we had to sit in bleachers and listen to instructions about nighttime combat. One thing we were taught to do was to identify sounds at night. Sound at night is more deceptive than it is during the day. We had to sit in the bleachers very quietly and identify among other things, a car door closing way off in the distance, several people whispering, a match striking, a rifle bolt being engaged, and a twig being broken. After each sound we had to guess what the sound was. The sound I could most readily recognize was the sound of the guy next to me snoring.

After the "night combat" lecture, we went to our platoon areas and set up our two-man pup tents. It was dark! Jack Hershey was my partner and we each had one small flashlight; however, since we were at "combat alert", we couldn't use them. One of the mysteries of the Army. We were always on "combat alert"; why then, did we have to even carry a flashlight with us?! We finally got the pup tent assembled and we "hit the sack" The last thing our Company Commander had told us was to get a good night's sleep because tomorrow was going to be a long and strenuous day. We were going on a *forced march.* "Get a good night's sleep", yah right. It was well after midnight when we got to bed and we were going to get up at 4:30am! To top it off, both Jack and I had to get up several times to go to the "latrine". What ever it was we had for dinner, it didn't agree with us. It was not fun digging holes in the dark!

After breakfast, which consisted of the ever-present s.o.s. and powdered eggs, we assumed "combat readiness". We were about to begin our forced march. And "Lefty" Weld was about to begin his worse *nightmare!*

We had been instructed that when in "combat alert" we were to march at "route-step" (that is, not in cadence) and not to be bunched up. If we were bunched up we were told that one grenade could get us all! We had also been instructed that when we were under attack from an airplane, we would be alerted by the platoon leader's two blasts on his whistle. At which point we were to *immediately* dive into the ditch along the side of the road.

We started off. We were well spread out, about ten yards apart. We carried our rifles at "port arms" across our chests *combat ready.* We were told we were in enemy territory and may be under attack at any moment. We didn't know what to expect, but we were ready. I expected maybe a sniper firing blanks at us, maybe a camouflaged machine gun nest, or maybe a mortar attack. What I wasn't expecting was an air attack! Suddenly, we heard two sharp blasts of a whistle from the head of the platoon. As we were instructed, we dived off the road into the ditch, and covered our heads. Two airplanes appeared out of nowhere and thundered very low over our heads simulating a strafing attack. After the second pass at our position, the planes flew away and in several minutes the "all clear" was sounded. We got up, reformed into our lines, and continued to march down the road. Since I didn't hear anyone cry for a medic, I assumed there were no casualties. I assumed wrong. Within an hour after our "strafing" by the enemy airplanes, "Lefty" Weld was hollering *"MEDIC!",* in the most pitiful voice I had ever heard! Since, we were still marching, I couldn't go back to see what was wrong with him. We were in alphabetical order so "Lefty" was behind me. Every five minutes or so, I heard this very pitiful little voice pleading, "I need a medic." The soldiers around him were trying to comfort him by telling him to hang tough until we took our next break. I figured if they weren't panicked, then "Lefty" must not be dying. Finally, we were given a break and a medic was sent back to see what was wrong with "Lefty". I went back as well and took one look at him. I knew immediately he was in serious trouble! "Lefty's" face was red and swollen and he said his throat was so swollen, he could hardly swallow. I was very concerned for "Lefty". Was he dying? Since we weren't really in combat, would he still get *The Purple Heart* if he did die? The only one who didn't seem overly concerned was the medic. He just smiled and said, "Private Weld (our rank and last name were stenciled on our shirts) looks like this bivouac is over for you. You have to go back to the company infirmary….you got you a bad dose of *poison oak!* Musta jumped in a batch of it when we had that air attack awhile back." The medic got on a walkie-talkie and within minutes a jeep came flying down the road. "Lefty" was loaded in the jeep and we didn't see him again until we got back from the bivouac several days later.

When we did get back and walked into our barracks, the first thing I noticed was that *something* was in "Lefty's" bunk. As I got closer, I realized that it was "Lefty"! What a sight he was! My first reaction was to laugh. I did, but I shouldn't have. "Lefty" was on the verge of tears. He mumbled, "It's not funny, Hadley." He was swollen up twice his normal size. He looked like one huge, blond haired *blister!* By this time, most of the platoon was gathered around "Lefty's" bunk. They all said he was the worse looking human being they had ever seen. The black kids were afraid they'd catch what ever it was Lefty had by breathing the same air. They wouldn't get near him. Everyone had a comment to make and to tell "Lefty" how bad he looked. By this time, he had tears in his eyes. I wanted to console him. I wanted to pat his shoulder and tell him that it'd be ok. But, I was afraid to touch him for fear he'd pop. He was lying on the bunk naked except for his military shorts; the legs of which had to be slit up the sides because his thighs were so badly swollen. Every part of his body looked to be one big mass of blisters. "Lefty" verified that *every part of his body was* a big blister. Every time he moved, a blister would pop and would spread the poison oak to some other part of his body. He even had it on his eyelids. He looked like he was Oriental. Now, come to think of it, he could have passed for a blond haired Sumo wrestler. The poor guy was like that for over a week. He had to stay in the barracks all day all by himself except for an occasional officer who walked through on an inspection tour and a medic who changed his sheets daily. The medic also applied calamine lotion to every part of "Lefty's" body. The medic always wore rubber gloves. The black kids never did come by to see how he was doing. After he was able to talk about it, he told us what had happened. He said that when he dived into the ditch, he must have hit a patch of poison oak as the medic had surmised. But, what got him in real trouble, he said, was when he noticed that some mint candies he had in his pocket had fallen on the ground. As he lay there waiting for the "all clear" to sound, he ate the mints! He had juice from the crushed poison oak leaves on his hands and fingers. He soon had it down his gullet!

Well, "Lefty" survived the ordeal. He never did get a *Purple Heart*. We all survived the eight weeks of basic training and knew that we were better men because of it. Nothing else of real importance happened after "Lefty's" bout with poison oak, though Jack Hershey did get in a pretty good fight with "Blade". Jack started it, I guess, when he told the black guys that they were cowards to not want anything to do with "Lefty", even after he had recovered. Bisbee kids were loyal to each other. "Blade" took exception to the comment and challenged Jack to meet him out behind the barracks. At first, Jack declined, "No way! You'll use your knife on me." But, "Blade" promised he wouldn't use it. He said, "Naw, man, I won't cut you. I promise." The fight was no contest. The tough *Puma* got the best of the fight right from the start. Jack had "Blade" on the ground really giving it to him when "Blade" tried to reach into his pocket, and said as he was doing so, "Hold on a minute Hershey, I'm gonna cut you just a little." One of the other black guys kicked the knife out of "Blades" hands and said that Jack had won fair and square. There'd be no cutting. Fight over.

Bisbee Junction never looked so good as it did that day in August of 1950 when the seven of us stepped off the train! We were hardened veterans of the toughest training any of us had ever gone through. We were so very thankful that we did not have to go to Korea. The Korean War became very personal to each of us. We knew that some of those men we had soldiered with were over there fighting and dying while we were safe at home playing football for Bisbee High School. We each had a greater love for America and appreciated more the freedoms we were blessed with.

BISBEE HIGH'S REAL WAR HEROES

I first heard the name *Art Benko* from my mother as I was growing up. I had known *Bee Benko* for several years. We became good friends in high school. Mother told me Art was Bee's father and that he was one of America's World War II war heroes. Mother remembered Art from his days as an all-around athlete at Bisbee High. They were schoolmates. Art was a dark, handsome, well-built young man, Mother recalls. He was an outstanding athlete at Bisbee High and was one of Arizona's best football players his senior year. Art was chosen the outstanding Puma player in the two games against Douglas High in 1929. He was recruited by several major universities his senior year. Jimmy Vercillino, Benko's *Puma* teammate in 1928, had gone to UCLA in Los Angeles on a football scholarship and almost talked Art into following in his footsteps. It is unclear why Art did not go on to college and pursue higher education. His records at Bisbee High indicate he was an above average student.

Maybe it was Art's love for the outdoors and the mountains of Southern Arizona that kept him at home. He was an avid hunter having learned to shoot at an early age. Mr. John Benko, Art's father had spent many hours teaching him the fine rudiments of pistol shooting and he even taught him how to use a bow and arrow. Art became a skilled hunter and downed his first deer with a bow and arrow at the age of sixteen. The Benko living room was a testament to Art's skill with pistol and rifle. He had over one hundred medals and trophies that he had won in competition throughout the state. One of his most prized medals was awarded to Art at the 1940 Arizona state rifle championships. He won second place for grand aggregate score. He was competing against adults who had years of experience on him. Another medal the Benko family was proud of was the "President's Hundred" medal awarded by the National Rifle Association in 1937 to the top one hundred marksmen in America. In just a few short years, Art was destined to use this God-given gift of marksmanship in defense of America over the skies of China and Japan.

Art worked as an electrician in the mines for several years after graduating from BHS. He also worked as a projectionist at The Lyric Theatre. It was while working at The Lyric that Art met Ester Fabio Romero. Ester was one of the ushers. They fell in love and were married in 1932. Their only child, Beatrice "Bee" Benko was born in 1933. Eight years later, Dec. 7, 1941 the Japanese bombed Pearl Harbor. The United States was at war and Art Benko became a man possessed with a deep seeded desire to be a part of it. He enlisted in the U.S. Air Force and the rest is history. Art Benko became a legend in the Air Force and one of America's most decorated war heroes.

Art and Ester divorced shortly after World War II broke out. Eight year old Bee was devastated by the divorce but has many fond memories of her father. In an Oct. 26, 1995 article of *The Bisbee News*, Bee recalls: "My father was a tall, handsome man. He was prematurely gray and had a deep voice. I still have little girl size skis he gave me, and I can vividly recall a lot of experiences with him." One of her fondest memories was the last time Bee saw him. He was home on leave before he was to go overseas. "I remember we went to the soda fountain downstairs in the PD Mercantile building. We were sitting on stools at the counter when a senior military officer came in. Dad immediately stood tall and erect and saluted. I was so impressed and proud of him." The next day Sgt. Art Benko, United States Air Force, left Bisbee, and his daughter Bee, for the last time.

Sgt. Benko was assigned to the 374th Bomb Squadron of the 308th Group, 14th Air Force under the leadership of the legendary Gen. Claire Chennault. Benko was a top gunner on a Consolidated Air Force B-24 Liberator known as *The Goon*. It didn't take long for Benko and *The Goon* to strike fear in the hearts of The Imperial Japanese Air Force. In one of his first missions it was reported that, "…a force of Liberator bombers with fighter escorts waded into a large formation of Japanese planes, shooting down thirty Zero fighters, and fourteen 'probables' over Indo-China. Benko got **seven** himself."

In the November 4, 1943 *Bisbee Daily Review* the headline read, **BISBEE'S BENKO IS TOP GUNNER.** The article reported how Art Benko had accounted for sixteen enemy planes shot down, disregarding "probables", which made him "high man" of the 14th U.S. Air Force operating out of China.

Just nineteen days later, November 23, 1943 the headlines read, **BENKO, BISBEE HERO, MISSING.** And, thus began a mystery which has never been satisfactorily explained. In a 1995 article in *The Bisbee News*, Mary Ellen Corbett reported:

> Arthur J. Benko, a Bisbee native son, a top turret gunner in the Air Force, and one of the greatest heroes of the war, was lost in a Hong Kong mission in October of 1943 and never heard from after. Here is what we do know: Sgt. Arthur J. Benko was posthumously honored in the mid-forties with the Legion of Merit and the Air Medal with two oak leaf clusters after being listed as presumed dead by the war department.

Mary Ellen Corbett quotes some recollections typed in 1993 by one of Art's Air Force buddies, Robert E. Cook of Rio Rancho, New Mexico. This is the most complete account of the fate of Benko that has come to surface so far. Cook's memories are as follows:

> Gentlemen/Ladies: In March of this year it will be fifty years since Arthur J. Benko arrived in China, you'll have to fill in the blanks from what we thought we knew: He was a full-blooded Indian (not true; according to daughter, Bee, he was Hungarian and German. hh), tribe unknown…we knew him in the squadron as a soldier's soldier, always neat and trim. His sixteen Jap kills came about by someone who knew just what his goal was and how to get it. He loaded his machine gun belts removing all tracers. He said he did not want his foe to know he was being fired at. But most important, tracer fire was false as the tracer round burned in flight, thus loosing weight. A tracer round would not have the same trajectory as the rest of the bullets, so he pulled them out of his belts.

Cook's letter concludes with this most interesting report:

> "Now I do not have the date, but the '*Goon*' was on a Hong Kong mission in October of 1943. They lost two engines coming off the target and could not maintain altitude and still had to cross a range of mountains to reach an air base. The pilot, Sam Skousen, asked the crew to bail out, which they did. Art and his bombardier, Lt. Malcolm S. Sanders, landed on the wrong side of the river and were captured by the Japanese. *A Catholic Missionary said they were crucified* (emphasis mine, hh).
>
> That was the sad end to the top Air Force gunner in all the air forces in World War II. He was a brave man and I was proud to have served with him.

It is interesting to me that a Catholic missionary was a witness to Art Benko's death. I can only surmise what happened. I know that Art's former wife came from a Catholic background and more than likely he would have worn a crucifix she gave him around his neck. Did the Japanese see this religious symbol of Christ's death and mock Art's faith by crucifying him? Did Benko and the missionary speak? We will never know.

His father in Bisbee fostered Art Benko's interest in weapons of all kinds at an early age. Art's skill with these weapons was honed to a fine degree in the mountains of Southern Arizona. John Benko, Art's father, had no way of knowing that what he was instilling in Art would someday be invaluable to America's domination over the skies of Japan and China. Early in his military career, Benko invented a sighting device to put on airplane machine guns, which aided the gunner in sighting in on enemy planes coming out of the bright sun. He was awarded the Legion of Merit for this contribution.

It is easy to picture Art Benko sighting in on the Japanese planes and blasting them out of the sky one after another; just like shooting ducks at a carnival shooting gallery.

Only in Art's case, the Japanese were shooting back!

Shortly after Art's death, a movement was started in Bisbee to have a memorial to Art Benko placed in the Evergreen Cemetery along with the one honoring the other Bisbee kids who were killed in World War II. That movement never got off the ground. I personally feel it would be a worthy thing to do. In fact, I feel the whole veterans' memorial at the cemetery could stand a complete face-lift. Over the past Memorial Day, May 31, 2004, Kathy Phillips, BHS '52 and I visited the veterans' memorial. I was shocked with what I found! Between 1941 and 1945, Bisbee lost **seventy-six** brave young men! The names on the plaque are difficult, at best, to read due to the effects of the weather. The two-wheeled cannon is not a fair representation of a World War II weapon. Much could be done to up-grade the whole area. It would be a wonderful project for a service organization to undertake. The beautifully and tastefully done memorial to **"The True Heroes…"** which was just dedicated last Memorial Day, 2004, would be an excellent model to copy. It can be found in the north Vista Park area, below the Loma Linda Lodge. Eagle Scout candidate Aaron Oertel, member of Boy Scout Troop 401, designed this memorial.

Ralph Echave, BHS '47 who served with the 1st Marine Division in Korea, lends some interesting insight into Bisbee High's contribution to World War II. Ralph recalls two large Foster signs next to the Bisbee Post Office which had the names of all those from Bisbee who served during World War II. One of the signs was completely full and the other was half full. Ralph states: "Bisbee probably had, per. capita, one of the largest number of volunteers and draftees than most any city in the country. They had to bring in soldier miners, draftees, to work the mines because all of our men were in the service."

Ralph remembered some former Pumas who gave the *ultimate sacrifice* for America. Ralph's cousin, William Webb, was killed in action in the battle of the Coral Sea. Webb went down with his ship. Earl Wood was killed on Iwo Jima in the battle for Mt. Suribachi. Probably the first Bisbee boy killed in World War II was Jimmy Murphy. Murphy, who attended Loretto Academy when it was a high school, was killed aboard the U.S. Arizona on December 7, 1941 at Pearl Harbor. Because military records confirm that Murphy's death was the first one on The U.S. Arizona, a minesweeper was built and christened *The U.S. Bisbee* in honor of Murphy's home town.

Pete Vucurevich, BHS '47 reminds us of one of the original *Goat Row Gang* members who was killed by "friendly fire" while in a prison camp in Italy. Gus Gaxiola grew up and lived on Cochise Row directly across the street from Pete. Gaxiola was captured by Germans during the Battle of the Bulge in Belgium. He was sent to a prison camp in Italy, which was unmarked as such in violation of the Geneva Convention. Our bombers housed in Northern Africa, thinking the prison camp was a German military instillation, targeted it during a bombing run. One of Gus's buddies was out of the particular building Gus was in when the raid took place. Gus's building took a direct hit, killing all those inside. When Gus' buddy was freed at the end of World War II, he notified the Gaxiola family about the incident. Johnny Lindholm was another former Puma whom Pete grew up with and who lost his life in World War II. Pete does not recall the particulars of Lindholm's death.

Frank Lee Adams, brother of Dolly Adams, BHS '52, is the first name listed on the memorial plaque in Evergreen Cemetery.

The BHS class of 1945 may have had the largest number of classmates who served during World War II. The 1945 yearbook, the *Cuprite,* devoted a full page to honor them.

On that page was a touching memorial to President Franklin Delano Roosevelt who died April 12,1945, just a month before the Cuprite was issued. The memorial read in part:

IN MEMORIAM

To our great leader and president
FRANKLIN DELANO ROOSEVELT
January, 1882–April, 1945

Every American and every Ally will remember and uphold his ideals and standards of democracy. Never have the people of the world had as great a champion of right and democracy as they have had in President Roosevelt. As long as "Old Glory" flies over a world of free people, they will remember and revere that memory of him.

Immediately following this tribute to President Roosevelt was this commemorative record of the young men who started out as freshmen at BHS in 1941:

To the boys well known by our class who have so courageously sacrificed their lives that we might continue our way of life-the American way.

NEWTON "Fig" WOLCOTT

U.S. Army, Infantry, in Germany

EARL NICHOLS

U.S. Marines on Iwo Jima

EARL WOOD

U.S. Marine Paratroops on Iwo Jima

We wish to express out deep regret that all you boys who started out with us four short years ago, were not here on the night of our graduation. It would have been wonderful if you could have stayed here and received your diplomas with us. Your are our friends and classmates from B.H.S.

ARMY—NAVY—MARINES—MERCHANT MARINES

*RAYMOND GALAZ—FRANK R.CLARK—GILBERT W. HILL—
BENITO OROZCO—WILLIAM McGUIRE—JAMES E. WARNE—
CLAYBORN COBB—EARL BARACKMAN—JACK A. GANNON—
EDWARD JACK BOWDEN—THOMAS LINDLY—MELVIN
MADDERN—BOBBY DEL SANTO—BRUCE WALKER—
FREDERICK GIBSON EHLER—THOMAS E. RUSHIN—
ALFONSO CORONA—WILLIAM NEEL*

The BHS class of 1945 paid homage to their absent classmates in this way. The weather beaten plaque in Evergreen Cemetery honors the other "war years" classes in yet another way. All were heroes. *Seventy-six* paid the full measure. Many more were willing to. The **B** did indeed shine brighter because of these brave young men of the BHS classes of 1941 to 1945. They sacrificed selflessly. They set the standard that others would follow; some in Korea; others Vietnam. As maudlin as it may sound, these young men took a part of Bisbee with them. These men were influenced, shaped and molded by many of the same people who touched all of our lives. They drove up and down the same streets we did. They played pool in Wallace's. They necked with their girl friends in the Lyric theatre. They went into the same classrooms we did. They spoke with the same teachers we did. They were *from Bisbee*. They served willingly. They could hardly wait to come home to Bisbee. Seventy-six didn't.

IN A LEAGUE OF THEIR OWN

Here is a trivia question for you: "Which Bisbee baseball player was the first and only Bisbeeite to hit a home run in *Yankee Stadium*?" The answer will be given later in this section.

The first time it happened, I was the most surprised guy in the park! It was my freshman year in high school. We had been practicing baseball and track for about a week. On this particular day, I had just hurried over to the Warren Ball-park from a brief work out with the track team in the Vista Park. I had put my baseball cleats on and Coach Dicus told me to get in the batting cage and take a few cuts. My Greenway buddy, George Bays was pitching. George had a pretty good curve. Since I had a *thing* about curve balls, I hated to bat against him, even in batting practice. As I got set in the batters' box not at all anxious to try to hit his curve, a deep female voice softly said "I'll tell George to groove a few fast balls before he throws you a curve." I looked at the catcher and was startled to realize that it was George's *sister!* Holy cow! What was going on?! A girl catcher! I couldn't believe it. Well, **Betty Bays** soon convinced me, as well as my teammates that she was not just a *girl catcher*. She was an outstanding *catcher*, period! Coach Dicus would recruit Betty to catch batting practice on a regular basis that season. She even played in some of our inter-squad games and more than held her own with the guys. She would dare the base runners to try to steal on her. Few did. Betty had a very strong arm.

Betty grew up playing softball in the sandlots around Bisbee. It was not until World War II broke out that Betty and other women started playing *baseball*. Softball and baseball are two completely different games. The most obvious difference is that a softball is pitched *under handed*, while a baseball is *thrown over handed*. A softball is larger in diameter than a baseball. The pitching mound is closer to the batter in softball and the ball is not thrown as fast. The bases are closer together in softball. At the risk of sounding sexist, I will say that baseball is a *man's game* while soft ball is a women's game that *old men* can play. Betty Bays was skilled in both sports. But, it was in baseball that Betty became a nationally known and well-paid professional.

During World War II while Bisbee men were stepping into harm's way, Bisbee women were stepping to the plate. A huge void had been created in the summer recreational activities of Bisbee due to the number of men who were in the military. In order to field teams in both the baseball and softball leagues, Bisbee went "coed". Women played beside men in both the baseball and softball leagues.

Ray Parker, a Bisbee businessman, was a scout for the national women's teams, which sprouted up across America during World War II. Ray traveled all over Arizona looking for talent. He found a lot of it in his own "back yard". In 1946, Ray signed Betty Bays and Ann Mihelich to play baseball in the national women's baseball league. According to an article written for the June 9, 2001 Bisbee Review by Cathy Murphy, both girls were sent to the mid-west to play in the very tough Mid-West Women's Baseball League. It was this league on which the 1991 movie *A League of Their Own* was based.

Betty's professional stint was from 1950 to 1951 during which time she played on three of the nine national women's teams. In an exhibition game in Yankee Stadium, Betty accomplished a feat no one else, male or female, from Bisbee has ever done. She hit a home run! The Yankees were so impressed with Betty's prowess that they gave her a bat autographed by Yankee players, Joe DiMaggio, Billy Martin (wonder if *he* knew Betty was from Bisbee?) and Johnny Mize.

The Bisbee Review article by Cathy Murphy points out another interesting aspect of Betty's professional career. Because Betty was such an attractive young lady, the management of her team, the Grand Rapid *Chicks*, had her take modeling lessons. Betty had been chosen to appear in publicity photos for the women's teams.

Like all professional sports organizations, The Mid-West Women's Baseball League was a money conscious, profit making organization. In order to spread her talent around, the Grand Rapid *Chicks* (Betty was voted *Rookie of the Year* for the entire nine team league with the *Chicks)* traded Betty to the Chicago *Coleens* in 1951. Because Betty was such a valuable commodity to the league, she was given a substantial pay raise from $500 a month to $650 a month. The pay raise made her one of the highest paid players in the league.

According to Cathy Murphy of the Bisbee Daily Review, in her playing days "Betty looked remarkably like today's actress and music star, Madonna. She could have easily doubled for the star in the 1991 film, *A League of Their Own* based on the women's baseball league." The producers of the movie even contacted Betty and offered her a substantial amount of money to serve as an "on the set" coach. For those of you who saw the movie, you are aware that some of the young actresses were not exactly suited to play baseball athletes. Betty would have been a great one to coach them. However, Betty was in ill health at that time and her husband, Greg Schuller, would not allow Betty to make the trip to Hollywood. To show their appreciation to Betty for her contribution to the women's baseball league, and the subsequent movie, the producers sent her a baseball cap showing the *League of Their Own* logo. Betty Bays Schuller, arguably the finest woman athlete to come out of Bisbee High School, died in April of 1992.

Another young Bisbee woman who made quite an impact on the Mid-West Women's Baseball League was Ann Milhlich. After being recruited by Ray Parker, Ann was assigned to play for the Rockford, Illinois *Peaches*. Ann was a slick fielding and power hitting first baseman. Ann's most memorable moment came when the *Peaches* played the national champion Muskegon, Michigan team in front of six thousand screaming fans. Ann said the noise sent shivers up her spine. Ann played two years in the national baseball league before returning to Arizona when the women's baseball league was disbanded. Ann continued her playing in The Arizona Women's Fast Pitch Softball League with the very strong Phoenix *Ramblers*. After a year with the *Ramblers*, Ann moved back to Bisbee and played for the Ray Parker coached Bisbee *Copper Queens's* fast pitch softball team. Under Ann's leadership and experience, and Parker's organization, the *Copper Queens* proved to be more than most of the teams throughout Arizona could handle.

Ray Parker had a knack of developing young players. He could always get the most out of them. Ray did not allow for any "cry baby" girls on his teams. If a girl got a small "oweee", a "strawberry" or even a bleeding cut, Ray would just say, "Spit on it and rub a little dirt on it. It is several feet from your heart. It won't kill you!" Ray's girls were tough competitors. Over a period from the early 1950's to the end of the decade, the *Copper Queens* won their league on a regular basis playing the strongest teams in Arizona. Ray would scout the grade school play grounds and if he spotted a young girl who showed promise, he would ask her parents if he could give the youngster a "try out" with the possibility of her eventually being able to play for the *Copper Queens*. Snoody Pelot was stealing bases for the *Copper Queens* when she was in the sixth grade. Luche Giacomino played third base for the *Copper Queens* for five years, beginning in the eighth grade. Jackie Heard and Thelma Crawley were slugging base hits as seventh graders. Lupe Sena pitched and played third for six years. She started in grade school as well.

Dale Hancock, BHS '57 reminds me of others who made the *Copper Queens* so powerful: Patty Bigham Loper started playing when she was in the sixth grade. Patty O'Brian, Jeannie Wright, Thelma Salas, Angela Dabecovich, and Bobbie Giacoletti all got their start under Ray Parker when they were in grade school. It should be mentioned here that Ray had quality help in molding the *Copper Queens* into a state powerhouse. Bob Henry had played professional baseball for a number of years for the Bisbee-Douglas *Copper Kings*. He married Ann Milelich after she returned from her sojourn in the women's professional baseball league. Bob's knowledge was invaluable to Ray. Angel Salas, a legend in southern Arizona and Mexico as an outstanding athlete, also helped Ray coach the girls.

Remember, these girls were competing and winning against the strongest teams in Arizona. They weren't just competing in the city recreational league! That has to say something for the legacy that Betty Bays and Ann Henry left for Ray Parker and his *Copper Queens* to continue. They were indeed in a *league of their own!*

**AUGUST 3, 1941
JIGGERVILLE, AZ**

WHERE THE HECK IS *JIGGERVILLE?!*

I always get a little nostalgic when I go back to visit my brother and his family in Warren. They live on 111 West Vista directly across the street from the Warren Ballpark. I have spent many hours sitting on their front porch reliving beautiful memories of growing up just across the street from where I was sitting. The copper water ditch was just behind me. I always think of Robert Thompson's numb head. It was impervious to bb's. He lived two houses down from where my brother now lives. Ken Hunt lived next door. The Vista Park and the Warren Ballpark are still there. What great memories. My visit home would not be quite the same without those memories. Others are not so blessed. I am saddened that so many who grew up in Bisbee cannot experience the joy of actually *tangibly seeing* those places which were so much a part of their child hood. Those people can still come *back to Bisbee.* They can still walk the streets of Bisbee, Lowell, and Warren. They can still *see* the old Lyric Theatre, the old BHS building, and other haunts that generate so many memories. Horace Mann Grade School is still there. St. Pat's is still there. Lowell Grade School is still there. Greenway Grade School is still there. *Jiggerville* is not still there. Yet, so many to this day, call Jiggerville *home.* They spent their formative years there developing friendships, which have lasted lifetimes even though Jiggerville itself has completely been wiped off the map! In its place remains a huge hole in the ground! Only the memories remain. I remember well the day when the top of the mountain, which once sheltered Jiggerville, was blasted away. I was a freshman in high school and the entire student body was taken to the roof of BHS so we could watch the mountaintop being blown away. Digging would soon begin on the new Lavender

Pit. I did not realize until all these emails started circulating, just how many childhood memories were being blown up that day.

It took the death and the resulting obituary of a former Jiggerville resident to open a floodgate of memories for many, many Bisbeeites scatted across the country. Earl Hindman was recognized all over America as *Wilson, the man behind the fence* in the TV comedy series, *Home Improvement*. Many Bisbeeites were not only saddened by his death, but were startled to read that he grew up in Bisbee. More specifically, that he grew up in *Jiggerville!* Many Bisbeeites read his obituary and commented "Jiggerville! Well, I'll be!" Many, many more Bisbeeites read his obituary and commented "Where the heck is *Jiggerville?*"

Dale Hancock, BHS '57 and Ed "Pappy" Swierc, BHS '53, both former Jiggerville residents, got the *memory train* rolling with this bit of email give and take: "I cannot recall Earl Hindman or his brother or his family, but that was such a long time ago that names and families escape me. I do remember the Jiggerville families because that was my home from somewhere around 1942 until they started Lavender pit and moved the homes to Saginaw…" wrote Dale. Ed responded: "I never read the part about Earl living in Jiggerville before, but when you told me about it, surprise!! I got a 'happy memory' thrill and, 'It's a small world' chill up my spine all at the same time. His brother, Ray Hindman, and I used to run together for the brief time he lived in Jiggerville! I remember really missing Ray after he moved out. I never saw him again or even heard of the Hindman's again until now. That's about fifty five years ago give or take a week or so. I didn't see an email address specifically pointing back to Ray's brother, but I sure would like to hear more of whatever happened to Ray."

Dale Hancock grew up in Bisbee, and lived in Arizona all his life. He had accumulated a long list of Bisbee acquaintances with whom he was in touch via email. Ed's note was passed on to Dale's list and the whole thing literally *exploded!* Those who responded with the question, "Where the heck is Jiggerville?" got their question answered many times over. Others responded with memories and questions of their own.

Carol Loy BHS, '57 sent a recent article from the Bisbee Review dated Sunday, May 09, 2004 written by Bisbee historian, Mary Frances Lynn. In it Mary Frances recalls her memories of the beginning of the demise of Jiggerville. Sacramento Pit had been a Bisbee landmark for years and Jiggerville was located near by. The Phelps Dodge Mining Company was planning to expand their development of Sacramento Pit to substantially increase the production of copper. Mary Frances Lynn writes "We knew that the PD was preparing for a large pit. Huge drayage trucks (large flat bed trucks to haul large loads, like complete houses! hh) were pulling houses from Johnson Addition, Jiggerville, and upper Lowell to a new section called 'Saginaw'". Saginaw was misnamed. In the Yaqui Indian language, "Saginaw" means *happy home*. Sadly, what the PD was doing was *uprooting* a lot of "happy homes". The PD gave the residents of Jiggerville two options, both of which were pretty traumatic; either sell the houses to the PD, or relocate where PD dumps them. Dale Hancock had no love for the move. He comments "Jiggerville was a special area and well designed and comfortable. They did us no favors by dropping our old frame homes down in Saginaw. Jiggerville had at one time been an upscale community for the Bisbee area where a lot of the bosses lived. They even had a trolley car service to take people from Jiggerville to Warren." Dale alludes to the fact that some thought that the PD did the people of Jiggerville a favor by moving them to Saginaw. It was not a "wonderful" thing that happened, but moving to "Saginaw was a situation we had to make the most of. It was the only place we had to live." It was better than being dropped into a huge hole that was going to be all that was left of Jiggerville when the PD got through digging. It was obvious to Dale that some bitter feelings were surfacing after all these years. "Some true feelings are coming out about the bitterness of Jiggerville being destroyed for the Lavendar pit. It (the many emails, hh) is the first time I have really seen or heard it expressed. It was within me, but I had not had the opportunity to discuss with others who felt the same way as I. Ed Swierc and I had shared between us, but not in this email circle we have going…Although we made the best of living in Saginaw, it was not anywhere close to the *Jiggerville experience.*"

You may be wondering what was so special about Jiggerville; *just what was this Jiggerville experience?* Here are just a few examples:

Not only did the families lose their homes but also the kids lost their *baseball diamond*. The diamond was a labor of love. Here is how Ed Swierc describes it:

"The 'big' baseball diamond was located right in front of my house at the folk's garage. We had a grandstand seat in back of home plate from our screened in porch. At first, home plate was right in front of the garage's tin doors and made a heck of a racket you could hear for half a mile when the ball hit it. Whether for noise abatement or scrap money, the garage was soon torn down and we had to then rustle up a tall pipe frame and put up some chicken wire for a backstop.

Now the big pusher behind creating our ball field was Clarence Dupnik. He had all the equipment, all the fielders' gloves, all the balls and bats. Everything we needed, Clarence had. Had his gloves been Toyotas, you'd have to say he got two hundred thousand miles out of them. The gloves got a dose of Neats foot oil every week and lasted for years. That kid loved to play ball!"

The manicured diamond was the envy of every professional baseball ground-skeeper in the southwest. It was more a trapezoid shape than a diamond. The ground rules had to be changed daily depending on the location of Old man McKeen's car and they definitely favored the home team. First base was a rock. A well placed bunt by a skilled Jiggerville veteran would bounce off the rock just as the first baseman reached for it. If the catcher was not alert as the ball bounced back in his direction, the bunter would be standing on second before a play could be made. Old man McKeen's corrugated garage was in foul territory near first base. The loud clanging sound of a ball hitting the garage announced to all that the ball was foul. Old man McKeen was awakened from many a nap by the foul ball announcement. A road was misplaced between first and second which necessitated the pitcher's mound being constructed almost on top of first base. Because baseballs were at a premium, any local dog was an automatic "shagger". Once, early in the days of the field, one of the "shaggers" was run over when Old man McKeen backed out of his garage to go to town. Had the pitcher at the time not been alert, he too would have been run over. Out of concern for future "shaggers" and pitchers, the pitcher's mound was moved closer to first base and an automatic "time out" was declared any time Old man McKeen cranked up his car. Second base was another rock right in the middle of the road. It was in direct line of sight from home plate through second to the fire hose cart in front of the Goar's wooden fence in dead center field. It was a good two hundred feet from home to the fence. Even with a good wind, few could hit it into Goar's yard.

Third base was really a "home field advantage". It was a piece of pipe sticking out of the ground about two inches high. The pipe was originally about a foot high but somewhere in the distant past before Dupnik was manager, someone had sawed part way through the pipe. Once in a grudge game between Bill Howard's Lowell *Looters* and Bill Decker's Jiggerville *Jocks,* an over exuberant young Jiggerville player, named Ignacious Dugie, tripped over the third base pipe nearly bending it in two. Dugie never made it to home and Jiggerville lost the game. Decker was immediately replaced as manager of the *Jocks.* The Jiggerville city council held an emergency meeting to appoint a new manager. Clarence Dupnik was the unanimous choice. Dupnik's first act was to bend and twist the third base pipe until it broke off two inches above ground. Dupnik made sure all Jiggerville players knew exactly where third base was. They held lengthy practices rounding third so they did not trip over the protrusion. Visiting teams often did. It was a decided advantage for the home team. It was not an advantage for adults however. Mr. B Hancock, Dales's dad, was a former professional player. He was used to rounding a base without looking at it. This was not a good idea on the Jiggerville diamond, and especially not a good idea when rounding third. B. was flying around third in one game when he did not look to see how close to the jagged edge he was stepping. His ankle was sliced up pretty good and had to have several stitches to close the wound. It might be mentioned here, too, that Jiggerfield players learned never to slide into third. To prevent any further serious injury from a miscalculated step, the jagged edge where the pipe had been ripped apart was hammered down. The ground rule at the time said that any hit directly over third and into Jay Howard's yard was a foul ball. If you hit the ball on the ground between second and third and it went into the short left field ditch, it was a hit and the batter could get all he could make. However, if the ball was hit in the air and it landed in Jay Howard's chicken coop, it was an out. Mr. Howard was a big brusque man who didn't approve of balls being hit in the chicken coop and scattering his chickens. He said it greatly reduced the egg producing capability of his hens; especially when the ball hit one of them. Mr. Howard was just not a real baseball fan.

Another problem was in short right field. Old man McKeen liked to irritate the kids by sometimes parking his Buick in front of his house instead of in his garage. When he did this, the back window of the car was only about twenty feet behind the pitcher and even closer to first base. I remember taking up collections twice to buy Old man McKeen a new back window for the Buick. If a ball hit his car and ricocheted back into play, it was all you could get. However, if the ball broke the back window, the batter was out.

Manager Clarence Dupnik had a very shrewd and organized baseball mind. He provided a two-page notebook for each visiting team, which listed all the ground rules. The notebook had to be updated on a daily basis. Soon, outside teams refused to travel to Jiggerville to play the *Jocks*. It was impossible for the visitors to remember and play by all the ground rules. The *Jocks'* did not have much of a travel budget, so after awhile all their games had to be inter-squad games. These games were better anyway. They could be pretty intense when it was family member against family member. I fondly remember some of the families, which were regular participants. It is amazing how almost every time we decided to play a game, ball players would magically appear. Dale and B Hancock, Harold and Art Welander, the Dupnik clan, most of Rica Hardt's family, miscellaneous neighbors and myself joined in as well. Harold and Art's sister, Ruth, was designated cheerleader. She cheered for which ever team was winning".

Ed concludes his musings about the Jiggerville ball diamond by extolling the skills which most of the players developed over the years. The more athletic of the bunch became expert place hitters. As Ed says "…for all practical purposes, a hitter on our ball field was limited to a thirty five degree cone of safety over second base where the ball could be hit. Dunno if Babe Ruth as a kid had to put up with those kinds of restrictions or not. He would have been a fantastic placement hitter if he had. Bet he didn't have any more fun than us, though."

Even before the PD started moving houses out of Jiggerville, there were a few abandoned houses kids could fool around in. One of them was Old man McKeen's house after he died. Evidently his sons did not want the house so they just left and abandoned it. That allowed for more base hits down the right field line. Another abandoned house that comes to Ed's mind was the one directly in front of Pug Whelan's house. All the windows and doors were gone. It was just an abandoned shell. These and a few other old vacant houses provided great places for generations of Jiggerville kids to roam around in.

Ed is reminded of the fact "...that each house in Jiggerville actually had two separate water systems. One was the Naco water system for drinking which everyone in Bisbee had. The second was the mine water feed with a tap at every house. The mine water wasn't fit to drink (it had an acid taste and left a bad sensation at the back of our throat), but it was great for watering the yard, the trees and gardens. Unlike the 'city water', the mine water was free. There was however, one minor problem in using the mine water around the yard. It was pumped at such a high pressure, that it would burst most normal water hoses sold around town. My dad solved that problem by using a one-inch high-pressure air line as a water hose. It worked great, but it was a chore for me to drag around."

In one of his first emails, Dale Hancock really got on a "roll" recalling the good old days in Jiggerville:

"...we played kick the can, hide and seek; we tried to communicate across ditches using tin cans and string; we hiked the surrounding mountains; we climbed the old dump and from on top we could see all over Jiggerville; we could fly our kites on a good windy day from on top of the dump and sometimes the kites would be so high they looked like they were over South Bisbee; we explored the old Sac Pit and the surrounding mine shafts; we found valuable treasures that only a kid would appreciate; to see who was the bravest, we would jump off of the cliffs that were everywhere; probably the stupidest thing we did was catch wild donkeys and take them into a tin shed and try to ride them. Wild donkeys don't like little kids. We got bitten, kicked and bucked off into the sides of the shed. It's a wonder we weren't killed. We walked to Lowell Grade School every day by a route that crossed several railroad tracks. On the way to school we would put pennies on the tracks and then see how flattened they were when we came home. On our way to Lowell Grade School we passed the Junction Yard front gate, the power plant, the bakery where we would get pieces of fresh warm bread from Mr.

Milovich; we always checked out the Lowell theatre to see what movies were coming. Once we found some condoms and thinking they were balloons, we blew them up and took them to school to show our friends. Some of our Jiggerville buddies had to walk to Bisbee to go to school at St. Pat's. They were the Dupnik kids and Ed Swierc. They had longer to walk. They had to walk the back route to Bisbee next to Sac Pit, and the Copper Queen Mine Shaft that is now a tourist attraction." Dale stops here to take a breath.

Here is how Ed describes his daily walk to St. Pat's:

"The walk to Bisbee every day seemed like it was five miles, but I think it was closer to maybe one and a half miles. Our walking path started from the 'high road' at the west edge of Jiggerville and followed the railroad tracks around Sacramento Pit, over the current location of the Copper Queen shaft, coming out behind the Bisbee Post Office. From there we had to walk up the alley behind the businesses on Main Street to St. Pat's. Sometimes we walked in the drainage ditch all the way. We got to know every step of that walk along with every railroad tie. We walked it day and night for years.

At night there was a street light at the last mineshaft after leaving Bisbee before getting to the Sacramento pit, and then it was totally dark until we got past the pit to the dump above Jiggerville. For a kid it was really scary to be going by the unlighted observation area at the Sac Pit. There was usually a car parked there in the blackness, sometimes with mysterious glows visible in the car window. You just knew someone was waiting for a scared kid to come by. Darn cars, should have stayed home. They couldn't see anything at that time of night anyway, especially with all their lights off!!"

Dale continues his memories:

"That is the same way we had to walk to go to the Lyric theatre on Saturdays. The Lyric was owned by the Diamos family and they always had good movies for us. We especially liked the cowboy heroes we got to see: Roy Rogers, Gene Autry, Lash LaRue, Tex Ritter, The Lone Ranger and Tonto, Tom Mix, Hopalong Cassidy, Johnny Mack Brown, Red Ryder and Little Beaver and others. We saw lots of cartoons; Mighty Mouse, Heckle and Jeckle, The Road Runner, and many more. We always felt very patriotic after we watched The Movie Tone News-Reels. There were some times when we went to the movies at night, but not too often because it was so scary walking home. It was very dark and there were no streetlights. We could go to the movie for a dime and for another dime we could get popcorn and a Coke. We built coasters and raced them down the main hill through Jiggerville.

Like other neighborhoods, Jiggerville was our 'hood'; a safe environment and a social center. We had no organized ball teams, leagues or recreation centers. We were our own social directors and parents were not involved except those young enough to play baseball with us. When the games were family member against family member, they were very competitive.

I remember playing in the Dupnik's yard when we heard via the radio that Babe Ruth had died. We went over to our diamond and each of us pretended we were the Babe."

Dale concluded with these recollections: "I can visually walk every street and road in Jiggerville and could even draw you a map of the lay out and the homes. I knew who lived in every one of them at the time, but could not tell you all the names now. Ed Swierc has been much better at names than me on Jiggerville. We made wooden 'rubber guns' and used old inner tubes from cars to cut out our 'bullets'. The rubber gun was cut out of wood in shape of a pistol or rifle and clothes pins were used as the firing pins after the rubber 'bullets' were doubled and stretched around the barrels and clasped in the clothespins. As we got older, we advanced to b.b. guns and played cowboys or war using b.b.s and actually shooting one another. We had to be a hardy bunch to survive. At times we used gasoline to kill ants. We poured the gasoline down the ant holes and lit it on fire. We even smoked 'weed' in those days. We got weed branches, which were hollow in the middle and smoked them. Do you remember the "cancer trees"? Do you remember Mrs. Bishop's beautiful house and yard? It had the biggest apricot tree I have ever seen. I was reminded of how the Churn Drills came in our neighborhood and how they gradually moved up the road and soon houses started to be moved out of our special place. WOW....did I get wound up or what?"

Ed noticed that Dale wrote about building coasters so his mind was joggled, and he responded:

"As we apparently grew up with deep wishes of self-destruction, we took note that the dirt roads of Jiggerville would be great for racing around. I never owned a bicycle to race around with, so a buddy and myself decided to build a neat coaster to ride down the steep hills. The coaster wasn't fancy like those used down Main Street in Bisbee on the Fourth of July, and in fact wouldn't have been allowed within the Bisbee City limits. The coaster consisted of a body made out of a long 2x12 plank pointed on the front end (air dynamics, ya know), with wheels and axles from either an old Radio Flyer wagon or lifted from a baby buggy. Steering was with a rope and there were no brakes. There was a stick nailed across in front to put your feet on. Having seen and envied our coaster, Clarence Dupnik and his friend also built a fast coaster they ran down a big hill by his friend's grandma's house. I don't recall Clarence's friend's name right now, but I believe he later became one of Bisbee's mayors for a term or two in the next thirty years. So Clarence's coaster and my coaster were in competition. The Hancock's (Dale's folks) also lived at the top of that hill right across the road from the grandmother. That was a BIG steep hill with no place to stop at the bottom. You first had to listen and look to see if any cars were coming before starting the coaster since nobody had any idea how to build any kind of brakes. Not only were cars possibly coming in from Lowell, but also there was another street blindly merging with the coaster-run at the bottom of the hill. If a car was coming, the only thing to do was to steer off the road to the right, which dropped steeply into a huge gully with big mesquite bushes about twenty feet down. You became airborne for a loooong ways. I remember Dale's little sister, Jan Hancock, taking that fast trip off the road one day. We thought for sure that she was dead the way she piled up. But, she couldn't have steered left at the bottom of the hill, because then she would have gone right into Pug Whelan's front porch. The ditch and bushes looked softer to her.

OUR coaster was designed extra fancy! I got the idea to put *four* wheels on the back plus the two in the front. I figured we needed to do this since my second bright idea was to nail down a three foot section of full sized steel railroad track on top of the coaster right between the driver's legs, right up in the crotch area. I figured we could get more speed that way with all the extra weight. In retrospect, it is a wonder any of us ever 'begat' any kids. We did indeed get a lot more speed, and we found out on our first run just how hard it was to stop that coaster just by dragging our feet.

It was always tough to find racing time on that hill. The coasters made a lot of racket going down hill on those rocks, and Dale Hancock's mom would invariably come out and chase us away. Since B Hancock worked the night shift and was sleeping, she didn't want us to wake him up. We got to wondering how come B was always sleeping. We suspected Mrs. Hancock stopped us just because she was afraid we'd kill ourselves.

The big problem we had with our coasters was that our axles were bending all the time. I remember heating up those axles over the gas stove at home to red-hot. Then I tried dipping them in oil and water trying to make them stronger. It never did any good. We usually got one or two rides and the wheels would then invariably splay out again. After about four times straightening them out they would break and the search was on for new equipment. When the parts finally ran out, that signaled the end of our coaster days.

Somehow *we survived Jiggerville, anyway!"*

Sue Cooke Ray, BHS '63 remembers with much sadness when her home in Jiggerville was moved. "When I was four, I started noticing the 'Churn Drills' showing up in the neighborhood. I never guessed they were there to destroy our wonderland. I remember walking past them many times. Does anyone remember the season they started moving us out? Mom and Dad were notified when they were ready to move our house. We watched as they placed the long metal rails under the house and slowly loaded it on the truck. Our house was #46 (the simple things I remember) and we were back in the corner next to the Hancock's. Our house was one of the first to be moved. The next morning after we watched them loading the house, Mom and Dad drove us back to Jiggerville. We parked at the top of the hill next to where Mrs. Bishop's house had been. I remember the devastation and destruction of our beautiful Jiggerville as I sat there and watched them come up the hill with our house. All the beauty and security was gone. Jiggerville looked as though it had been bombed. I remember looking around and seeing nothing familiar. So vivid the memory and I was only five years old when it was finally over. That memory will be there forever. Thank you all for sharing your stories and reinforcing the memories I was gradually forgetting."

A number of respondents to the question about the origin of the term *Jiggerville* were able to shed a bit of light on it. However, what most came up with was that *Jiggerville* was named after the *jigger bosses* who first lived there. But, nobody could satisfactorily tell what a *jigger boss* was. After reading all the weak attempts to define the term, I decided to put the question to bed once and for all. I consulted with none other than Mr. Daniel Webster and here is what he says a *jigger* is: *(1) a plate, box or open frame for holding work and for guiding a machine tool to the work. (2) an apparatus for washing coal or separating ore from gangue by shaking and washing.* So there you have it. A *jigger-boss* was an under-paid miner who stood around all day and watched a big box full of rocks being shaken and washed, so that the copper could be separated from the gangue. For the Lowell Grade School graduates, *gangue* is "rock or mineral matter of no value."

At the beginning of this section on *Where the Heck is Jiggerville?*, Ed Swierc recalled for us how surprised he was to find out that "The man behind the fence" was the brother of his good friend from Jiggerville days, Ray Hindman. Well, Friday, May 7, 2004 was a very special day for Ed Swierc. After losing touch with each other for fifty-five years, Ed and Ray Hindman were united again via the telephone! I'll let Ed tell you about it:

"Friday was a special day for me as I talked over the phone with Ray Hindman for the first time since 1949. He and I shared many good times in the last days of Jiggerville, up until the time he and his family moved away. It was only months after he moved, that Jiggerville itself was moved away as well. It was interesting to learn that while we had similar interests as kids with crystal sets, coasters and roaming the hills, this similarity of interests continued well past those childhood days. When we both joined the military, he in the Air Force, me in the Navy, both of us were assigned to attend electronic schools. We both were interested in airplanes and both of us learned to fly them. My flying was curtailed by an overseas assignment, while he pursued it further. Ray got his commercial pilots license. While we ended up in different career fields, we both opted for an early retirement. I don't know if we can blame that last decision on our Jiggerville connection, but why not?

Talking with Ray really made the years dissolve away, pretty much as the exchange of Bisbee memories serves to do for all of us. I hope everyone can make at lest one re-connection with a special long ago family as I have. It is a great feeling!

At the end of our talk, I also had a few words with a very special lady, Ray's mother. She always welcomed me into her home, treating me like on of her own. She commented as we talked that she is now eighty-eight years old. I told her if she keeps that up she is going to fool around and get old soon. That got a laugh from her. It was a good end to a good day for me."

In Earl Hindman's obituary a "Dean Shields" was mentioned. An article written by "Dean Shields" accompanied the obituary. As one reads the article it becomes obvious that "Dean Shields" is a close relative; one would assume a male relative. Through the many twists and turns all these hundreds of emails have made, "Dean Shields" has surfaced! "Dean Shields" is *Deanie Hindman Shields,* the *sister* of "the man behind the fence" and sister of Ed's buddy, Ray Hindman. Deanie, too, has been in touch with many of her Jiggerville friends since Dale and Ed started this email *train* rolling. Deanie lives in the Payson, Arizona area. It is only fitting that a note she wrote should end this section on Jiggerville:

"When the Payson Roundup ran the story about Jiggerville and Earl, they also include the photo of Jiggerville. I loved what the editor wrote beneath the photo. The text read *The Lost Village of Jiggerville. I*'ve been thinking about that. I wonder just how many little towns in the U.S. have actually been picked up and moved to another location like Jiggerville was? And I wonder how many towns have ever had a group of people like you all who are getting together with memories that go back forty or fifty years; who write about the memories, and plan a reunion for everyone that was there in the 50's? I'll bet this is a very unique happening. It is so good that everything is getting down on paper and flying through cyberspace."

Ok, so, *where the heck is Jiggerville?* It is right there. Right where it has always been. Only now you can't see it. But, it is still there none the less.

FUZZY

"Eoo, kalook, kalook, kalook!" I have no clue what that means. But, we heard it frequently during football practices at BHS whenever something stellar happened. When a back would make a good run, or a defensive back would deliver a vicious tackle; whenever a BHS *Puma* did something that got Coach Fuzzy Warren excited, we could expect to hear that enthusiastic voice of his yelling out, "Eoo, kalook, kalook, kalook!" All the time Fuzzy was yelling, he would be sprinting towards the honored player. Fuzzy would grab him, hug him and swing him off the ground. It was an honor that only Coach Fuzzy could bestow. When he got excited we knew it! He was one who was not afraid to show his emotions. When he was happy we knew it! When he approved of what we did we knew it!

But, we frequently saw the other side of Coach Fuzzy Warren as well! He had a temper that caused him and others a lot of grief over the years. Fuzzy had been fired from Douglas High School before he came to BHS. His anger had gotten the best of him. Nobody seemed to know just what it was that had caused his firing at Douglas. Many rumors circulated over the years as to what he had done. We never knew what the infraction was. Nor, did we care. Fuzzy was a *Puma*. His past did not matter to us. We loved him. Douglas' loss was Bisbee's gain.

Unforgiveness is a terrible burden for one to carry. It eats at you. It can cause one to lose track of reality. Sadly, Fuzzy was carrying around a lot of unforgiveness in his heart. Towards what or whom, I never knew. I do know that it had something to do with how he was treated by Douglas. He hated Douglas with a passion. I never heard him say anything good about a Douglas person. Even Gib Dawson, a Douglas great, one of Arizona's all time best football players, could never garner respect from Fuzzy. Every running back who ever played for BHS was a better back than *Douglas'* Gib Dawson, in Fuzzy's mind.

Fuzzy loved to beat Douglas in *anything.* Come to think of it, he loved to beat *anybody* in *anything*! He was a vicious competitor; he would go for the jugular! If we had a team down by several touchdowns and just a few minutes to play, most coaches would put in some of the second team. Not Fuzzy! If it was up to him, the starters would still be in the game going for more points! That is why Fuzzy was never a head coach. He had no compassion for the opponents. He loved winners. He could not tolerate losers.

I knew Fuzzy for many years. His wife, Wilma, was my Uncle Don Fergus' sister in law. My parents often included Fuzzy and Wilma and their young daughter, Linda, in family gatherings. Yet, I never *really knew* Fuzzy. Looking back on it, he was an enigma to me. At that time in my youth, Fuzzy was just *Fuzzy*. I loved him. He was my coach whom I respected very much. Yet, I never knew much more than that about him. He was my coach, period. He was such a complex personality. How I wish I would have taken the time to peel away some of his self-evident exterior and gotten to know the *real Fuzzy Warren*. He had a heart of gold...for those he liked. His dislikes were fairly obvious.

Probably the people who got the closest to the real Fuzzy were the students in his chemistry class or the ones he taught to drive in his Driver Training classes. Kathy Phillips, BHS '52 tells of her learning to drive the hard way. After a traumatic experience with her dad in which Kathy and the family car ended up in a ditch upside down and the car totaled, Mr. Phillips decided to turn the job of teaching Kathy to drive over to Fuzzy. Mr. Phillips had Kathy enroll in Drivers' Education. Kathy was pretty much a basket case after her experience with her dad and had decided she would walk the rest of her life. However, she said that "Fuzzy took me out every day. He was pretty tough with me, but was kind and patient. I loved him for that. Had it not been for Fuzzy, I probably would be walking instead of driving today!"

Jean Silvey Olander, BHS [47] tells us "My best friend, Ruby Barrow Rhodes and I were in our early 20's and we had not learned to drive well enough to get our driver's license. I got my learners permit but tore it to pieces once when I was driving with my husband, Phil. He got mad and I got mad every time he tried to teach me to parallel park, etc. Mr. Warren took Ruby and me out every evening for a couple of weeks in the high school's training car. I don't know who laughed the most, him or us. All our silly mistakes only made him smile and he had the utmost patience with us. So, had it not been for him, I probably would be walking with Kathy!"

Wanda Talley Owens, BHS '52 remembers Fuzzy teaching her how to negotiate "Curve Street" where a driver had to slow down and honk before going around the curve. "I remember Fuzzy setting up a coke bottle on the floorboard in the back and if the coke bottle fell over as you drove around Curve Street, you failed your test. But, if we passed his class, we got our license to drive without going to DMV." When Fuzzy taught you, you were *taught!*

Susan Ridgway, BHS '67 has fond memories of Fuzzy's chemistry class. "He was my chemistry teacher in 1966. I remember the sense of fun Fuzzy generated in class. I also remember some of the things we did that would not happen today: We examined the properties of mercury. We thought it great that we could turn our gold rings to silver by rubbing mercury on them. WOW. Some girls volunteered to sniff laughing gas and apparently got too much, becoming hysterical and needing the attention of an ambulance crew (I don't think we had paramedics in Bisbee at that time). Fuzzy left immediately to follow them to the hospital.

Some clowns at the lab tables next to mine mixed chemicals that had a major adverse reaction and we didn't wear protective goggles then. But, my favorite memory was the day he decided we needed to pay less attention to him than to the clock. He moved a lab stool in front of the clock and climbed on to it; he ceremoniously yanked the clock off the wall, locking it in the closet. It never returned."

Mrs. Jane (Al) Ridgway was a big fan of Fuzzy's. "Fuzzy coached with Al and we were close friends. He always found a way to help a kid who was having trouble in class and he did all he could to help the kid pass. He was a great teacher at BHS and was thought a lot of by his students."

Jim "Lefty" Weld and I were two of those students Jane Ridgway spoke of. We struggled in his class learning to "balance equations" in chemistry. Fuzzy made us come to his class early in the mornings all one semester. He made sure we "learned" how to balance the equations! We never could explain "equations", but we "passed".

Fritz Kuehnlenz, BHS '53 remembers coming back from Korea and talking with Fuzzy several times at Wallaces' Pool Hall. They talked about military matters. Fuzzy had been a lieutenant colonel in World War II and was highly decorated. I wish I knew *that* story! I know this. Fuzzy was one man I would have wanted on my side in time of war!

Sam Kitterman, BHS '47 remembers Fuzzy's temper getting out of control in class and Fuzzy having to grab on to a bar he had attached over his desk. Fuzzy would pull on the bar until he calmed down.

Quite a few tracksters at BHS recall being chased around the Warren Ball Park with Fuzzy in hot pursuit firing his starter's pistol at them; firing blanks, of course. He even "shot" Bill Howard while Bill and several others were showering after practice one day. The echo in the shower room was deafening!

At a track meet in Tucson one day I was *broad* jumping (that word became politically incorrect and the event today is known as "long jumping.") and I got off what appeared to be a pretty good jump. Fuzzy was in the habit of placing a white handkerchief in the sand measured to designate the state record. I had cleared the handkerchief, but had stepped over the take-off board. The official at the broad jump pit correctly called "foul". It was obvious to all that I had fouled on the jump, but Fuzzy wanted the official to measure my jump anyway. The official wouldn't do it. "No sense measuring it, Coach. He fouled." the official said. Fuzzy insisted "Measure the jump. I want to see how far it was." Again, the official said "He fouled, Coach. I will not measure it!" With that, Fuzzy came unglued! He picked up a rake and started after the official. Fuzzy chased the guy around the pit a time or two before cooler heads stepped in. They grabbed Fuzzy before he could further convince the official that he was serious about wanting the jump measured. "He cheated you, Hadley! That was a state record!" Fuzzy screamed. I started to say "But, Fuzz, I fouled." I didn't say it though because Fuzz still had the rake in his hand.

My uncle, Don Fergus, Fuzzy's brother in law, told me that Fuzzy was an outstanding football and track performer at Missouri State University in his college days. He was an all conference running back and a superb low hurdler. Fuzzy was still a very fast runner when he coached at BHS. He often would run wind sprints with us after practice and could hold his own with all of us. When he would win, and he sometimes would, he would prance around, his knees pumping waist high and that exuberant "Eoo kalook, kalook, kalook!" reverberating around the field. He was quite a guy.

The last time I saw Fuzz he was confined to bed at Tucson Medical Center. It was in 1983, the year he died. I had been to a BHS Boosters' Club Banquet as quest speaker. The Boosters' Club had named Fuzz as their "Booster of The Year" and had a beautiful red and gray blanket to award him. Since he could not be there, I was asked if I would deliver it to him on my way back to Flagstaff. Of course I said I would be pleased and honored to present the blanket to him. When I walked into his hospital room, his eyes lit up. It had been many years since I had seen him, but he still recognized me. He smiled and said "Hey, number twenty, you look good." The voice was weak, but the same; the smile was the same, but he was just a shell of the Fuzzy Warren three decades of BHS students all knew and loved. He was pleased that the Boosters remembered him. He weakly said, "That was nice of them." I only stayed for five or ten minutes. For some reason I just felt uncomfortable. I shouldn't have, I know. I should have stayed longer. I should have asked him questions about *him*. I should have asked him what happened in Douglas. I should have asked him about his military record. I should have asked him about the family he came from. I should have gotten to know *him*. I should have told him how much

I loved and appreciated *him*. I didn't even ask him what "Eoo kalook, kalook, kalook" means. I should have.

"WELL, PIN A ROSE ON ME NELLIE". COACH DICUS

Coach Waldo Dicus had more of a positive impact on me than any other man I have ever known. I feel certain that any number of other young men who came in contact with Coach Dicus can say the same thing. This is one section of the book I have struggled with. How do I begin to put into words just how much Coach Dicus has meant to me and to so many others? So much can, and should be said about him. I will begin by quoting some comments that Lou Pavlovich, BHS '46 wrote about him. Lou was sports editor for the *Tucson Citizen* for many years and is now retired and living in Tucson. Lou owned and wrote for the nationally distributed *Collegiate Baseball* newspaper before retiring. Lou has "Bisbee blood" pumping strongly through his veins. Here are some of his comments regarding Coach Dicus that he wrote in a sports column in 1952 titled, *A Profound Personality:*

> A sports writer hears a lot of scuttlebutt in his daily meanderings. He can pretty well tell you how this coach or that player ranks in the eyes of others.
>
> A fellow makes his mark in this world and when it is especially good and worthwhile, we think everyone should know about it.
>
> Take Waldo Dicus, for instance. Here is a man who was an outstanding athlete at the University of Arizona. He was well liked, captained a few teams, set a record or two, and then went on his way into the coaching game.
>
> **At Jerome High** he started out as a typical coach. Before long he built up outstanding teams and made, generally, a very successful record. But like all mentors, he didn't escape criticisms. (Who the heck, especially a coach, ever escapes criticisms?)
>
> His outstanding record earned him a job at a bigger school, **Bisbee,** where he became football coach, athletic director, etc. The years went by and Dike compiled more outstanding records, even though he scheduled as many Class A opponents as he could find for his Class B school.
>
> This year Dike was named superintendent of schools at Ajo and his successor at Bisbee was Max Spilsbury, one of his outstanding athletic pupils.
>
> Max, in succeeding Dicus, made the remark: 'Dicus is the greatest man I've ever known and I will try in every way that I know to pattern my coaching and my living after him.'
>
> These quotes, as far as this writer knows, never got into print at that time. It could have been a lot of smoke-but it wasn't.

Next comes Hugh Crawford, another former Dicus performer at Bisbee, who is now head football coach at Patagonia High School. Crawford made the news recently when he banished his first two teams off the Patagonia squad for breaking training regulations.

He penned a letter to this writer last week, explaining his actions. Among other things, he wrote: 'It sure is hard to play with eleven boys, five who are freshman. But I will play as I played under Dicus in Bisbee, or not at all.'

And then there is Ted James, another Dicus protégé who is now head coach at Valley Union High School. Ted's comments about Dicus, as told to this writer last week, went like this: 'Dicus was an outstanding high school coach. He was well liked by his boys and highly respected, on and off the field. I find myself using his philosophy on my teams.'

This is just a sample of some of the things you hear. And when you collect them and put them together, it makes a real nice tribute to Waldo Dicus-a guy who somewhere along the way caught the spark of greatness.

Waldo Dicus-a guy who somewhere along the way caught the spark of greatness. I like that. Somewhere along the way he caught the spark of greatness and over a span of forty three years Coach Dicus used this God given spark to ignite various fires under untold hundreds of others; who in turn ignited a fire in others; who in turn, etc., etc. You get the picture. Coach Dicus' influence will never stop impacting others. There is a young man today, coaching track at Chaparral High School in Scottsdale, Arizona who has that spark. He has been named Teacher of the Year several times and has had successful track programs. He was born with that spark. His name is Brad Dicus, grandson of Waldo Dicus; son of Robert Dicus, Scottsdale, Arizona dentist.

The degree to which his spark of greatness is caught varies from one to another. For some under Coach Dicus' charge, the spark was never caught. For others, such as Al Ridgway and Max Spilsbury, the spark was caught and fanned into a raging inferno.

It used to be that in our society, the term "coach" attached to a person's name denoted *respect* and *honor* which is due that person. That is not true anymore and I want to touch on that point later in this book. But, for now, when I was growing up, "coach" carried almost a *divine* connotation to it. We looked upon *Coach* Dicus, *Coach* Ridgway, *Coach* Warren, with *respect*; we *honored* them as our authorities. Sure, we *liked* or *disliked* them depending on how much we *thought* they "liked" or "disliked" us; or, how much we got to play. But, like or dislike them, we respected and honored them.

"Coach" as defined by Webster is *a person who* **trains** *an athlete or team.* Therefore, anyone can be a "coach": the Little League *coach*; the drama *coach*; dad, you are a *coach.* The key word in the definition of "coach" is the word, **train.**

Again, as defined by Webster, **train** is *to develop or form the habits, thoughts or behavior by discipline and instruction.*

In The Bible, Proverbs 22:6 says, *Train up a child in the way he should go, even when he is old he will not depart from it.*

Coach Dicus was a *great* coach! He **trained** us. Quite obviously, he trained us to play the game (football, basketball, and baseball). I can honestly say that under Coach Dicus, I never went into a contest where the team, or I did not feel we were prepared to play the game to the best of our abilities. There were some coaches I played under in later years where I could not say that.

More importantly, and as trite as it may sound, Coach Dicus trained us for the game of *life.* If we caught the spark, it was there for life. It guided us through the good times and the bad times. And, it guided us to the degree, which *we* deemed it important. He taught us the values of *fair play, good sportsmanship, respect for our elders, honesty, respect for our teammates,* and, yes, *respect for ourselves...* And I could go on and on. Coach Dicus, by his very example, showed us what a life worth living is all about. We all became better citizens, more productive citizens, than had our lives never been touched by Coach Dicus.

Lou Pavlovich, in his article, *A Profound Personality* alluded to the fact that Coach Dicus had his critics. Even some of his former players have, in retrospect, been critical of his coaching philosophies. Sam Kitterman, BHS '47 a very fine athlete for the Pumas, commented that Coach Dicus was rather predictable. He had very few plays and the opponents could anticipate the ones he did have. Ralph Echave, BHS '47 said Coach Dicus was "from the old school...three yards and a cloud of dust." That "We practice our pass plays every day but come game time, I believe I had three passes to me in three years and I played end." Bennie Hamrick, BHS '47 (what was it about the year 1947?) criticized Coach Dicus for making him run laps when he couldn't practice due to an injured elbow. "What the hell good did it do my elbow to make me run laps?" complained Hamrick.

But, you know what? Every one of those guys went on to extol Coach Dicus' virtues. They all said that "he was a good man", that he was honest; that he taught good sportsmanship. Pete Vucurevich, BHS '47 said that Coach Dicus "...changed the direction of my life. He talked me into going out for football my sophomore year. I hated school and was ready to quit until he talked to me." Bill Monahan, BHS '52 credits Coach Dicus for keeping him out of the Army for Bill's senior year in high school. Bill's good buddy and football teammate, Bob White had Bill talked into joining the Army with him until Coach Dicus heard of it. Bill said "…and you know how persuasive Coach was!" Bill did not go in the Army. The Korean War was at its height at that time. Bob White was killed just six months later. Howard Loper, BHS '52 gave Coach Dicus the credit for keeping him in school. Howard had decided that he was quitting and did not show up for school one Monday morning. Coach Dicus heard that Howard was quitting and going into the military. The military lost another warm body thanks to Coach Dicus. Coach went to Howard's house and literally pulled him out of bed and made him get to school; much to the relief of Mrs. Loper! Howard graduated in 1952.

Yes, we were trained by Coach Dicus. Our habits, our thoughts, and our behavior were developed by the discipline and example Coach Dicus exhibited. I was coached and trained by a number of other men during my post-BHS years as an athlete and a teacher/coach. Most of them were very good with the X's and O's; that is, the fundamentals of the game. However, *only two* in the many years I played and coached were of the same ilk as Coach Dicus. And, only one of them is relevant to this book; his name was Dan Yurkovich. I coached for six years at Carmel High School in Carmel, California in the early 1960's. Dan Yurkovich was the basketball coach at Carmel High. He got me my first teaching/coaching job there. Dan had played for Coach Dicus when they were both at Jerome High School. Later, before he came to Carmel, Dan was the basketball coach at Ajo High School; there he was under the leadership of Superintendent of Schools, Waldo Dicus. Dan Yurkovich was well trained under Coach Dicus!

Coach Dicus trained boys on how to become men. Coach Dicus was a *leader.* I have always felt that he would have been an outstanding military leader. When I saw George C. Scott play the part of *Patton*, I saw *Waldo Dicus!* The military bearing that George C. Scott brought to the role of *Patton* had *Waldo Dicus* written all over it! There was one slight difference however; Coach Dicus never swore! I never heard him once cuss or use The Lord's Name in vein. Though I did remember him telling Bill Howard once to "knock him on his butt" in reference to a blocking technique.

Coach Dicus was not a "jock". He came to school every day dressed in a two piece suit and a freshly ironed white shirt and a tie that always had some pattern colored with red and gray. I don't remember him ever in the halls of BHS in anything other than his suit and tie. Coach Dicus had *class*. He was a picture of dignity, poise and pride; pride in BHS and her students, pride in himself and in the position God had placed him. Our academic records and our graduation dates were more important to Coach Dicus than was his won-loss record. Upon his death in September 1985 newspapers all across Arizona carried his obituary. Not one of them mentioned his won-loss record, yet they all alluded to his leadership and his love for people. It just wasn't that important to Coach Dicus how many games he won or lost in his career. What was important was the legacy he left.

Coach Dicus was a *big* man. He was big in the impact he made on the lives of young people and he was big in stature. He was six feet, three inches tall and weighed two hundred and fifteen pounds when he played football and basketball at the University of Arizona. He captained both teams his senior year at the UofA; he was all-Border Conference in both sports. When Coach Dicus walked into a room, his very presence was felt by all. Yet, he was very unassuming. He was modest about his own many achievements, but was quick to heap praises on others. I never heard him speak in a demeaning way toward anybody. His philosophy was "If you can't say anything good about someone, don't say anything at all." There was one slight exception to that. At times, and especially the week of a Bisbee-Douglas game, he was known to refer to Douglas folks as "...just a dog of a different breed."

In a subtle way, without making a player feel "put down", Coach Dicus would get it across loud and clear that he was not pleased with the effort or the result of what a player had just done. In one scrimmage my freshman year, a bunch of us scrubs were scrimmaging the first string. Jerry Ballard was a tough, hard-nosed runner and he was coming through the line directly at Don Mangham and me. I was a step or two behind Mangum. Mangham was a tough kid himself, but when he gathered himself to tackle Ballard, Ballard lowered his shoulder and blasted Mangham to the ground. Ballard continued on down the field for a good gain. In the meantime, where was I? Well, when I saw Mangham ready to hit Ballard, I stopped and figured that Ballard was going down; Mangham would tackle him; the play would be over. By the time I recovered from my surprise that Mangham did not make the tackle, Ballard was too far away for me to chase. So I just stood there. Coach Dicus, for what seemed like an hour, just looked at me. Finally, he said, "Hadley, my boy. Why did you stop? Why didn't *you* tackle Mr. Ballard?" I said, "Well, Coach, I just figured that Don would get him." With that Coach Dicus became as sarcastic as he ever got. He said, "**Well, pin a rose on me Nellie!** Hadley, my boy, the rule book *does not* say it is illegal for *two* players to tackle a ball carrier."

Coach Dicus had a way of making a point and teaching valuable lessons by "coming in the back door", so to speak. In my freshman year we played Phoenix Union High School at the Warren Park. We gave the heavily favored *Coyotes* a good game only to lose a heart breaker, 19-7. The state newspapers the next day was full of glowing plaudits about the "plucky" *Pumas* who outplayed the *Coyotes* only to lose on bad breaks. I scored our only touchdown in the game on a ninety two-yard kick off return. Here is how I remember the run: I took the kick on our eight-yard line and started up the middle as *I had been instructed to do.* Then I broke to my left; *as I had been instructed to do.* About that time I remember seeing two huge Phoenix Union players coming at me from my right side. I remember flinching, expecting to get clobbered. Nothing happened. I ran the rest of the way unmolested. Ninety-two yards for a touchdown by the skinny fourteen-year-old freshman! *Alright!* I was pretty good! I remember walking off the field after the game and absorbing all the pats on the back by the *thousands* of adoring fans; most of them girls. I was grinning from ear to ear. And we had lost 19-7. But, hey, I had scored on a ninety two-yard touchdown run! A kick off return, at that; against a much superior team! After most games, Coach Dicus had a few words to say to the team. Man, I could hardly wait! I would try to look humble. Well, sure enough, he called the team together and spoke to us. He started off by complimenting us on our aggressive and tough play; on our "never say die" attitude. Then he got into the game itself. He said, "Men, we *should have* won that game 7-0. Our defense played well enough to win. Our offense made a few mistakes is all. (I think someone had told me once that the quarterback runs the offense. I was the quarterback) Had we not **had two passes intercepted** (I vaguely remember throwing at least *two* bad passes) and a fumble on a **bad handoff** (I was the guy doing the handing off) we would have won it. That kick off return by Hadley was a thing of beauty," Dicus continued. Alright! Here it comes! I sat up a little straighter and got an, "Aw, shucks" look on my face. "Hadley, you ran it exactly the way *Coach Fuzzy* drew it up. And, *Monahan,* you threw one of the most devastating blocks I have ever seen! If you hadn't gotten those two guys (I remember seeing two guys coming straight at me, but nothing happened) we'd have had to pick the skinny freshman up with a blotter on about the twenty five-yard line! Great block, Johnny Monahan!" Well, I learned a few lessons. I was playing on a *team.* The team was comprised of other players all pulling together. No one player is bigger or more important than the other players are. Coach Dicus did not belittle me, yet in a rather round about way, he let me know that *we* win and lose as *a team.* Later, when I walked by him on my way to shower, he looked at me, winked and said, "Good game." I loved that man.

Rob Dicus, Coach's number two son, told me recently that the Bisbee-Douglas game my freshman year was Coach Dicus' most memorable game. We had been underdogs to the heavily favored Gib Dawson-led Douglas *Bulldogs.* We won the game 25-0. Another highlight of Coach's career was the Pumas' 20-12 win over a strong Tucson High team in 1951. It was the first Bisbee High win over Tucson High since 1934!

Coach Dicus' most heart breaking game was my senior year when we lost to Carver High School in the state basketball championships at Arizona State College in Flagstaff. Carver High was an all black high school in Phoenix with some outstanding players who would go on to college and have excellent careers. The best player on their team was a young man named Charles Christopher. He had a promising career at Arizona State College at Tempe in his future. He passed away on the operating table during knee surgery his freshman year. Two others on that team who had the college scouts drooling were Robert Green, a huge six foot, four inch, two hundred and fifteen-pound center, and Charles Lucky, a gifted six foot, two inch forward. They were tall and fast and outstanding shooters. We were the decided underdog even though we came into the game with a 20-2 record. Coach Dicus knew that we could not run with them. They were very fast and excellent ball handlers. They were taller than we were as well. We had two tall players, "Hooty" Howell at six feet, four inches and Bill Wagner at six feet, three inches. We went down hill from there, height wise; Ron Haynes was six foot even. I was five eleven and Vince Romero was a five foot eight inch freshman. Vince was the state's leading scorer as a freshman averaging twenty-five points a game. Coach Dicus had a great game plan. We opened the game playing very deliberately. We were not to shoot unless we had a wide open shot. We were to pass the ball around their tenacious zone defense and try to get Vince open for a shot, or feed it to one of our big guys underneath. At the end of the first quarter, we had outscored Carver 20-12. Then Coach Dicus made his big mistake. He got a little over confident and felt that now we could run with them. We went away from what was working and tried to play their game. They out scored us 28-8 the second quarter! By the time we could get reorganized at half time, they led 40-29 and went on to win 74-62. Coach Dicus took full blame for that loss. He said publicly in the newspapers, and in front of our student body that had he stayed with the original game plan, and had more patience, we could have won. I learned another valuable lesson that day. Great coaches never blame their players for a loss!

Vince Romero was on fire that game. He scored 32 points in a losing effort. One can only wonder how many points Vince would have scored in his BHS career had the three-point circle had been in play. He was the best outside shooter I ever saw; high school or college.

Coach Dicus was born in Jerome, Arizona in 1906. His father came to Jerome at the turn of the century and worked as a blacksmith his first few years in Jerome. He later became an automobile dealer and up until the 1970's the building where Mr. Dicus, Sr. had his blacksmith shop and later his automobile dealership was still standing. An observant driver through downtown Jerome could see the name *Dicus* in fading lettering on the side of the building.

Upon his graduation from Jerome High School, Coach Dicus worked for a year in the mines to save money for school. After a year of work, Coach enrolled at The University of Arizona and almost immediately broke his leg at football practice. Coach Dicus claims he was The UofA's first "red shirt" football player as they granted him another year of eligibility in lieu of the season he had to sit out due to the broken leg. Coach Dicus would say in later years that those two "lost" years, the year he worked after high school graduation, and his "red shirt" year, were the best things that could have happened to him at that time. He got bigger, stronger and more mature. Coach Dicus went on to become one of The University of Arizona's greatest athletes. Old timers in the Tucson area will tell you that he was one of the most rugged rebounders of his era. They also give him the dubious distinction of being the first UofA basketballer to be thrown out of a game in "Bear Down" Gymnasium. Coach Dicus adamantly denies that. He says he may have been the first to *foul out* of a game, as he did that frequently, but he said he was never *thrown out* of a game! "Bear Down" Gym incidentally was given that name because of a death bed utterance by a Bisbee boy, "Button" Salmon. As he lay dying, "Button" Salmon told his coach, "Pop" McKale, to "Tell the players to *bear down*."

Coach Dicus was enshrined in the UofA's Athletic Hall of Fame as a charter member. He is recognized for his achievements in both football and basketball. He also received numerous academic honors while at The UofA. He was inducted into national education honorary Phi Delta Kappa for his post-graduate work.

He said many times that it wasn't his athletic or academic achievements, as wonderful as they were, that was the most significant result of his two "lost years". What made the most lasting impact on his life was how much a Jerome girl named Francis D'Arcy had grown up. He had known her for years as they both grew up in Jerome. Francis was a skinny little grade school girl when Coach Dicus graduated from Jerome High School. Then he noticed her again when she enrolled at The UofA as a freshman in Coach Dicus' junior year; my or my, it was love at first sight! They were married in 1936 and lived together as a model husband and wife for 39 years.

Coach Dicus was a *gentleman*. He emphasized to his players that we should always be gentlemen, as well. More importantly and more emphatically, he *demonstrated* that trait by how he treated Fran, the love of his life. One could tell by observing his relationship with Fran that she was not just his wife, but that she was an integral part of him. He treated her as his *queen*. Coach was more proud of her accomplishments than he was of his own. And, Fran had many accomplishments of which to be proud. I remember Coach telling all who would listen, how she won the Women's' Golf Championship of the Warren Country Club by beating Margaret Holt in a two-hole play off. Fran was a physical education major at the UofA and came by her athletic talents naturally. At one time, Fran was considered one of the top lady golfers in Arizona. Coach always said she could beat him at golf; and he was no slouch as a golfer, either. He and Angel Salas were two of the better men golfers in Bisbee. Coach played a round of golf with only three clubs; a driver, a 5 iron, and a putter.

I got to know Fran well the summer between my freshman year and my sophomore year. Coach Dicus called me over to his house shortly after school had let out for the summer of 1949. He informed me that he was thinking about the possibility of moving me to halfback, instead of quarterback, but, that he still wanted me to call the plays in the huddle. I wasn't so sure of that move, but as Bill Monahan, BHS '52 said, "You know how persuasive he is!" I spent a number of evenings that summer helping Coach Dicus and Fran pick tics out of their cocker spaniel all the while talking football and how to best utilize the talents of the individual team members when calling plays. Fran was always present with her contagious smile and kind words. She usually had a plate of cookies and a glass of milk available. It was Fran's confidence in Coach and his decisions that helped convince me that I could play halfback and call plays, too. However, to this day I do not believe that it is a good idea for a halfback to call plays. He will either call his *own* plays too often, or too seldom. It is better for a quarterback to designate who should and should not get the ball at any one particular time. That is just about the only criticism I have of Coach Dicus' coaching!

Coach Dicus retired from coaching and from Bisbee High School in 1952. He made the announcement of his retirement to the football team in the locker room after we had beaten Douglas 14-7 in the annual *Copper Pick* game on Thanksgiving Day. The locker room after that game was a bedlam of noise. Bill Monahan was the hero of that game. He returned a Douglas fumble fifty-seven yards for the deciding score. It took Bill only a few seconds to run the fifty-seven yards, but it took him a good fifteen minutes in the locker room to replay the run for all that would listen. He was excited! It is interesting as I think back on my football career at BHS, that a *Monahan* was there blocking for me when I scored my *first* BHS touchdown and my *last* BHS touchdown. Johnny's life saving block on my kick off return against Phoenix Union my freshman year; then in this last game against Douglas, Johnny's brother, Bill, was a key blocker for my one touchdown that day. And to be perfectly honest, Bill Monahan was instrumental in almost every touchdown I ever scored for BHS!

After we had celebrated our win, and after Coach Dicus had gone around and personally congratulated each player, he quieted us down. As he spoke, we could tell Coach was choked up. We knew something was amiss. He seldom got emotional. He then told us that he was "hanging it up". That his coaching days were over and that he was taking a job in Ajo as superintendent of schools. He told us how proud of us he was and what a great "going away" present we had just given him. He then addressed the nine graduating seniors again, and said, "Men, we are going out together and we are going out winners." To the rest of the team he said, "The 'B' will continue to shine brightly. You will see to it." We were all in tears when he had finished speaking. Bisbee's loss was to be Ajo's gain. He would serve Ajo for twenty-two years with the same intense integrity he served Bisbee.

Coach retired from the Ajo school system in 1975 at which time he and Fran moved back to Bisbee and lived on El Rancho de la Requesta on Purdy Lane. They had privacy and could look across the valley into Mexico with a clear view of the Huachuca Mountains. They had lived there just a few months before Coach's beloved Fran passed away on Memorial Day weekend 1975. Coach then moved back to Ajo and said at the time that there was such a void in his life with Fran gone that he could not stay in Bisbee with all those memories the two of them shared. They shared wonderful memories in Ajo as well, but they were not as involved with the "kids" there as they were in Bisbee.

Coach Dicus died in September of 1985 of a heart attack on his way from Ajo to watch a UofA football game. I attended his funeral in Cottonwood. The church was full. It was like a Bisbee High School reunion. I can't begin to name all the Bisbee people who were there. Bill Williams, BHS '56 and I drove down from Flagstaff together. Max Spilsbury was there with his lovely wife, Ginger. Max gave a beautiful, heart felt eulogy. Nick and Steve Balich were there. Bill Penn was there. Al and Mike Marusich were there. Marty Ryan, wife of Charlie Ryan, was there. Bob Browder was there. Bill Reeves, Ajo and UofA basketball star was there. So many were there to pay their last respects to a great man; a man of integrity who touched so many lives. I agree with Max when he said in his eulogy to Coach, "He is the finest man it has ever been my privilege to know; who has dedicated his life to bring out he very best in every boy; who has always championed the real, the good, the gentlemen; a man who inspired men and boys alike to do better than they can…"

One story I want to relate before I close this section on Coach Dicus. It shows the heart Coach and Fran had for hurting kids. There was a youngster who had played one season of football at BHS, and who would have to leave Bisbee because his family was moving away. The kid was heart broken. He loved Bisbee

High and did not want to move. Coach and Fran opened their home to this kid so he could continue at BHS. He lived with the Dicus' his entire junior year. That football season, he made all-state as a defensive end. Though he was just a junior, he would never play another game for Bisbee High. He joined the Marines that summer and was seriously wounded in the battle of Guam. His knee was almost blown away and the kid had to live the rest of his life with a metal plate holding his knee together. Some said he would never play football again. The kid's name was Max Spilsbury.

SEMPER FIDELIS. MAX SPILSBURY

The United States' Marine Corps recruiting poster proudly proclaims, *WE WANT JUST A FEW GOOD MEN!*

Max Spilsbury was one of those *few good men.* He was born to be a United States Marine! Max epitomized the very heart of The Corps; he was tough, he was loyal, he loved America. He was a protégé of Coach Waldo Dicus. I heard Max tell a heart-wrenching story *that says it all.* I will attempt to tell it as closely as I can to the way Max related it at a gathering at Northern Arizona University in the 1970's:

Max was wounded in the battle for Guam. He had been a replacement for the Marine 4th Raiders who were pretty well depleted after the battle of Guadalcanal. Max and a close buddy were in the first wave of Marines to land on Guam. They made it though the landing in spite of overwhelming Japanese resistance. Their assignment was to recapture the Marine barracks on the island that the Japanese had occupied for several months. As Max and his buddy were inching their way on their bellies towards the captured barracks, a mortar round landed between Max and his buddy. Max said his last conscious remembrance was of a deafening explosion and seeing his buddy blown into the air just feet away from Max. When Max regained consciousness he was in a Marine first aid tent behind the lines. He did not know the whereabouts of his buddy. Max was told he had been killed. Max was then sent back to the States to recuperate and the war ended before he could be redeployed into combat.

Fast forward now about fifteen years when Max was Head Football Coach at Arizona State College in Flagstaff. One of Max's football players was a very bright student named Brad Luckingham. Brad had his heart set on becoming a lawyer when he graduated from college. One evening as Brad was walking the campus of ASC, he was struck by a car and seriously injured. He lost a leg and was in critical condition for several weeks. During that time, Max initiated numerous fund raising projects to help defray Brad's medical costs. The most notable fundraiser was Max's "wheelbarrow walk". Max started at the campus of ASC and proceeded to push a wheelbarrow to the Flagstaff Hospital, several miles from campus. Max took one step every time somebody would put a dollar bill in the wheelbarrow. It took Max many hours to complete the walk, but when he reached the hospital, he had received several thousand dollars towards Brad's medical costs.

Brad's mental condition was at rock bottom. He saw no hope of ever becoming a lawyer. He only had one leg. Brad was in a state of complete mental depression. It was during this time that Max and his wife, Ginger, went to see the movie, *The Men* in which Marlon Brando played the part of a paraplegic in a hospital full of paraplegics. As Max and Ginger watched the movie, Max suddenly sat bolt upright! There on the screen in a wheelchair was Max's buddy from Guam! Max couldn't believe his eyes! Max somehow got in touch with his buddy through the studio what produced the movie. Max corresponded with him and found out that his buddy had lost *both legs* in that mortar blast on Guam. Max told him about Brad Luckingham and convinced the buddy to fly to Flagstaff and to try to lift Brad's spirits. When Max wheeled his buddy into Brad's room, a transformation soon took place in Brad's countenance. Max's buddy gave Brad a severe tongue-lashing and told him to "…quit feeling sorry for yourself! Get your butt out of this hospital and get on with life". Brad Luckingham went on to finish college and get a law degree. God certainly works in strange ways!

Max Spilsbury was born in Hachita, New Mexico. But, his parents moved to Mexico when Max was a small child. He went to early grade school in Mexico, and moved to Bisbee when he was in the sixth grade where he attended Hoarse Mann. In 1941 when Max was a freshman at Bisbee High School, Coach Dicus, ever on the lookout for football players, saw *something* in Max that he liked. When Coach Dicus approached Max about trying out for the football team, Max told Coach Dicus that *basketball* was his sport and not football. But, as many Bisbee students found out over the years, Coach Dicus was very persuasive. Max soon found himself playing defensive end for the *Pumas* and lettering his freshman year. Max went on and became an all-state performer for the *Pumas* his junior year. World War II was raging and Max felt a call to join the Marines. He had three brothers and a sister already in the service so he felt it was his obligation to serve his country just as they were. Max joined the Marines because "that's where the tough guys go." His senior year in Bisbee High School was put on hold.

To verify that there are people *from Bisbee everywhere*, Max ran across Carl Wood one of his BHS teammates on the 1942 *Puma* football team. They ran into each other by accident when Max was being loaded on a hospital ship headed for Hawaii and Carl was just landing on Guam. Both men survived World War II.

Max came back to Bisbee and completed his senior year. He graduated with the class of 1946. The Marine Corps had been good for Max. He had a much more mature outlook on life. He was more disciplined and being a Marine, he wanted everybody to experience that discipline. Max had no patience for an undisciplined person, adult or child. He was to exhibit that trait, that Marine training, many times over his lifetime. Some would accuse Max of being "too tough, too mean." Yet, what he expected in others, he displayed in himself.

When Max graduated from Bisbee High, a recruiting war ensued for his services. Coach Dicus felt Max would be a good fit for The UofA. Former BHS all-staters Garner Barnett and Mark Kalastro were at Arizona State College at Tempe and had other ideas. They had told ASC Coach Steve Coutchie about this tough Marine. Coach Coutchie visited Max at BHS several times and almost, I said *almost,* talked Max into becoming an ASC *Bulldog* (before they were "Sun Devils"). Coach Coutchie made a fatal mistake, however. He told Max that if he went to The UofA he would just sit the bench his first year; if he went to ASC, would play immediately. No Marine would back down from a challenge like that! Max went to The UofA and *played, and lettered* his *first year!* Plus, Max found out just how persuasive Coach Dicus could be.

Max became a "living legend" while at The UofA. He soon became known as the "toughest guy on campus", not just because of his rugged, Marine style of play on the football field, but he did a few other things most students did not have the intestinal fortitude to undertake. Max did these *all at the same time and with a metal plate in his knee!* Max would practice *football* in the afternoons, go to the *boxing ring* in the evenings, and would *rodeo* on the weekends!! One year, just for variety sake, and to prove he could do it, Max went out for basketball and *lettered!* He was the heavy weight boxing champion at The UofA *all four years!* He boxed in the heavy weight category though he never tipped the scales over one hundred eighty-five pounds! The metal plate in his knee accounted for some of that weight, I am sure. He wasn't very big by today's standards. He stood about six feet, two inches and weighed maybe one hundred eighty five pounds. The old adage, once a Marine, always a Marine (Max did not like to be called "an x-Marine". He would always be *a Marine)* certainly applied; you don't have to be big, but you better be tough! You talk about *tough,* Max was TOUGH!

Two of Max's BHS buddies, Lou Pavlovich and Hugh Keyes, were Max's constant companions at the University of Arizona. The three were easy to spot amongst the swarms of students walking to and from classes each day. These three were not your typical "Three Amigos" college students. First of all they were *from Bisbee,* secondly, their leader was *a Marine,* thirdly, one of them was in a wheel chair. They were not content to merely stroll to and from class; they played *games.* One of their favorites was "wheel chair wheelies". They would take turns seeing which one could get Hugh going the fastest and farthest on the *back wheels only.* At times, they used Hugh as a *battering ram* when they wanted to get through the throngs of students. Hugh loved every minute of it. He had to laugh, or Max would call him "chicken". It was Max who insisted that Hugh go on a geology class field trip to Colossal Cave. Hugh had his doubts about being able to negotiate the many ups and downs necessary to explore the many deep, dark confines of the huge cavern. Max and Lou went with Hugh that day and with their help, Hugh Keyes became the first handicapped student to complete the several hours' long hike. Max always said that Hugh Keys would have made a great Marine! He had courage!

One day as the three Bisbee buddies were on their way to class, playing "closest to the curb" with Hugh, a young coed was almost run over by the "out of control" wheel chair. As she nimbly dodged out of the way, Max apologized and the three continued on down the sidewalk. As they carried Hugh up the steps to his class, Max told his buddies that the girl they almost ran over was the one he was going to marry. He didn't know her name, but he would find out.

Well, true to Marine tradition, Max saw an objective and set out to conquer it! Max's two buddies became a two man reconnaissance patrol. Each time one of them saw the cute coed he would notify Max. Soon Max pretty much knew the girl's route to and from classes. He managed to just *happen to be* walking the same route and would drum up the courage to speak to her. The *intel.* (Marine talk for "intelligence information") had revealed that her name was *Virginia Edge.*

Well, Virginia had her *intel.* sources as well. They told Virginia that Max was a football player and was therefore off limits to a girl from the "hick" town of Winslow, Arizona. Virginia's friends soon found out that she loved a challenge! She said to her girl friends, "Just give me two weeks."

In the meantime, Max had found out that a Bisbee friend, Virginia Markam, was his "objective's" Senior sponsor. From her, Max found out particulars, which would make the "objective" easier to approach. You need to remember that in Max's Marine Training Manual they did not have a section on "Over powering, winning and wooing the prettiest girl on campus". Max was a novice at this kind of thing. He had to improvise. He went about winning the "objective" in pretty much the same way he did everything else. He "advanced forward at double time"! The first time he saw her after he had found out her name, Max went up to her and said, "Your name is Virginia Edge and I would like to walk you to your dorm." He correctly assumed that Virginia already knew his name.

Max told her that that weekend the football team was flying to Lansing, Michigan to play Michigan State University, but when he got back he would be in touch. Virginia was never one to let any grass grow under her feet. She had a date with another guy that weekend.

That Sunday afternoon when the team returned from Lansing, Max made a beeline to Virginia's dorm. She almost didn't recognize him when she came down to the dorm lobby to see "her visitor"! There to greet her was this guy with tape holding his nose in place and his face a bruised and bloody mess! And, "he had the nerve to ask me not to date anyone else!" Virginia said incredulously. Max's intentions obviously got through to Virginia, because "to make a long story short, it was in the spring when we went to Bisbee to meet Coach and Fran. I am glad they approved." As Virginia explained, "...they were Max's family; they were the ones who had to approve of our marriage." Those Marines do move fast! And, they always respect their *chain of command!*

Max graduated from The UofA "on time" in 1950, and was immediately hired by Globe High School to be their head football coach. Max and Virginia were in Globe for two years, 1950–51 to 1951–52. When Coach Dicus took the job as superintendent of schools in Ajo, there was never any doubt who would replace him. The Bisbee School Board did not conduct a statewide search for a new football coach. Numerous candidates applied but were not interviewed. Coach Dicus and Max had been in touch all season long and Max knew that if and when Coach moved on, that he, Max, would be the next *head Puma!* A job he eagerly looked forward to.

Though Max looked upon Coach Dicus as his surrogate father, and emulated Coach Dicus in numerous ways, Max was his *own man* when it came to running a football program. The ever-present ache in his knee was a constant reminder of what he had gone though on Guam; Max believed if he did not make football as demanding as the Marine Corps had been for him, he would be cheating the kids he coached. Max had an insatiable drive to instill in his kids the Marine motto *Semper Fidelis,* "Always Faithful". Max believed, as the Marines did, that the harder one worked at a task the harder it would be for that person to give up that task. Bleeding and sweating side by side with buddies would cause you to remain *faithful* to them no matter how tough the circumstances.

Ted Sorich, BHS '57 played for Spilsbury at BHS and at Arizona State College in Flagstaff. He also coached with him at ASC. Ted lent some good insight into Max's philosophy:

"What I remember most about Coach Spils at BHS was the love that he had for football. He truly believed that every boy in school would benefit from having played what he called 'the greatest game on God's green earth'. His Marine Ranger background shaped his coaching persona. He was one tough, hard-nosed football coach who tried to instill that same attitude in his players. 'Through these doors walk the toughest football players alive' read the sign at the entrance to our locker room. It was a testament to Coach Spils' work ethic and Marine background. He truly believed that winning on the field was a direct result of winning the physical battles. There was never a time that a Spilsbury coached team wasn't physically ready for an opponent; he simply would not let it happen! Looking back in retrospect, I truly believe that some of our conditioning was quite typical of a Marine boot camp! Once you get a bunch of young men physically and mentally prepared to play that kind of football, it didn't matter who we played; we went into every single game expecting to physically whip our opponent, including the "Big Red Machine" from Tucson High. We beat them two straight years, 12-6 and 7-0.

The 12-6 game was played in Bisbee before a packed house; kind of like a Douglas game! And the 7-0 game was played in Tucson. I can remember in the pre game warm-ups THS coming out of their tunnel under that concrete stadium in single file. One hundred thirty in number and stretching from end zone to end zone! Thank goodness that they could put only eleven of them on the field at one time! Most teams that played there at THS were probably intimidated by this show of imaginary strength; but not these confident Pumas who were ready to 'kick some butt' once the game started.

As a side note to the 12-7 game in Bisbee, I can remember Coach Spils concluding his pre game talk with, 'Just remember this. Those guys over in the other locker room put their pants on the same way that you do; one leg at a time.' To which Louie Reyna replied, 'Si, Coach, but did you see the size of some of those legs?!' Talk about a tension buster. It cracked everybody up including Coach Spils!"

George Hershey, BHS '57 remembers the 7-0 game very well. He modestly wrote to inform me that when Paul Renner, BHS '57 ran 70 yards for the only score of the game, that it was George who led the way by blocking several of the huge Tucson *Badgers* and then out running Paul to the goal line. George says he was "the fastest pulling guard in the state". That is probably a true statement; one might question Coach Spilsbury's assessment of personnel when he would put the fastest guy on the team at *a guard position*. Does this say something about Coach Spilsbury's ability to judge personnel? No, it says something about George's ability to hold on to the ball! His hands were bricks! But, he was tough and he could run!

Being coached by Max was fun. His players knew it was fun because all the time he was playing "drill sergeant" with the guys, *he* was laughing! The guys weren't laughing; they were as close to the threshold of death as one can possibly get without crossing over! Max ended every practice with the team running *ten one hundred-yard sprints;* this was *after* the team had gone through their *conditioning* drills! If a coach today did what Max did routinely, the coach would have his socks sued off!

Since most of Max's football players were excused from taking Physical Education, Max made sure that the young men in his PE classes were not deprived of his brand of Marine Corps training. Here is how Dale Hancock, BHS '57 describes a typical *Spilsbury PE experience*:

"As a freshman taking PE from the Maxer, I suffered a lot of pain in that old BHS gym! One day while we were doing our Marine calisthenics to warm up for the class, Clarence Dupnik came in with a question for Coach about a football play; while Coach was explaining it to him, we were making noise and laughing while doing the exercises. He punished us by making us get in the pushup position with only our feet and hands touching the floor. We had to remain in that position with out moving for a long time. If we moved we got one of his famous raps on the head with his big key chain that hurt like hell and would bring tears to our eyes. He had a Spanish word for those raps on the head. They were *chingosos,* but I don't know how to spell it. Then we had to run down the hill to the parking lot and back *up* the hill to the gym.

I remember another PE activity he dreamed up. Coach Max put up a barrel strung up on four cables or ropes, which were hung from the ceiling. We had to get on this smooth barrel with a rope tied around it and the rest of the class would get on the ropes holding it up from the ceiling. They would pull and shake the ropes to simulate the barrel as a bucking bull. Most of us came flying off pretty quick.

Coach also used the gym stage to help young men finish a school fight. If you got into a fight with someone at school, Coach would take the participants up on the stage and close the curtains. He would put heavy boxing gloves on them and tell them to 'go at it'. Pretty soon they would be so tired they could hardly lift their hands to swing. He would say 'Do not stop until I tell you to. You wanted to fight, so fight!' He would also put on staged fights as fundraisers for the Lettermen's Club. He opened these fights to the public and sold tickets. He raised lots of money for the Lettermen's Club that way! Another thing he would do with these gloves was to play 'battle ball' in PE class. We would put one glove on our non-dominate hand and play a brand of basketball where 'anything' went. You could slug the opponents with the gloved hand while dribbling the ball with the dominant hand. He soon added another game by putting a football-tackling dummy in the center circle and a glove on each of our hands. He would then call out two numbers and the two guys who had those numbers had to run to the center and try to haul the blocking dummy back to their respective sides. Again, 'anything' went. At times he would call out four numbers at once. You can imagine the chaos that caused!" That was PE 101 Spilsbury style! Of course, this was an approved State of Arizona PE curriculum.

Max told me once that his grading system was pretty simple. When he gave written exams in class he graded them by throwing the papers *up* a set of stairs. The papers that landed on the top step were given A's in the class; those, which landed on the second step, were given B's, etc. Nobody flunked unless they just never showed up for class. Nobody ever ditched class. They were afraid they might miss something *educational!*

After a successful tenure at BHS, Max took a job coaching football with Coach Warren Woodson at The University of Arizona in 1955. That job lasted one year. Coach Woodson's style did not jive well with Max's philosophy. He applied for and got the head football job at Arizona State College at Flagstaff in 1956. He soon became a legend in Northern Arizona! Max led the Arizona State *Lumberjacks* to national prominence. The '*Jacks* played football the *Spilsbury* way.

When Max took the job at ASC he recruited a bunch of "no name" players mostly from Arizona and a large number of them were *from Bisbee!* Some of the former *Pumas* were: Cecil Nelson; Al Alvarez; Louie Reyna; Ted Sorich; Brian Phillips; Nate Hickman; Mike Garcia; Dale Hancock; Paul Renner; Jerry Loper; Charlie Ham; and Glen Morgan, to name a few. Morgan had an outstanding career at ASC. He was named small college All America two consecutive years. Sorich was an outstanding quarterback and was recently (2003) named to the NAU Football Hall of Fame.

Max's *Axers* had the distinction of being the first Arizona football team to play in a nationally televised bowl game. The game was played in St. Petersburg, Florida in 1958. This was the first time most of the players had ever flown. They felt it was a great honor to represent Arizona in a nationally televised game. The week before the game, the practices at Lumberjack Stadium on the campus of ASC were probably the most intense any Max had ever conducted. Even the team managers were feeling the tension. Max had called the two young managers into his office on Monday of that week. He sadly told them that "…due to financial restraints, I will only be able to take *one* of you on the trip." To decide which one was to go, Max said "You two go into that closet over there and which ever one of you is the first to come out *standing* will be the one we take." This was not much of a surprise to the two managers. They had been around Max long enough to know that this was "the Spilsbury way" of doing things. Only the toughest could go. The two both had grim looks on their faces; when Max closed the door behind them, mayhem broke out inside that closet! Max said the racket inside the closet was deafening. After several minutes the door opened and one battered and bloody manager staggered out. He found Max and his assistants in stitches laughing. Tears were running down their faces. Max couldn't speak, he was laughing so hard. When he was finally able to say something he said, "I was only kidding. We are going to take *both* of you!"

I remember watching that game on television from my home in Carmel, California. I do not even remember who won the game, but I do remember how proud I was of Max's *Axers*.

Once during Max's tenure at ASC, The *Lumberjacks* made a trip to Northern California to play Santa Clara University. A fellow teacher from Carmel High School and I drove up to the game and we were given sideline passes by Max. My Bisbee buddy, Ted Sorich, BHS '57 was an assistant coach with Max at that time and it was great fun eating and visiting with Ted and the team both before and after the game. I was surprised to see a Bisbee kid I hadn't seen in years. "The Yo-Yo Kid" was there. As a grade school youngster, Eddie Minor had performed tricks with his yo-yo at half times of BHS basketball games. He could literally make that yo-yo sing! Eddie was one of the first ones I saw when my friend and I walked into the hotel where the *Lumberjacks* were staying. Eddie was as surprised to see me as I was to see him. Eddie was a running back and punter for the 'Jacks. We had a great time talking "old times". Eddie's sister, Barbara Minor was a year behind me at BHS.

I will recount one more *Spilsbury* story to verify Max's acute desire to win, and his intense disdain for those who don't share his passion. I witnessed this event at the Santa Clara game. My friend and I were on the *'Jacks* sideline as I have mentioned. The team bench was close to the visitor's bleachers and we could easily see and hear the few fans that were there to root for the *'Jacks*. Early in the first quarter Santa Clara jumped out to a two-touchdown lead. It looked like a long night for the *'Jacks*. Toward the end of the first quarter when it was obvious that Santa Clara was getting the better of the game, a loud voice from the middle of the

'Jacks' fans yelled a plea to "Put LeRoy in!" It only got worse in the second quarter. Santa Clara was running away with the game. And the vociferous voice was getting even louder and more frequent. "Put LeRoy in!" "Come on coach, put LeRoy in!!" Half time came. I was apprehensive about going into the *'Jacks'* locker room. I had never witnessed a Spilsbury tirade. As my friend and I neared the locker room door, Ted motioned to us to stay outside. We did. I don't know what transpired inside the locker room but what ever it was, it didn't do much good. The third quarter was more of the same. Santa Clara went up and down the field at will. And LeRoy's fan club got even more adamant about putting LeRoy in! The third quarter came and went, and still, no LeRoy. As the seconds ticked off the fourth quarter, not only was it evident that the *'Jacks'* were out manned in this game, but it was also evident that LeRoy was destined to finish the game on the bench. His fan club became almost belligerent. Their screams of "Put LeRoy in!!" became more and more hysterical. They continued up until the last play of the game. Mercifully the game ended. As Max and his team dejectedly walked off the field, I noticed LeRoy's fan club waiting near the gate the team had to walk through to get to the locker room. Oh, oh. It might turn ugly! Max was not in a good mood, and anything the LeRoy fan club might say would only add fuel to the already very smoldering Max Spilsbury. Sure enough, as Max walked by, one of LeRoy's fans, probably his dad, said "COACH! WHY DIDN'T YOU PUT LEROY IN?!" To which Max simply replied, "Because he isn't worth a s---!" and kept on walking. Case closed. I have a feeling that LeRoy's fan club did not vote for Max Spilsbury to be Coach of the Year.

The flap over Max's dismissal from ASC as head football coach in 1964 reverberated all across Arizona. Max was unquestionably the most popular college football coach to ever grace the gridirons of Arizona up to that time. The administration at the college took a lot of heat from ASC alumni all over the state as well as across the country. The case against Max was pretty well documented. It was his failure to abide by college rules regarding student class attendance. They said Max gave grades to students who never attended a class. True enough, I suppose. A young married kid that I had coached at Carmel High School in Carmel, California was one of those students whom Max doled out a grade to and who did not attend the required class. The young man's name was Jim Kelley and he was awarded a football scholarship to ASC by Max. Jim played for the *Lumberjacks* his first semester and then got married to his high school sweetheart during semester break. Upon returning to campus to start the second semester, Jim informed Max that he would need to find a part time job to support his wife and himself. Several weeks into the semester, Jim's wife became pregnant. Jim told

Max that he would need to get more hours to support his growing family. Max obliged by telling Jim to work during the time period he was registered for Max's class. Other students over a period of a year or so were in the same category as Jim Kelley. Max's love for his kids and yes, his disobedience to his authorities, caused him to lose his job. This occurred in 1964. Every year since, some where in Arizona, a group of Max' *Axers* get together for a reunion. They don't meet every five years or every ten years, they meet *every year*. That's how much his players loved him. For many years Max and Virginia would return for the reunion. As the years went by and age took its toll, Max and Virginia were unable to attend the yearly reunions. So what did the Max's *Axers* do? On a number of occasions they took the reunion to Max and Virginia in Mexico.

One might think that when Max was dismissed from ASC that he would just "hang it up"; find a ranch somewhere and retire. Well, he found a ranch somewhere alright, but he **did not retire!** Here is how Max's wife, Virginia, describes their life after leaving Arizona:

"Max's brothers and sisters wanted him to come to Mexico and take over the family ranch. We felt we couldn't do it unless Max was able to get a job teaching at Juarez Academy. The academy was in Colonia Juarez near the family ranch and after talking to the headman in Mexico City, Max was offered a job as director of the schools, which included two grade schools and a high school. After a couple of years of coaching just basketball and track for the boys, Max introduced American football. This was quite a job as most of the students had never even seen American football on TV, much less in person. With a lot of help from many of Max's Arizona coaching friends, he was able to outfit not only his team, but also several other schools in the area. Max's Arizona friends sent him crates and crates of discarded football equipment. When Max first started the kids playing they couldn't get enough of it! They would show up in Levis, no pads and play until the allotted time was up and then they would beg Max to let them play another quarter. Over the years Max's team would venture outside Mexico to play teams in Texas, New Mexico and Arizona. Plus, of course, they played the teams in Mexico on a regular basis. The year Max quit coaching, just a few years ago, his team went undefeated and ended the season by beating Willcox. Our youngest son, Max Kortny had been helping Max and he took over when Max quit coaching. Max always felt that football helped build young men and he wanted the boys here to have that opportunity. His willingness to volunteer his time has influenced a lot of young men in this area."

Virgina, that is a huge understatement! We all know that Max's influence has had *a tremendous* impact on multitudes of young kids in Mexico, just as it has

done in Arizona! Max's legacy will be passed on to generations of Mexican families just as it is being passed on to generations of Arizona families. Max Spilsbury,
simper fidelis, always faithful!

As a closing comment on Max, it is interesting that as I wrote this on June 16,
2004, that this year's reunion of Max's *Axers* was to be held in Globe, Arizona at the
Apache Gold Resort on June 18 and 19. My good friend, Ted Sorich will be there
and so will a number of other former Bisbee *Pumas.* Max's *Axers,* simper fidelis!

Max Spilsbury. Some said he would never play football again.

Top Left to Right:
Bill Plumb——pre "Wake Island", Jerome Biddle, *Peachy* McKay, Patsy Brashear,
Bottom Left to Right:
Haddie Hicks,?, Mary Kay Plumb, Peter Biddle, Jack Brashear

Left to Right: Bob Browder——"He knew things", Charlie Ryan——"He REALLY knew things", Jim Baker

Jim *Lefty* Weld——He unrolled his.

Wally Quayle——He never left home without it.

Waldo and Fran Dicus on their honeymoon
at Oak Creek Canyon.

Betty Bays——In a league of her own.

Fuzzy Warren, Jack *the Rock* Miller,
Waldo Dicus.

Hugh Keyes, courage on wheels,
with Jim Monahan.

3

1960's

JUST CALL ME "AL"

How many fathers would wait up for their daughter's curfew looking out the window until the car drove up? Quite a few would. How many fathers would flip the porch lights off and on if the daughter didn't get out of the car *immediately* after it stopped? Some would, but not many. How many fathers would walk out on the porch *in their underwear* if the daughter wasn't out of the car when the porch lights were flipped on and off that first time? *Only one would; and he did.* You can just call him *Al.*

This story is attested to by Al Ridgway's daughter, Susan Ridgway, BHS '67. Al only did it *once*. He only *had* to do it once. Susan was a Greenway Grade School graduate. She was a quick learner.

When Max Spilsbury replaced Waldo Dicus in 1952 as head BHS football coach he thought it would be appropriate if he introduced himself and his assistant coaches to the team. Wally Quayle, BHS '53 was at the introductory meeting and this is how he remembers the coaches introducing themselves:

"My name is Max Spilsbury. You are to address me as 'Coach', or 'Coach Spilsbury.'"

"My name is Garner Barnett. You can address me as 'Coach' or 'Coach Barnett.'"

"My name is Al Ridgway. You can just call me 'Al'.

My relationship with Al Ridgway goes back to 1946 when I was a seventh grader at Greenway Grade School and Al had just been discharged from the U.S. Navy. We were told one Friday that fall that we would have a new PE teacher with us on the following Monday. We were excited because our PE periods had been pretty lackadaisical up to that point. They had been pretty much your typical grade school *recess;* do your own thing and don't get hurt. Our principal Mr.

Nedolski, or one of our teachers would kind of stand around to see that thirty year old Alejandro Morales or one of the other "big" kids didn't get too rough. Now we would have a PE teacher! Maybe we could bring out a couple of footballs we could play with. Maybe we wouldn't have to play kick the ball and "Red Rover, Red Rover" with the girls. Maybe, just maybe we could get to play those cocky eighth graders in football. Don Manghaum, Bill Phillips, Duke Milovich, Ken Hunt, Robert Thompson, Bobby Vucurevich, George Blagovich, Johnny Wilcox; they thought they were so tough. We could beat them any day; even if they did have thirty-year-old "Hondro"!

Monday finally came. I can still see our new PE teacher as he came on to our huge Greenway play ground. He came that afternoon after spending the morning at Lowell Grade School. We figured that since he had been at Lowell, he'd be in a bad mood. Our new PE teacher no doubt had his hands full with those rowdy Lowell thugs. They weren't cool and suave like we were. Two things really surprised us when we first saw our new PE teacher: he was riding a motorcycle and he was *old*. We could tell he was old because he didn't have any hair. He was *bald* as a rock! But, for an old man, he sure had a neat motorcycle! Mr. Nedolski was there to introduce us to him. The entire seventh and eighth grades were on the pavement by the steps when he was introduced. Some of the silly, immature eighth grade girls were giggling because they thought he was so cute. Charlotte Caldwell, Elaine Jay, Lorraine McCollum and Louise Hendricks especially, were not acting their age. Couldn't they see he was just a bald, old man? Mr. Nedolski said, "Boys and girls, this is your new PE teacher, Mr. Al Ridgway." Mr. Ridgway looked at us and smiled. He said, "Just call me, Al". I don't know what Mr. Nedolski thought about that, but we liked it. We liked his smile and we liked him; even if he was a bald, old man. We didn't realize until years later, but Al Ridgway became a part of our lives at that moment. We soon realized too, that he wasn't old. He was bald though; that wouldn't get any better over the years!

Al and Jane Ridgway

Al Ridgway was born in Bisbee in 1920; he was raised and attended school in Bisbee; he raised his family in Bisbee; he coached, taught and was an administrator in Bisbee; he died in Bisbee on May 17, 2004. More than any of our coaches, more than Coach Dicus, more than Max Spilsbury, more that Fuzzy Warren, Al demonstrated a Bisbee pride which was exclusively his. We sensed that pride when he told us that he was going to teach us how to play football *just like the Pumas*. As a result, we started going to more Puma practices than we had previously. We would hurry down to the Warren Ballpark the minute school was out. In the past when we would go to a practice, we were always treated as just a bunch of little kids who got in the way. Now when we went, Al would greet us and we were "Al's kids"; we felt we could stay as long as we wanted. We stayed until we had learned all we could for that day and then we would head for the Vista Park where we'd practice the plays that Al had taught us that day. We really felt sorry for the other grade school kids. All the Lowell kids had to do after school was beg for ice chunks to chew on from the Bisbee Ice Plant. The Horace Mann kids were too busy throwing rocks at the St. Pat's kids to practice football. Another big advantage we had over the other grade schools was that Al could get us old discarded Puma football equipment. We were sure lucky Al was our PE teacher and that he coached the Pumas.

Most grade school kids like to sleep in on Saturday mornings. After Al became our PE teacher, we never slept in on Saturday mornings again! He saw to that. We got up early and headed down to the Warren Ballpark where we had a game scheduled to play one of the other grade school teams. I have already told you about the Greenway Grade School *Jets*. Everybody knew we were the best. Now, most of you will not believe this, but there was one year when Lowell was the best, thanks to Al! Of course, it was long after the Jets had gone on to bigger and better things. It was in 1953. Here is how Dale Hancock, BHS '57 remembers that memorable year: "Al was our PE coach at Lowell. He was also PE coach at Greenway, though I do not know why anyone would want to do that. I remember the Saturday morning games between each of the other grade schools at the Warren Ballpark. Al coached us during PE during the week and then on Saturdays he was neutral. My eighth grade year we won the city championship with the likes of C.W. McElyea, Jimmy Elkins, Charlie Herrera, Dane Randolph, and others, myself included. I remember the big gun for Greenway was Les Fenderson ("Hondro" had developed arthritis so badly by this time that he couldn't play anymore. hh). We had a lot of razzle-dazzle plays and scored a touchdown with one against Greenway to beat them. C.W. flipped the ball behind his back without looking, going in one direction. Speedy Jimmy Elkins was going the other way around end and he caught the lateral from C.W. for a touchdown!" I can understand Hancock remembering this so well. Lowell very seldom won and when they did, it was a pretty big deal.

One day we found out that Al could make jewelry! He took us down in the basement of the eastern most building at Greenway. There he had a table set up with lots of lapidary equipment. He instructed us in making copper bracelets, belts, and rings. We did that off and on for a month or so before the basement somehow got flooded. Much of the equipment was underwater. We never did go back to making jewelry. Jewelry making became a hobby for Al, which he became very skilled at. He often made jewelry for his friends.

I will never forget the day I found out that Al was married. What a shock! I was in the Warren Drug Store drinking a cherry phosphate when Al came in with a *beautiful* lady! When he introduced me to the lady he said, "This is my wife, Jane." I know my jaw must have hung down to my waist. I couldn't believe it. This lady was beautiful and Al was bald! All I could do was stare. I developed an immediate crush on her. That crush has lasted for fifty-eight years. Jane Ridgway is still beautiful and as vivacious as she was that day I first saw her in 1947!

In a recent email, Jane shared how she and Al met. Jane said she first saw Al in 1943 when she was a freshman at Arizona State College in Tempe and Al was a senior. She doubted that Al even knew she existed. Al graduated and immediately joined the U.S. Navy. "In 1945," Jane elaborates, "I was living in Bisbee with my sister and her husband and working at the Douglas Army Air Base. One Saturday when Al was home on leave from the Navy, I was walking down Main Street in Bisbee and Al saw me from across the street. He came across to where I was and said, 'I know you.' He asked me for a date and of course, I said 'no'. When I saw him again a day later he asked if I would go to a football game in Douglas (my future!!). I agreed. That was the start of our relationship."

Jane and Al were married when he was discharged from the Navy in 1946 and they lived in Bisbee ever since. They raised two beautiful daughters in Bisbee, Judy and Susan. They had a wonderful fifty-six years together. It was a wonderful fifty-six years for Bisbee as well, I might add.

When I was a freshman and playing football for Bisbee High, I had to wear large bulky prescription goggles because I was as blind as a bat! I couldn't see a thing without my glasses. In one game, I got smashed in the face and the goggles caused a cut over one eye. It was bleeding profusely. Al led me to the bench and told me to sit down, lean back with my head over the back of the bench and look at the sky. I couldn't see a thing due to all the blood in my eyes. But, I could still hear, and the first voice I remember hearing said, "OH! HONEY! You are bleeding!" I forced open my eyes and there was my mother with tears in her eyes looking at my bloody face. She was down on the field behind our bench! Mothers were supposed to stay in the bleachers. How embarrassing! Al finally persuaded Mother to get back to her seat. He told her that I would be ok.

That incident with the bulky goggles made Al talk to Coach Dicus to see if they couldn't somehow modify the goggles. What Al did was to call a long time Bisbee ophthalmologist, Dr. Piepergerdes who had relocated in Phoenix. "Piep", as he was called for obvious reasons, told Al about a new invention called "contact lenses". Al and Coach Dicus convinced my parents to give them a try. My mother and I flew to Phoenix several times that summer of 1949. My eyeballs were measured, tested, etc. Finally the day came when they were ready to put the lenses in to see if I could see. They forced my eyelids open and stuck two chunks of glass in my eyes and asked how they felt. Those things hurt something terrible and my eyes were so full of tears that it took several minutes to dry them. I could see better though, and Dr. Piep said I would get used to the feel of them. He lied. I never did get used to them. I hated them!

For the next three years Al Ridgway became my personal "contact" coach. Most practices and every game Al did "surgery" on my eyes. It took him awhile to get the procedure down pat, but he finally did. What he had to do was get me to lie down on the training table after I was completely dressed with my pads on. Then he would get my contact lens box which was an empty band aid can where I kept all the necessary contact lens stuff. He would take the suction cup applicator, put one of the lenses on the tip and then pry my eye lid open. That was tough to do as I did all I could to keep him from getting the lid open and keeping it open. When he had my eye-lid open with one hand, he took the suction cup applicator in his other hand and tried to plop the hated contact down in the dead center of my eye. It usually took several attempts and an explicative or two by Al to get the lens centered; I blinked so much and was not very cooperating. I hated those contact lenses and I know Al probably hated them worse than I did. Al's job was usually not finished when he got them in because the contacts usually slipped "off center" a couple of times per. practice and game. Most of the time I could slide them back on center with my finger; sometimes, though, they would get stuck in the side of my eye and Al had to probe around with his finger to find the elusive lens. Once he found it, he could slide it back to dead center. Al and I became a pretty good team in keeping my lenses functioning properly. It was not unusual for one of my lenses to slide "off center" during a game; usually, I could readjust it myself. If I couldn't, I had to run to the sidelines and have Al dig around in my eye for it. He got so good at it that I could run over to him, have the lens centered and get back to the team without missing a play. Once, and I want to emphasize **once,** I lost a contact during a game and it could not be found. I had to play the last quarter of the game blind in one eye. I wish I could count the number of times over the years I have had somebody tell me they were *at the game* in Morenci, or Nogales, or Douglas, or wherever, when I lost a contact lens. Chloe Ella Noble Cavanaugh's late husband, Cliff, even took credit for being the guy who tackled me so hard that the contact came out. Ok, here is the true story. I lost a contact during a game **one time.** We were playing **at** Tucson High in 1951, my senior year (we beat them 20-12!). During a time out I had gone over to the official to ask him if he wanted a drink of water as Coach Dicus had always instructed us to do. "Those guys get thirsty, too." he had said. As I was walking back to our huddle, the contact in my right eye just plopped out. No rhyme or reason. It just plopped out. We had to call a time out and both teams got on hands and knees to look for it. The four officials even got in the hunt. The lens was never found. Tucson High coach, Jason "Red" Greer even had his PE classes look for it on Monday. I was the first high school athlete in Arizona to wear contact lenses so I got a lot of "press" because of that. Then it became really big news when I lost one during **that** game. It seems that more people remembered the fact I lost a contact lens than that we upset Tucson High that night. I am sure that all those people who said they "saw me lose a contact" at Morenci, or Nogales or somewhere, remembered Al digging around in my eye repositioning one. He did that frequently; once or twice each game.

When Coach Dicus quit coaching to go to Ajo, Al stayed on to be an assistant for Max Spilsbury. Al was very content to be an assistant coach. He could have had the head job at a number of high schools across the state, but Al was *from Bisbee*. He wasn't going anywhere. Al had the most important and necessary quality to be a great assistant coach. He had an intense loyalty to the head coach and to Bisbee High. Plus, he loved the kids he worked with! Max only stayed at BHS for three years; from 1952 until 1955. Again, the Bisbee School Board did not do a large search for the head coach. They only had one man in mind. After much soul searching, Al relented and agreed to become the head football coach. Al served as BHS head football coach from 1955 to 1965, ten very memorable years. Al stayed on at BHS as athletic director and assistant principal until 1981 when he retired from education entirely. Shortly after Al retired he was named to the Arizona Coaches' Football Hall of Fame. He had been recognized twice by his fellow coaches as Arizona's Football Coach of the Year.

Al had many *crowning moments* during his illustrious career. The one that is foremost in Jane's memory and the one she says he was always so proud of was the huge upset by Al's BHS Pumas of the undefeated Douglas Bulldogs in a classic "Turkey Day" encounter. The game was played Nov. 30, 1961. This win was arguably a bigger win than the upset by the Pumas of the Dawson-led Bulldogs in 1948. In the '48 game, Douglas never got going. They were out of the game from the "get-go". It was a different story in 1961. Douglas came out of the locker room on fire! They completely dominated the first half and led 12-0 at the end of the second quarter. The *Pumas* could not get untracked. They were a dejected bunch when they left the field at half time. Al Ridgway breathed new life into the Pumas at half time; the second half was all Bisbee! Led offensively by Bob "Ripper" Sanders and Ray Johnson, the Pumas completely dominated the Chuck Willingham coached *Bulldogs*. The Pumas scored twenty unanswered points! The *Puma* defense led by Roy Barrow, Joe Stock and Don White shut down the high powered Douglas attack. The *Pumas* won 20-12. The Douglas paper, *The Graphic* heaped glowing praise on the Al Ridgway coached *Pumas*. They said the *Pumas* victory was "the biggest win of 1961 in all of Arizona high school football" and that Al Ridgway should be voted "Man of the Year" for the brilliant coaching job. The paper featured a picture of Al hugging his biggest fan, Jane! Another picture the paper had was one I would love to have. It showed Al with his big *Al grin*, his arm around a *Puma*, and Fuzzy Warren in the background waiting to take his turn to hug the kid. Priceless!

Al Ridgway stories are many among Bisbee minions. The one I like the most shows Al's love and concern for "his kids". The story involves a young man I knew when I was in school, though he was quite a few years behind me. His name is Nate Hickman. Nate was a good, tough running back for both Max Spilsbury and Al Ridgway. Ted Sorich, a friend of Nate's tells the story: "A few years after Nate's playing days were over, he developed a rather nasty habit of going through some of the bars in Brewery Gulch looking for a fight. From what I understand, it became a weekly ritual. Nate would get tanked up, walk into a bar looking to clean the place out. The police would be called. More often than not, they had a very difficult time getting Nate's cooperation to leave the bar and go home! Someone put a bug in the police chief's ear about how much respect Nate had for Al Ridgway. So the chief called Al and asked him to have a talk with Nate. Al did, and from that point on whenever Nate decided that it was 'time to go clean out the gulch', the bar owners would call Al for help, rather than the police. Al would walk into the bar and say, 'Nate, it's time to go home'. Nate would quietly leave the bar and Al would drive him home!" Nate still lives close to Bisbee and is a solid citizen. His respect for Al Ridgway is undying.

Jane Ridgway tells about the time that Al took his team to a pre-game meal at the swank Santa Rita Hotel in Tucson. The team had pre-called their orders in; the meals and tables were ready and waiting for them when the team walked in. However, the manager of the hotel saw that one of the *Pumas* was a black kid. He informed Al that the kid would have to eat in the kitchen. Al did not argue. He merely told his team to get up, that they were leaving. He then turned to the manager and said, "You are going to have a lot of meals to eat!" Al and the team walked out. They never did pay for those meals!

Al's sarcasm was notorious and biting! He could get his point across with just a few words and sometimes a huge smile. Dale Hancock, BHS '57 remembers several times at football practice when Al said, "My god. Hancock made a down field block! Will wonders never cease!" Those comments were accompanied by a huge smile. I remember two other sarcastic comments that were *not* accompanied by a smile. In 1951 in the *Puma* locker room before our game with Douglas several of our alumni were walking through wishing us good luck. Coach Dicus encouraged alumni to come back whenever they could. One particular guy who had played the year before, was being rather obnoxious by letting us know how great he had been; he kept telling us how sorry he was that he couldn't suit up and help us in this game. He was going from player to player patting us on the back and wishing us good luck. With each pat on the back he said, "Boy, I wish I could play today!" After about five minutes of this, Al had about all he could take. The next time the alumnus said, "I wish I could play today", Al turned to him and said with a disgusted look, "Why the hell didn't you play last year when you had the chance?" If I am not mistaken, the alumnus left the locker room shortly after that!

Then there was the time when I had been in the military for a year or so and was home on furlough. I went to the Globe High game at Globe. Al invited me to be on the sideline with the team and I was delighted. Al gave me a very nice introduction to the team and I felt pretty good about my self. I had played a couple of seasons of college football and one season in the military so I was a big "stud" and wanted to impress the team with that fact. I also wanted to impress the team with my knowledge of the game and my poise during the heat of battle. I stayed as close to Al as I could. I was almost in his back pocket as we walked up and down the sideline. As the game progressed it became obvious that it would be a close, hard fought game. The Globe *Tigers* were playing at home and the fans were loudly supporting them. It appeared at times that the officials were possibly favoring the home team on some key infractions. On the first couple dubious calls, Al was pretty cool about them. But finally one huge unnecessary roughness call against the Pumas really hurt and Al had had enough of the "homers". Al called time out and asked to talk to the official who had made the bad call. I couldn't go out on the field, but Al and the official were close enough for me to hear the dialogue between the two of them. The official explained to Al what the penalty was all about and Al's parting words were less than complimentary; he ended with commenting to the official, "Ref., you can't call that. That was poor!" The game continued, but Al was still pretty hot. I was close behind him and every several steps I would call out to the official, "Ref., you can't call that!" For varieties sake, I would inform Al so all the team could hear me, "Al, he can't call that! He can't call that, Al!" I finally got under Al's skin. He turned to me and said, "Hadley, the man has a whistle and a flag. He can call anything he damn well wants to call." In other words, "Hicks, shut up. I have a game to worry about. I can't listen to you belly-ache all night long." I didn't say another word; except, "Good game" when the *Pumas* won.

Like Dicus and Spilsbury before him, Al Ridgway left his special brand on many Bisbee High students. Lenard "Red" Loper expressed his feelings toward Al very poignantly, "Al Ridgway was vice-principal and head football and baseball coach while I was in high school. I played for him in both sports from 1958 to 1962. I can honestly say this: he was the only reason I graduated from high school in 1962, and I would like to tell you how he did it. I was in the second semester of my senior year, and was in Mrs. Medigovich's English class. Well, I got into some trouble outside of school that required me to leave school several times a week for several weeks. One of the times that I had to leave was during

Mrs. Medigovich's class. So I told her I had something I had to do and asked to be excuse. She refused to excuse me from class, so I just walked out and left. She responded by throwing me out of her class. Now, without senior English, I couldn't graduate. Well, I was out for about a week, when one day Al found me walking the hallways during the English period and asked me what the hell I was doing out of class. I explained to him that Mrs. Medigovich had thrown me out of English. He wanted to know why and what I had been doing. I told him it was a private matter and that I couldn't tell him. He thought about it for a minute, and told me that he would talk to Mrs. Medigovich and try to smooth it over, and for me to go back to her class the next day. Well, the next day I went to her class and peeked in the door so that she could see me. She looked up and exclaimed 'Well! Mr. Loper! Please come in! We've missed you!!' I managed to pull a passing grade and graduated with all my schoolmates on time. For Forty years I have wanted to thank Al for what he did for me. I even got to see him and visit with him at Jerry's funeral, but never quite got up the courage to say 'Thanks for the diploma' Maybe you could forward this note to his family to let them know how much I appreciated what Al did for me."

"Red's" brother, Jerry Loper, BHS '57 was killed tragically in an automobile accident several years ago. Loper had distinguished himself as one of Arizona's greatest high school coaches. Shortly before he was killed, Jerry Loper told Dale Hancock, BHS '57 that Al Ridgway "was the biggest influence" in his life for him becoming a football coach. Loper said Al's style of handling athletes and people was what he patterned his coaching techniques after. Dale shared with us that "it was fitting that Al could be at the ceremony on the football field to memorialize Jerry. I shared with the crowd in attendance and with Al, that story of how much Al had influenced Jerry's coaching. I am glad Al got to hear it."

Wally Quayle, BHS '53 succinctly summed up the feelings of so many of us who knew Al: "So many things I remember…he spent a lot of time with me. I needed it, and I needed him. He was there for me." That was the legacy Al left for so many. *He was there for us.*

DRIVING THROUGH LOWELL

My wife and I *really* do love it here in Sterling, Kansas. There *really* is a lot to do. Well, there really isn't much to do *in Sterling itself*; but, we can always drive to Hutchinson or Wichita and find lots to do. People *drive through* Sterling all the time. Ed "Pappy" Swierc, BHS '53 drives through Sterling almost every summer.

He visits his sister and brother-in-law in Hutchinson just twenty five miles from Sterling. He never stops to see me. He never even honks when he drives by. Highway 14 runs through the middle of Sterling just a block from my house. Some say that the best thing to come out of Sterling is Highway 14. Some refer to Sterling as "drive through country". You just drive through it.

I have to be honest with you. That was how I viewed Lowell when I was growing. Lowell was what we *drove through* on our way to Bisbee; or, what we drove through on our way to Warren. Nobody really lived there. Oh sure, we knew that *someone* lived there. We played against them on Saturdays. We knew there was a school there. But, those who lived there didn't really *live*. There just wasn't anything to do in Lowell. Unlike, Ed who never stops in Sterling, I would stop sometimes in Lowell. Johnny Caldwell had a drug store there where he sold great sporting goods. I would stop sometimes if I *had* to buy something. I would go to a movie at the Lowell Theatre sometimes when the Lyric Theatre in Bisbee was closed to repair the screen. Sometimes a drunken soldier from Ft. Huachuca would throw a beer bottle through the screen. My parents and I would go to Lowell and eat dinner at the White House Restaurant once or twice a month. When I was a real little kid; about in the 4th or 5th grades, I looked forward to eating at the White House because my dad always left a bunch of change for a tip. When we were getting out of our booth to leave, dad and mom were always busy talking to Ted Safferovich and I would steal some of the money dad left for a tip. I never did get caught. We liked going to dinner there in the spring time. After dinner we would drive to Bisbee and check out all the senior pictures is Art Blunt's window. When we stopped in Lowell, we never stayed longer than we had to. Even when we walked from Greenway Grade School to Lowell Auditorium for some kind of special kids' performance, we didn't stay longer than necessary. When the performance was over, we got out of there. There just wasn't much to do in Lowell.

It wasn't until just recently that I began to realize that people *really did live* in Lowell and that they really did *like living in Lowell*. Some people actually drove from Warren or Bisbee and *stopped* in Lowell because they lived there. I have found out recently that **lots** of people *kind of lived in Lowell*. It was just like those of us who lived in Warren and went to Bisbee High School could say we *lived in Bisbee*. Well, those who lived in Jiggerville, Saginaw, South Bisbee, Galena, Biggs, Tin Town, Winwood, Don Luis, Huachuca Terrace, Upper Lowell, German Town, Johnson Addition, Double Adobe, Sulfur Springs Valley, Bisbee Junction and most of Bakerville could say *they lived in Lowell!* Those kids went to Lowell Grade School! With all that area to recruit from it is no wonder Lowell Grade

School won the city grade school football championship once. I hate to admit it, but more people lived in Lowell than lived in Warren! And, you know what? Those people *had a life!*

For some in Lowell it was an adventure just going to the bathroom! In Warren we had indoor facilities. All our homes had flush toilets. Not so in Lowell! Ed "Pappy" Swierc, BHS '53 will, to this day, sit and reminisce about sitting and reminiscing in the old outhouse outside his "little green house" in Lowell:

"…if you walked out the back door of that green house, the iron cemetery fence (with those sharp points on top) was about six feet in front of you, with a path and many, many creepy tombstones immediately beyond. To the right of the porch was a heavy honeysuckle vine so thick you couldn't see what was hiding there; and to the left was a path about fifty feet long leading to the fence…and, *the outhouse which sat in the corner.* Yes, as close as we were to Lowell School, that little green house had no indoor facilities and day or night, that's where we went when we had to go. Now in the daytime, that wasn't too bad. But there were no streetlights in the area and going out there at night with the cemetery so close was not much fun. There were lights out there past that fence, and things that made noises, and things you just knew were gonna come right through the spaces between the cemetery's fence bars and get you. All the scary stories you ever heard about that cemetery at night are true, believe me.

To show the path at night, a clothesline was strung from the porch to the out-house, and an electric wire was tied onto this line to a point halfway out to the outhouse where it ended at a bare light bulb hanging over the path. When you had to go out at night, you switched on the light (one of those old round rotary knob switches) at the porch. You went out and did your duty and then switched the light off when you safely made it back to the porch. Now this lighting arrangement helped some, but not entirely. If you have ever been around a bare light bulb at night, you may have noticed that it blinds you so you can't see much past the bulb into the darkness. That makes the sounds even louder coming from behind that iron cemetery fence. The inside of the outhouse had no light, so I always had to reach out, open the door and let out whatever got in there before me. One night a bat suddenly flew off in the dark and I almost became the first six-year-old in Bisbee to suffer a heart attack. Then there was the time somebody at the house turned off the light, not knowing I was still out there. I screamed for help when I saw how dark it was and I ran full blast into a tree before I got to the porch.

It got to be fun in the daytime, too. I still remember sitting on that hole in the outhouse leaning close to admire that shiny little black spider with the red hour-glass on its belly. Its web was about six inches from my eyes. I've often wondered if that spider was there at night, as well. Somehow I survived.

That little green house held a couple of memories I'll likely never forget. It was the first place we lived in Bisbee when we moved from Panhandle, Texas in 1941. This was before we moved to Cowan Ridge and Jiggerville. For a six-year-old kid fresh off the farm, that little green house next to the Evergreen Cemetery was about as scary as it could get.

The little green house was located no more than a few hundred yards from Lowell School. If you look straight out the front door of Lowell School, then you will see the green iron fence of the cemetery. If you follow the fence to the left, you quickly will come to an outside corner of the fence as it turns to the right. About a hundred and fifty yards on down the fence will make another turn. On the inside corner of the fence at that turn was where our little green house was."

When Janet Humphries Crabaugh, BHS '49 found out that Ed had lived in that "little green house" she wrote him to tell Ed how lucky he was: "Ed, when you went out the back door of your little green house, you were looking through the fence at my Grandpa, and if you had known him you would have been **REALLY** scared! Grandpa Albert was a big, tall, very strict Swede who ruled the roost with an iron hand. I know of absolutely no photographs of him that show a smile. After Grandma died and she was placed there in the cemetery beside him, he might have mellowed a little, but I doubt it."

Ed continues, "Like many little boys of that time, I learned the joys of tying thread to a June bug's legs and letting him fly around tethered to my little 'leash'. That was great fun. One day when I was swatting down my flying pet of the day, I accidentally knocked down one of those giant yellow bumblebees instead of the June bug I was aiming at. Being a pretty bright kid, I knew this was a potentially bad situation. When that big bee woke up, I was going to be in big trouble. So I did what any Lowell kid would have done. I pulled the bee's head off. After about five minutes that bee hadn't moved and I began to feel safe. In another few minutes I got to feeling bad about what I had done to that bee. To make things right, I decided I would repair that bee and let him go on his way. I went into the house and got some glue. I glued the bee's head back on. I was not stupid and knew that when that bee came back to life he would take after me. I ran and hid while the glue set. I did not want that bee coming after me when he woke up. Naturally, nothing happened and young "Frankenstein's" career was squelched before it even got started. I was really disappointed about that bee though, and it took another few years before I finally figured out what went wrong that day (Ed was a freshman in Bisbee High School taking Mr. Curtis's General Science class when he finally figured it out. hh)

Another exciting thing I remember about that little green house was when I heard my mom scream in the other room. When I jumped up to check it out, there was my eighteen-year-old sister, Sylvia, talking to my mom. There was a strange man in the room, too. I'd never seen him before. Boy, was my mother carrying on and crying! I heard my sister say the words, "Momma, Warren and I got married today!" followed by another scream from my mom. I didn't know what to think or do. Should I hit the guy or hug him? So I waited for the full story.

My sister had a job as a waitress in the little restaurant that used to be located in the building to the right of the Lyric Theater in Bisbee. She had met a young man from Kansas named Warren. He was working in the mines in Bisbee and lived near the café. So they became infatuated with each other and secretly had run off to Lordsburg, New Mexico and tied the knot. Up to that point, she hadn't even told mom she had a boyfriend.

Well, things worked out with my sister and Warren from Kansas. They were married at St. Patrick's in a quiet ceremony and went off to live happily ever after. They celebrated their sixty-third anniversary with their children, grand children and great grandchildren. I would say it worked out just fine. Good ol' Bisbee!"

Ed lived in that little green house for a few years before the family moved just up the road to Jiggerville. He was living in Jiggerville, but he was still *from Lowell.*

Just a few years ago, Ed visited Lowell after many years' absence. He drove down "...the narrow road by the cemetery and the little green house was still there! Of course it was in great disrepair. *Awesome!* After all these years and that close to the cemetery, that green house is no doubt haunted and cursed and will remain there forever. My sister must have used up the last of the house's good luck finding her husband of sixty three years; and that bumblebee I decapitated was the victim of the first of the bad luck Anybody who tears that house down now is doomed to have one of his parents born sterile."

Dale Hancock, BHS '57 is a pretty good guy for a Lowell kid. He goes so far as to admit that the other grade schools in Bisbee were "good" schools. But, he says "...the shining light was the working man's blue collar school that set aside the Lowell traffic circle" He was referring of course, to Lowell Grade School. Read what Dale says in his own words what that "shining light" consisted of:

"For many years my classroom at Lowell was on the side of the building where I could look out on *the Ice Plant and watch the doings of the day*. It was exciting to watch the loading of the large columns of ice onto trucks and watch the ice come shooting out of the little door with the flap onto the dock to be loaded. Guys with ice tongs and rubberized aprons and long sleeves shirts were tugging and pulling the ice onto trucks; and every once in awhile an ice pick was pulled out to split up the size of the ice column." If Dale calls that "exciting", he must not have been watching the day Sammy Sorich, BHS '53 kicked at one of those ice blocks. His foot slipped off onto the circular saw that cut those ice blocks into squares. Sammy lost two toes that day; plus, a perfectly good right boot.

Dale got pretty nostalgic remembering all he learned his early years at Lowell Grade School by "looking out on the Ice Plant…"

It was at Lowell Grade School where Dale was "taught and learned more than I ever realized when later in life I had to extend myself. I made associations and friendships that endure to this day. Many influenced my life and direction." The massive brick building is still vivid in Dale's memory. He remembers the bolted down desks that had inkwells. They were neatly lined up in the spacious class-rooms. Some of the special teachers Dale remembers are: "Little" Miss Regan, "Big" Miss Regan, Miss Molly Bendixen and a "beautiful student teacher named Jackie", Mrs. Jim McNulty, wife of a new Bisbee lawyer Jim McNulty. Dale credits Miss Bendixen with contributing greatly to the outstanding career he had as a public school administrator. "She was tough, hard and demanding and she probably never felt she reached me or that I would amount to anything. But she sure poured a lot of knowledge and skills into me that I never knew latched on to me. She was up to the task however, and we all walked a fine line in her class and to the orders of her drum beat. When I became an educator, I gained a whole new respect for what she had contributed to my success."

Dale had a lot of respect for Mr. Herman Price, the Lowell Grade School principal. He was strict and could wield the whipping paddle with the best of them. The rumors circulated around for years that he had a "whipping machine" hidden in the closet in his office. Fortunately, Mr. Price never had to use the "whipping machine". His hand operated paddle worked most effectively.

Lowell Grade School was no different than many schools. If you wanted to get something done, even the principal and the teachers went to the *school custodian*. Lowell Grade School had one of the best custodians. Pop McGeary was loved by all who knew him. He had been custodian at Lowell Grade School for as long as anyone can remember. Dale describes Pop this way: "….I remember Pop McGeary and his engineer hat and striped work overalls and his bad eye. He was always most willing to play his favorite musical instruments, his spoons! And, what an honor to be picked by him to help him pick up trash and clean up!" Junie Hamrick Schaub BHS '65 adds to what Dale said about Pop. "We all LOVED Pop McGeary. He was the nicest guy to all the kids. He had a little black figure on a stick that he would make dance. That wouldn't be politically correct today, but we loved to see Pop make that little figure dance on his knee. He kept the school so clean. I loved the smell of that red oil he used to on the dust mop when he dusted the halls to a beautiful shine. It was spotless."

Next to Naco, the Lowell Grade School Auditorium was the cultural center of Bisbee. All of the grade school kids in Bisbee were first introduced to large group gatherings, plays, music concerts, graduation ceremonies, etc. in the Lowell Auditorium. There were many adult cultural events there as well. Opera companies from the University of Arizona were regular features in the Lowell Auditorium. The Phoenix Philharmonic Orchestra performed there once. I didn't go, but I remember my mother being in awe over it.

As Dale said, "When we were small the auditorium seemed larger than life." The school was two stories high as Dale remembers, but where the beautiful auditorium was, it had three stories counting the large spacious balcony. Dale "…thought of it as a place of splendor and elegance…the wooden theatre seats, the stately and massive curtains…!" Those of us in Greenway secretly envied the Lowell kids because they had such a beautiful auditorium at their school. We never admitted it though.

I really don't think the Lowell kids had as much fun at recess as we did at Greenway. They played such dumb games. And their play ground area resembled a prison exercise yard that I saw in a movie once. There wasn't a blade of grass to be found anywhere near Lowell Grade School, except on some of the gravesites across the street in the cemetery. When the Lowell kids ate lunch, they picked up their milk inside and then went out into a fenced in area where a teacher stood guard duty. The kids had to eat sitting on the hard cement basketball court. When they finished lunch, they had to walk through a narrow gate to get to the playground. Before being allowed through the gate they had to make sure that they threw their trash in a barrel that Pop McGeary had put near by. That is the way Dale and Ed "Pappy" Swierc described it. Doesn't that sound just like a prison? Then when they were inside the play area they could "play the various games or just sit and talk or walk around." Now, that doesn't sound like much fun to me. Their whole school had a fence all the way around it! I don't remember them saying anything about spotlights on the corners or guard dogs, though. And what dumb games they played! The boys played normal games sometimes, but they wouldn't practice as much as we Greenway kids did. They played a game called "buck-buck" which sounded weird to me. One team would hold on to each other's waists, bend over, and the other team would run and jump on the backs of the ones bent over. If the "jumpers" could break the hold on the ones bent over, they won. If a "jumper" was bucked off, the bent over ones won. Weird! Dale and Ed admitted that the Lowell kids were "status seekers" which Greenway kids weren't. The Lowell kids set up their "pecking order" based on who had won the most marbles at the end of any given day. We played marbles at Greenway also, but we never had to worry about who had the most at the end of any day. "Hondro" always won. The two Lowell scribes both admitted to sneaking under the street bridge over the water drainage ditch between the school and the Standard Station. They would sometimes do this during lunch hour when they were in the seventh and eighth grades. And do you know what they would do under there? They would SMOKE CIGARETTES! Cigarettes that they had *stolen* from their parents! Greenway kids **never** smoked! No wonder the Lowell kids never won any games. They were all out of shape! Dale ends his confession with this revelation: "If they had expelled us boys for smoking in the ditch when I was going to school there, they would have wiped out 80% of the 8th grade boys. We did this almost every day. We got the cigarettes from our parents. I got some *Cools* one time to see if the menthol really did make them cool. It did. I cannot believe the teachers did not know we were all there! How does a large group of boys walk off the school grounds and go under the bridge to smoke and never get caught!?" Could it possibly be that the teachers were *glad* that that bunch of "ornery seventh and eight grade kids" as Dale called them, were off the school grounds?

There was a murder in Lowell once. I mean a *real murder* where someone kills someone else; not the kind we used to do to the Lowell kids all the time at the Warren Park. And you know something else? I didn't even know it until I read some emails from folks who remember the murder. Or, I should say, "They *think* they remember." Well, I don't remember it at all and I was around at that time. But, remember, I used to just drive through Lowell. I even knew the Cunningham kids. Chuck Cunningham was one of the Horace Mann terrorists. Chuck's sister, Charlene was a waitress at the Toot-N'-Tell-Em restaurant in Warren. Billy Cunningham was the youngest Cunningham. He was a few years younger than I. Most people who "remember" the murder say that it was Chuck's, Charlene's, and Billy's dad who killed a guy. Pat Harris Flick, BHS '31[1] verifies that it was Mr. Allen Cunningham, former owner of the Toot'n Tellem in Warren, who killed a man outside a bar in Lowell. Pat is related to the Cunningham's and should know.

Wally Quayle, BHS '53 remembers the murder in vivid detail: "Me and McElyea were coming out of the bakery and we saw a guy shoot another guy several times."

Julian Courteol BHS '48 does a little better than Wally. Julian says "I'm not sure of the dates, but it was in the late '40's; perhaps '47 or '48, there was a murder on Lowell Main Street. Seems there was some bad blood between Mr. Cunningham and another man (perhaps a business associate) who made some rather gross and suggestive threats regarding Cunningham's daughter, Charlene. Mr. Cunningham caught the man leaving a bar, pulled a gun and shot him dead and he lay in the gutter. This would have been a few doors east of the Lowell Drug Store. I think it was a Sunday night and I was going through Lowell (See what I mean? "going through Lowell". hh) with Clyde Ward, headed to Bisbee from Bakerville to pick up something at First Baptist Church in Bisbee for a youth meeting being held at that moment. This was before the bypass that goes around Lowell (They don't even *drive through* Lowell anymore. They *bypass* it. hh). We drove by the spot; the body was in the gutter, people milling around. I think there was a lot of sympathy for Mr. Cunningham. I'm pretty sure I was still in high school so that seems to date it for me."

Tom Vercellino, '55 recalls that "Cunningham was the guy doing the shooting. Don't know who the victim was. It happened on main street on the north side of the Office Bar. I think it happened in the afternoon around 4:00pm."

Junie Hamrick Schaub, BHS '65 says that her dad, Bennie Hamrick, was a witness to the murder. He was coming out of the bakery (wonder if he saw Quayle and McElyea?) and witnessed one man shoot another man and kill him. They were both Bisbee guys, according to Bennie Hamrick. Hamrick was called as a witness at the trial. I wonder why Wally Quayle and Ken McElyea weren't called as witnesses?

Kathy Phillips, BHS '52 gets in the act with a woman's insight into the murder. She romanticizes the whole thing as women are likely to do. "I think the shooting...happened at the Lowell Women's' Club. There was a dance going on and some people got into a fight. Jack Bennett had been hired to keep the peace. He took out his gun and in the shuffle two innocent guys were shot. I remember

---

1.   Pat is not really that old. She just never puts her graduation date by her name when she signs off. I wanted to teach her a lesson. Plus, I wanted to have one footnote in the book. It adds a touch of professionalism.

my mom saying her and dad were sitting in their car on the parking lot there in Lowell watching the traffic, like they often did. The guy who died fell against their car. Mom said he had on a white shirt and it was completely red with blood. I used to know the names because my dad knew both of them, but can't seem to recall them. Everyone said Jack Bennett was devastated and was never quite the same after that."

After thinking it over for several months, Wally Quayle got back in the mix and sent this updated report on the murder: "Their names were Allen and Cunningham. Very unfortunate. Allen was a womanizer who owned the Toot'n Tellem across from the Warren Ballpark. Allen liked to go after married women. As a result Cunningham came after him and called him out of the Office Bar in Lowell and shot him, emptied his gun on him and cursed him out. Some of us were waiting for a bus in front of the bakery when it happened. I think he got something like five years. The Cunningham's were a good family. The boys, Chuck, class of '51, Bill, class of '54 were good students and pretty good athletes. Their daughter was a very cute girl. She was a waitress at the Toot'n Tellem in Warren. Bill died of heart failure. I was very saddened by his death."

So there you have it. Six very reputable Bisbee High graduates who offered us first hand testimony to a murder in Lowell. When you piece it all together the scenario looks something like this:

There was a big dance at the Lowell Women's Club. It was a Sunday afternoon about 4:00pm. Julian Courteol and Clyde Ward were driving through Lowell on their way to The First Baptist Church youth meeting, which was in progress in Bisbee. Bennie Hamrick, Wally Quayle, Ken McElyea and others were coming out of the Lowell bakery, which stayed open on Sundays. Mr. and Mrs. Phillips were spending a typical Sunday afternoon watching the traffic go through Lowell. They were parked in the Women's Club parking lot so they could listen to the music coming from the dance while they watched the traffic go through Lowell. Suddenly, Jack Bennett who had been hired by the Women's Club to keep things peaceful, tried to break up a fight by brandishing his pistol. Two innocent by-standers were shot when his gun went off. One of the innocent by standers staggered out to the parking lot where he fell across the Phillips' car getting blood all over the place. Meanwhile, down the street a block or so away from the Women's Club, in front of the Office Bar, Mr. Allen insulted Mr. Cunningham by making disparaging remarks about Mr. Cunningham's daughter. Mr. Allen and Mr. Cunningham were co-owners of the Toot 'En Tell 'Em restaurant in Warren. Mr. Cunningham shot Mr. Allen and since Mr. Allen was a known womanizer, Mr. Cunningham got off with a five-year sentence. Though there were many witnesses to the murder, only Bennie Hamrick was called to testify at the trial.

I have to admit that I am confused. I guess I really shouldn't be as I am writing this book about "memories", not "facts". **If** Pat Harris Flick remembers her relative, Mr. Allen Cunningham shooting a guy she can't remember the name of, and **if** Wally Quayle remembers Mr. Cunningham shooting Mr. Allen in front of numerous witnesses who were eating donuts they bought at the Lowell Bakery Sunday afternoon just as Julian Courteol and Clyde Ward were going through Lowell on their way to a youth meeting at The First Baptist Church in Bisbee, **AND IF** Tom Vercellino remembers it being 4:00 p.m. Sunday afternoon, and **if** Kathy Phillips remembers her mom remembering the dance at the Lowell Women's Club when Jack Bennett shot two innocent by standers, one of which got blood all over the Phillips car, **if** that is the way they remember it, **then, so be it!** That's good enough for me.

"SIXTEEN TONS AND WHAT DO YOU GET?"

It would be hard to find a Bisbee landmark, which symbolizes the legacy of Bisbee, any more succinctly than *The Iron Man* statue. For more than six decades the Iron Man has greeted visitors to Bisbee from his lofty pedestal just below St. Patrick's Church at the conflux of Bisbee Road and Clawson Avenue. To the casual observer, the Iron Man is merely a statue, a sculpture of an old fashioned "hard rock miner"; nothing more. To generations, literally hundreds upon hundreds of Bisbee High School students, the Iron Man is so much more. I believe that an article by Bisbeeite, Ralph Ladner says in just a few heart-felt words exactly what the Iron Man represents. This article was made available to us by Ron Sanders, BHS '56.

I grew up in Old Bisbee. When it comes to the Iron Man, I guess its beauty is in the eye of the beholder.

When I was young, it was just another statue. But one evening, as all young boys do, I asked my dad what he did for a living. I recall clearly, and how with great pride, he explained that he was an underground miner, a 'raise miner' driving tunnels straight up through the ground. He took a piece of paper from my notebook where I was doing my sixth grade homework and explained how to drill, blast, and timber raise; stull, crib and six post. He explained how to safely reenter a raise and make it safe after a fresh blast when there was no timber, and all the loose, broken rock was hanging over your head in a 6 by 11 foot area, and anything that fell could kill you.

I remember the day he came home upset because his young partner was hit in the eye with a piece of steel that splintered from the bit while drilling. I remember a couple weeks later when the same young man, sitting in our living room in Moon Canyon, blind in that eye, personally came to thank my father for saving his life. He said, when the steel entered his eye he panicked and ran, blinded by the blood and sweat, and my father grabbed him, calming him, and narrowly kept him from falling seventy feet to his death.

I remember the day Dad got hurt and his partner hoisted him on his shoulders and carried him down eighty feet of ladders, out of harms way. That evening, as we sat together at the kitchen table, he also explained that he did this so his kids could have a good education and a better way of life. It wasn't until I was older, when I went to work underground myself that I fully understood. **It was Dad, and all the miners like him, that truly were the Iron Men; heroes in their own right.**

In that statue I see my father. In my father I see that statue. It stands as a tribute to him and all the miners like him, a source of pride to those like me who were lucky enough to have shared their lives and benefited from them.

The Iron Man represents a legacy; a legacy of freedom and a better way of life. The Statue of Liberty has these words inscribed on her base, written by a young Jewess, Emma Lazaurs: *Give me your tired, your poor, your huddled masses yearning to breathe free…*Much like that majestic lady in New York harbor who has welcomed millions to the shores of The United States of America with those words, The Iron Man has represented that same greeting and way of life to thousands who made Bisbee their home; many of whom were immigrants from other countries. To the families of those immigrants, the Iron Man personifies their loved ones.

The Iron Man represents *Eli Vuksanovich* an immigrant from Yugloslavia who raised his family in Bisbee and was crushed to death in the old Calumet-Arizona mineshaft in 1922. His grandson, Sam Borozan, a Flagstaff resident, visits Bisbee several times a year. Each time he visits, he stops at the Iron Man to pray silently and thank God for his grandfather and the way of life Bisbee provided for his family. Sam sees his father and his grandfather in the Iron Man.

The Iron Man represents *Sam Sorich, Sr.* His sons, Sam, Jr. and Ted, hold their father in high esteem. Sam Sorich, Sr. immigrated to America from Yugoslavia just before the start of World War I. He felt he had an obligation to "fight for his country" so he enlisted and served America honorably. Upon his discharge he promptly returned to Bisbee and went to work for Phelps Dodge. Ted Sorich BHS '57 remembers his dad telling him how grateful he was that Phelps Dodge provided *a better way of life for him and his family.* "I have no idea how much he was being paid, but in his own mind, he considered himself to be 'well off' compared to where he was in *the old country.*"

Pete Vucurevich BHS '47 proudly recalls his father as well: "My father was seventy seven when he died in 1942 from complications from an automobile accident. I remember him well, but only as an old, old man. He was sixty-five when I was born. I was twelve when he died. My mom survived him by eighteen years." Pete shares a most interesting story about his dad and mother. It seems that Pete's mother was a "mail order bride"! Here is how Pete tells the story:

> Dad came to America in 1909 and settled in Lead, South Dakota. There he met and fell in love with an Italian woman. The lady soon left Lead and headed for Bisbee, Arizona. Dad had a small business in Lead, which he left with a young teenage nephew. Dad then packed up and followed the lady to Bisbee. Upon arriving in Bisbee, dad found out that the lady had left for San Francisco. At this point, dad gave up the chase. He heard from some of the old 'hunkies' that lived in Bisbee about a family in Yugoslavia that had a couple of eligible daughters. In 1912 he sent for my mother and she came. He was forty-nine and she was twenty. Smart man! They started their family and had nine children over a span of about fifteen years. I happened to be the youngest because of an accident. Let me clarify that. My brother Danny's first name is *Miaden,* which translated to English is derived from the word 'youngest'. In other words Danny was supposed to have been the last child. Then the accident and here I am.
>
> It was common in those days for men to marry young women. The tradition carried on for years. Even my oldest two sisters married men that were much older. Both are still alive and have been widowed for over forty years!
>
> My family has been fortunate in that, of the nine, seven of us are still kicking. The oldest is a sister and is ninety, a brother is eighty nine, a sister is eighty eight, a brother seventy nine and one soon to be seventy six (Danny) and me at seventy four. Not bad for longevity. As Paul Harvey says, 'and that is the rest of the story.

The legacy of the Iron Man is meaningful to Jane Ridgway because of her husband, Al's, tie to the making of the statue. Al's dad was a blacksmith for the Phelps Dodge Mining Company. He made the tools the Iron Man is holding. For those of us who knew Al as a teacher, or coach, or administrator, will surely remember his thumb that was merely a stub. Remember how he used it as a "weapon"? When he dug that stub into us we were quick to yell, *uncle!* Al lost that part of his thumb in a mining accident the year he worked underground.

It is sad to some that the Iron Man has been spray-pointed *copper* in recent years. I am sure who ever authorized the painting of the Iron Man had good intentions. They wanted to "spruce him up", I am sure. But as Sam Borozan said "I think every miner's child sees their father in the miner's statue…I was saddened on my last visit to Bisbee that it had been spray painted copper…it is what I call the desecration of the Iron Man…I came to know and love that *weathered statue…*"

Sam Borozan's feelings speak for many. Children and grandchildren of miners who toiled in the Bisbee mines did not remember their loved ones as "spruced up", squeaky clean, 8:00am-5:00pm workers. Those miners worked in the bowels of the earth where conditions were, at best, miserable and severe. Serious, incapacitating injuries were common place. Death was always a possibility. Bennie Hamrick, BHS '47 remembers Louie Perez, an immigrant from Mexico who was killed in 1949 while working the night shift at the Shattuck-Denn shaft. Bennie said that Louie was a great guy, a great miner and full of laughter. Bennie's usual partner was Rudy Silva, but that night he was with Louie. A strictly enforced rule that all underground miners adhered to was **never, never look over the edge of the shaft; neither up or down!** The cages, which brought miners and equipment down to their levels, or up to the surface, traveled at high rate of speed. It was so noisy working under-ground that one could not hear the cages as they approached. There was, at most, a three-inch space between the shaft and the rock wall. That night, Louie broke the rule. For some reason, he looked down the shaft. He couldn't hear the rapidly descending cage. Louie was decapitated and his body thrown into the cage as it sped past. Louie had a young wife. She left Bisbee and returned to Mexico shortly after Louie was killed; the Perez's dream of "a better way of life" in America was never realized.

Pete Vucurevich, BHS '47 says "at one point, a life was lost about every two to three years." Pete had two experiences with "cave ins" he won't forget. "In my own experience…, I came close two times. Once, a big slab of rock fell and brushed my shoulder enough to push me aside. Had it been directly over head, *goodbye!* The other time, I was about ten feet off to the side when about twenty to thirty tons of rock came down. I guess it just wasn't my time in either case, but it came close…"

Sam Moore, BHS '56 remembers his dad telling about a miner being killed who worked with Mr. Moore. A cave in had occurred and Mr. Moore was the shift boss who was sent to look for a missing miner. When Mr. Moore uncovered the man, "…his face was up and his eyes were wide open. Dad said he had dreams of seeing those eyes for a long time." Two other times, Mr. Moore had to retrieve two miners who had suffocated due to lack of oxygen in their stope.

With the constant threat of death and serious injury always present, miners became very superstitious. If one miner was paired off with another and the two of them had "good luck" than those two did everything possible to see to it that they were paired together each shift. If one miner got the reputation of causing "bad luck" he was shunned like the plague. Ralph Echave was one such example of a "carrier" of bad luck. Here is his story of the events, which caused his banishment from the good graces of all the miners: "While I was working in the Cole shaft, I was working in a stope, which caved in. My partner and I were seven levels high when the rocks started coming down. The 10x10 timbers were popping like the sound of .22 shells going off. The falling rocks were momentarily held back by the timber above us. My partner shouted, 'Let's get the hell out of here! She's coming down.' Down she did come, and fortunately I got a burst of adrenaline-induced speed and we both sat in the drift gagging on the dust. Several weeks later, I was in another stope with another partner and that stope came down. This was an area, which we were not timbering. It was a huge slab that fell this time. Again, we were unharmed in the drift gagging with the dust....the word spread throughout the mine and NO MINER WOULD HAVE ME AS A PARTNER. Miners were extreme believers in the mysteries of the unknown. They just would not take chances with a known carrier of bad luck".

People from all over the country and from all over the world came to Bisbee on the promise of a better way of life and a degree of security that could not found where they had come from. The flow of immigrants from Europe began in earnest in the early 1900's. Pete Vucurevich, BHS '47 and Sam Borozan have already attested to that. The family roots of the Sorich's, the Balich's, the Blagovich's, the Verbica's, the Milovich's, the Dabovich's and so many other Serbian families, can be traced back for generations to "the old country." They came because of the mines; the promises that the copper rich Mule Mountains tendered allowed these immigrants to dream of better lives for their children than what had been available in the 'old country".

During the Great Depression years of the 1930's, Bisbee began to see more of an influx of families from destitute regions of The United States. Again it was primarily the allure of the promise of work in the mines, which drew them here. Tony Carretto, a second generation Italian, came to Bisbee from the Bronx in New York. He worked in the mines for many years before his death in the late 1950's. Robert French mined in Bisbee for eighteen years before he died of "consumption" in 1943. He left Minnesota to come to Bisbee. It is pretty safe to say that the majority of native Bisbeeite families were drawn to Bisbee by that promise the Iron Man represents. My father, Dr. Hadley H. Hicks was drawn to Bisbee in the late 1920's because Bisbee's rapid and steady growth promised a good clientele for his dental practice. My grandfather, Robert Fergus, Sr. a first generation Scotsman, left New Jersey to work as an accountant for The Phelps Dodge Company. My uncle, Robert Fergus, Jr. came *back* to Bisbee after serving in the U.S. Army for the same reason my dad came *to* Bisbee; he saw the possibility of a good dental practice. Families who had suffered great loss during the "Dust Bowl" years also found their way to Bisbee. The George Thomas family pulled up stakes in Oklahoma for the mines; Edgar Bauchnett and his two children left a failing Kansas farm for the mines. Bauchnett was a widower. And on and on it goes. Family after family found a new life in Bisbee. The Iron Man represents all of them.

The father of Bisbee author, JAJance, aka Judy Busk, BHS, '64, came to Bisbee from South Dakota. Here is how JAJance tells the story of her insight into the degree to which her dad had sacrificed for his family:

> While visiting the Dueches Museum in Munich, Germany in 1965, I visited a display that included life-sized dioramas of mines through the ages from a Roman salt mine right through a modern copper mine. And it was while I walked through that display that I realized what my father, a lifelong farmer from South Dakota, had sacrificed for his children when he went to work in the copper mines in Bisbee in 1948.
>
> He had been stricken with rheumatoid arthritis while living in South Dakota and had moved to Bisbee for his health; which he recovered completely.
>
> When he first went to work underground, his legs were still so weak he had to pull himself up and down the ladders with his arms. Yes, underground miners were indeed Iron Men!!"

I believe it is safe to say that the Iron Man statue is a reminder for JAJance of that sacrifice her father made many years ago.

It has been a wonderful education for me to read and write about the Phelps Dodge Company and the influence it had on all of us growing up in Bisbee. I was completely oblivious to what Phelps Dodge meant to Bisbee. I was aware of the fact that most of my friends were somehow connected to the PD. Either their fathers worked for the PD directly as a miner, an office worker or an administrator, or else their livelihood was earned indirectly from the PD. My father's dental practice had its ups and downs directly concurrent with the PD's financial ups and downs, as did my uncle Robert Fergus' dental practice. The Copper Queen

Hospital's doctors and nurses were paid out of the PD's coffers. The entire economy of Bisbee was solely dependent on the Phelps Dodge Company. I did not grasp the significance of that as a kid growing up in Bisbee. The PD had always been there, and in my mind, would always be there. To me, the PD was no "big deal". My outlook, I know, would have been quite a bit different had my dad been a miner; or had I worked underground in the summers like some of my friends did. Ed "Pappy" Swierc, BHS '53, in his light hearted manner, wrote a brilliant treatise on the life of a young miner. This is a fascinating account of what those miners went through on a daily basis for years. Ed just did it for a few months. Imagine having to do this day in and day out **for years!** Ed wrote:

> When I got out of the service, I came back to Bisbee and went looking for a job with the PD, waiting for the fall school term that was to begin in nine months. I used the 'regular' way to get hired at the PD, which was to join others in a line outside the hiring office near the Junction every morning, waiting until the hiring agent would come out at 7:00am and announce who, in anybody, was to be hired that day. This kind of job hunting was called 'rustling'. Once you got hired, you took a physical, bought some most necessary steel-toed shoes and the PD would give you perhaps your most prized possession; *your brown miners' hard hat.* You needed the hat not only to protect your noggin, but you needed it to clamp your underground light to.
>
> I had a big problem the first day. I was hired and almost 'unhired' the same day. It seems that the PD, with all its millions of dollars in equipment, didn't have a hard-hat to fit my big head (I'm not gonna tell ya what size I wore, but it is much more reasonable now that I am bald). No hard-hat, no work. It wasn't until late afternoon that first day when somebody finally discovered that they had a **white** colored hat that would fit me (instead of a brown one like everybody else wore), and the big shots then gave approval for me to wear it underground. With that decided, they called me back in, gave me my new hat and finished my processing to start work the next day. So I was marked right off the bat to be the only one working underground with a white hat.
>
> When I was hired-on, the pay for a 'mucker' was $16.00 per day and we worked a six-day week. (Out of curiosity, I looked up the word *mucker* to see how Mr. Daniel Webster defined it. Webster says a mucker is, among other things, "of no value", a mucker is "filth", a mucker is a "bungler". Let's just say that when Ed was hired on as a mucker, he was hired on as a "rookie". Sam Moore, BHS '56 is much kinder and gentler in his definition of a mucker. Sam calls them "jack of all trades" hh) If you were lucky enough to work 'partners' with a good, experienced miner who was making a bonus for exceeding his ore quota, then you could make a few bucks or so above your wage. That rarely happened to us lowly ones. In regards to that regular pay, to this day I still unconsciously judge the priced of things against that $16.00 wage; wondering whether something like a $5.50 hamburger, for example, is worth

almost three hours of heavy picking and shoveling. I don't think so. At that time $16.00 a day was a decent wage.

When that whistle blew to start our shift, down you went jammed in one of those multiple-deck cages (elevators) with a dozen or so other men and your body was only inches from the exposed side of the mineshaft. The cage dropped at almost free fall speed until it got close to its designated level. Each level in the mine had a well-lighted disembarking station with a 20 ft. high portal, and those you didn't stop at appeared only as quick passing blinks as the cage sped by; that and the wind and our ears popping were enough to wake you up good every morning.

I remember very well my first big day underground, helping "pipe and trackman" and trying to keep stooped over every time I had to move to keep from hitting my head on the low ceiling. At six feet four inches tall, I tended to bump my head more than most. I soon learned the value of my hard-hat even if it was white. It was a very trying day for me. When I got home I immediately fell asleep and didn't wake until it was time for work again.

Those 'old men' working in the mines were a tough bunch of critters, and it took a week or so before a young pup like me could begin to keep up with them. The first time I had to help lift one of those big air-drilling machines up on its stand, I could hardly raise up my end. After a few months, I discovered I could pick the whole thing up by myself and set it up there with no help.

The lonely *track cleaning detail, which* I was put on at times, always reminded me of that "Sixteen tons" song. They told me that one of those ore cars held two tons, and with nothing better to do, I usually tried to fill up around eight of them during a shift. For those of you who went to Lowell Grade School, 2 tons x 8 tons = 16 tons! If I stopped working and sat for a while, it only took a few minutes in that drift air before all your sweat dried up. If the shift boss picked that time to come by, he could take one look at you and see that you were not sweating, and assume, every time, that you had been goofing off. Of course, being the diligent, hard working young man that I was, I was always sweating.

One of the better jobs a mucker could get was 'swamping', clearing the surface which was helping out on the underground ore car train that transported the mined rock from the working areas (stopes) to the storage areas near the mine shaft. The cage operators would later on, usually on the midnight shift, attach big buckets, called 'skips', under the cage, and haul the ore in these 'skips' to the processing. The 'swamper's job on the train was to fill each mine car with ore from a chute that came from the stopes from where the miners worked to a position just above the tracks. I know this sounds complicated, but bare with me.

As the motorman, or driver, on the train positioned each car under this chute per your headshaking signal with your light, it was your job to stand up on a board high above the track, to open a crude chute door, let the broken rock ore fill the car and then to shut the door quickly before the car overflowed. Fine. But it didn't always work out the way it was supposed to. Those loose rocks in the chute above you weighed many tons and had a lot of energy behind them. Once that rock started moving down, they wanted to keep moving and sometimes they didn't care whether you closed that little chute door or not, especially if the rock was wet. In that case it might just keep flowing right over the top of that door. Sometimes, too, you would close that chute door onto a big boulder, and all the loose stuff just kept flowing around it until you got that boulder out of there. In either case, the ore car would overflow onto the tracks, covering the tracks and wheels and maybe even half the car if your luck was really bad that day. Now you're back to a track cleaning detail again, because if that train moves six inches over that spill, its gonna derail and then you're really in big trouble.

The time or two that I got a bad spill, I was always fortunate to be working with the heaviest, widest motorman in the mines, who couldn't possibly make his way past all those cars in that narrow drift (tunnel) to help me dig out. Such was the life of a mucker.

One of the jobs a mucker had to do when working with a miner in a stope was to get the dynamite and blasting cap fuses that would be needed toward the end of his shift. You had spent the entire day drilling a series of deep holes into the rock work face and now it was time to blast. The miner had to figure how many sticks of dynamite were needed and how many fuses. The fuses had blasting caps attached on one end that detonated the dynamite when the flame reached the cap. So, off to the powder magazine you went where the Powder Man would load you up with canvas sacks of dynamite sticks, plus one separate sack with the fuses and caps.

Once the mucker made it back to the working place with the dynamite, usually struggling up a ladder or two, then the holes that had been drilled that day were loaded with the sticks and tamped tight with a long wooden broomstick' looking pole. The initial (bottom) dynamite stick put in each hole was first prepared by punching a hole into it with a sharp wooden dowel (that looked exactly like a Sugar Daddy stick) for insertion of a fuse and blasting cap. With all the holes tamped tightly with dynamite which hole he wanted to blow up first. In a rock faced stope, usually the center hole had the shortest fuse so it would go off first, then the next ring of holes nearest the center hole was next, and fuses hanging out, the miner would then cut off pieces of each fuse according to so on, until the outer ring of holes went off last. The theory was that consecutive blasts would all break the rock nicely toward that center hole, getting maximum efficiency and rock breakup of the blasting round. All the cut fuse ends were placed in a thin board with a slot in it, so that all the ends faced the miner, all lined up evenly like ducks in a row. What remained was to light the fuse and bug out....quickly and with haste!

Usually by this time the miserable phenomenon called a 'powder headache' had set in for us non-career workers. The headache was caused by the fumes from the dynamite raising cain with our blood circulation system. It is a piercing headache that ended once you got away from the dynamite, but meanwhile it really got your attention.

Once the proper time arrived, usually just at quitting time, the fuses are lit with a 'spitter' (which looks exactly like the sparklers kids play with on the 4th of July), and the miner and his trusty helper quickly depart the scene a safe distance away. Their last jobs were to guard all access to the area, making sure that no one walked into the blast. A person walking into the blast area would likely get more than a 'powder headache'! The second part of that job was to count all the individual 'booms' and report the count to the boss if it appears one of those holes laden with dynamited failed to go off. Because *counting* was so important, you can see why only St. Patrick Grade School graduates were used for this job. It wouldn't be pretty if the next crew dug into the unexploded dynamite. If a crew did so, it meant instant loss of their jobs!

One of the miners I was fortunate to have worked with during my time was Dale Hancock's dad, B. Hancock. From our ball field days together in Jiggerville, to years later working together in the mines drilling holes with a 'stoper' machine, was quite a connection! Naturally, we got along great and even tried to get hooked up for a longer period, but it was not to be. In about two weeks his regular partner came back and I was tossed back into the mucker bucket. If I'm not mistaken the powder man at the time who was in charge of the nearest dynamite storage area was Sam Sorich, Sr., Sam and Ted Sorich's dad.

I also managed to meet my own dad one day, despite the fact he worked at the Junction and I was working at the Campbell shaft. For some reason I had been sent down a long drift looking for something, and after about the third set of air doors I went through, there he was! That was a thrill for me. I remember him showing me a Timex pocket watch that was nailed to a timber by where we were was standing. The watch was nailed with a 50-penny nail right through its center. A 50-penny nail is a big one; almost like a spike. It seems that one of the pranks miners did to one another when one of them left his watch laying around or had lost a watch, the finder would nail it down on a post in full view so it didn't get lost again.

I had two close calls while in the mines. One involved a big, wet 8-inch by 8-inch timber post. That sucker must have weighed well over a hundred pounds. I had just 'handed' it up to my partner who was at the top of a ladder at our working area, when it slipped from his hands, dropped five feet and nailed me square on top of my hard hat. The concussion drove all the metal retaining clips holding my hatband down on my head like a crown of thorns, and rung my bell pretty good. Being the tough guy I am, I never reported it; years later a chiropractor examining my spine wondered how its curvature got so out of whack. I knew instantly.

A second bad incident I had was when my partner and I were sent into a caved in area to check it out and bar down any dangerous rock accumulation. We saw that a huge slab of solid rock about 9 feet high by 15 feet wide and about 4 feet thick had fallen onto its edge and probably needed to be taken care of. My partner went around back of it to look at conditions there, while I stayed in front. As I was looking up at the top of that slab, I saw it start o move towards me, followed a split-second late by my partner hollering, 'LOOK OUT!'

I was in excellent condition at the time, as only a twenty two-year-old working hard in the mines for six months could be. Instinctively, I made one humongous jump sideways and landed just barely outside of where that entire huge slab impacted a half-second later. When the dust had cleared and my partner found me, we estimated that somehow I had jumped flatfooted almost ten feet. Every muscle in both my legs and hip were severely cramped and I couldn't walk at all for the next two hours. But, I didn't have a scratch on me. Lucky? Well, I guess!!

During the two hours I was recovering, we sat in the drift talking about my near miss, and got to experimenting with our hat lamps. As there is no other illumination except for those lights we carried, I got to wondering if there was any ambient 'glow' or phosphorescent light in those mines. So we both turned off out battery lights and sat there for half an hour letting our eyes adjust; trying to see something. Let me tell you, I knew then what DARK meant! There was absolutely no light available whatsoever.

At the end of a hard day's work, most miners came back to the top absolutely black dirty! Those air drills lubricated with oil bottles did a great job of spray painting you, and the heavy rock dust mixed with water and sweat totally saturates your clothes. Once worn for a few shifts, a miner's pants can literally stand up in the locker on their own. The only thing I found that would really clean the body was liquid detergent. It burned the eyes, but it got the job done. And, it helped the smell!

After working night shift at the Campbell shaft, I quickly learned the value of liquid replenishment from a long day of sweating. So, I would hurry through the shower, jump into my car and haul off for the Hitching Post. I could usually get a cold six-pack before closing time.

That just about does it for Ed's experiences in working underground; except for one thing. Ed acquired a nickname while he was there. Since Ed was going to school that fall, he never joined the union. The miners were used to students doing that, but it still irritated them. The students didn't have union dues taken out of their checks. Ed became better known than most of the students because of his *white hard-hat!* Ed became known as **"the scab in the white hat"**. A "scab" was a non-union miner or a miner who would not participate in a strike; one who would cross the picket line to work. They were looked upon with disdain by the striking miners.

Any discussion of Phelps Dodge, the mines, and Bisbee would not be complete without briefly mentioning the affects that strikes, lay-offs or shut-downs had on the economy and morale of Bisbee.

Paul, BHS, '56, Renner's father was injured early in his career with PD so he worked most of his career as a "watchman". He did not go underground and therefore would work all the strikes and shutdowns. The Renner family was not hurt financially when a strike or shutdown occurred, but it was very hard on Mr. Renner emotionally. Most of his friends were on strike; they were walking the picket line and Mr. Renner had to "cross the picket line" often at the risk of physical abuse. On paydays, Mr. Renner would give his friends who were striking a five-dollar bill to buy coffee, donuts, etc.

Sam Sorich, BHS '53 and Ted Sorich, BHS '57 tell us their father would not participate in a strike. Ted writes:

> Our father refused to strike whenever one was called by the union leaders. He was one of the "scabs" who crossed the picket line. He was called every name in the book by those who manned the line. He was humiliated by the name calling, but with courage, he walked quietly through the line, put in his eight-hour shift and returned home, many times on the verge of tears, because of the stress that he was put under. He was one of the few who brought home that paycheck every week. No need to worry about meals, clothing and shelter for the Sorich family. We were, indeed, fortunate. When things got really tough for some of the strikers who had little or no income and the situation was getting desperate, I can remember some of them coming to our house, "hat in hand" so to speak, to borrow some money from our Dad. Not one time did Dad refuse to lend the money, even to those who disagreed with his "crossing the line". And according to our Dad, every cent that was borrowed was eventually paid back!

Sam Moore, BHS '56 remembers how difficult the strike in 1949 was on his family. Sam said the strike lasted almost a year and up to that point was one of the longest strikes on record, His family had to move to Abilene, Texas where Mr. Moore owned a small service station. When the strike was over, the family moved back to Bisbee. Except for that short stint in Texas, Mr. Moore worked under ground for over forty years!

Dale Hancock, BHS '57 and his family had to resort to picking cotton in the Elfrida valley during one long strike. Dale's sister, Janice, BHS '60 had to help the family financially by baby-sitting. She was seven or eight at the time.

JAJance, well-known Bisbee author, aka Judy Busk, BHS, '63, recalls the strikes being very hard on her fathers' life insurance business. "With seven kids to feed, I am not sure how my parents weathered some of those tough times. My mother did a lot of canning."

Like everybody else in Bisbee during a strike, my family was affected. I was not aware of it though, except I do remember times when my parents had an abundance of Mexican food on hand, and when I did not have as much work to do in our yard; Dad had "helpers" available, usually high school students. You see, Dad had an agreement with his dental patients that he would do their dental work and they would work off the bill by giving us food or working around our yard. It was a great deal for me. Lots of good food and no work in the yard! One time one of his patients gave him half a deer. We ate a lot of venison for several months.

In spite of the strikes, the lay-offs, and what some considered low pay, the PD was good for Bisbee. Pete Vucurevich, BHS '47, records some "positives" based on his experiences: "PD was 'the' economy in Bisbee for years......Families depended on the company for their livelihood. The pay, in general, was not all that good, but with fringe benefits such as health care and retirement, the jobs were not that bad. Local taxes the company paid went a long way in funding our schools. The company maintained an irrigation system in Warren, including the Vista Park for years, using wastewater that was pumped from the underground mines. They maintained the Country Club in Naco and the golf course irrigation for years as well. They owned and operated the hospital and mercantile stores in Bisbee and Warren."

The PD was indeed the lifeblood of Bisbee.

When I started writing this book on February 5, 2004, I wrote JAJance popular Bisbee author and asked her how best to go about writing a book. She is the experienced professional and I am the bumbling novice. I wanted her wisdom gleaned over many years; and I wanted it given to me simply, concisely and thoroughly. I expected at the very least a two or three page "how to" pamphlet. Do you know what she told me? JAJance, the accomplished professional, simply said "just write". Well, that is what I have been doing and so far I have seldom been at a loss for words. *However, I am now at a loss for words!* In the last two days I have had a complete transformation in my thoughts about the PD and the mines! As I read and reread the numerous emails from those who had worked in the mines and/or came from a family of miners, I have gained a respect, an admiration for those of whom the Iron Man speaks. I am struggling to put those feelings into words, so I will take the advice of JAJance, and *just write.*

I have to admit when I read Sam Borozan's touching tribute to his grandfather, Eli Vucksanovich, my first thoughts were, "Come on, Sam. Don't get emotional on us!" Then as I read Sam and Ted Sorich's and Pete Vucurevich's tributes to their dads, I began to feel some of what they were conveying. Then as

I read Ed Swierc's account of his nine-month stint as a miner, it began to dawn on me that these men put their lives on the line daily. Most of them for a much longer time than the nine months Ed put in. Twice in those nine months Ed almost died. Pete had several brushes with death; as did Ralph Echave, BHS '47. Louie Perez did die; as did Eli Vucksanovich. I cannot imagine thirty or forty years of that kind of life. In my self-absorbed life, I have never had to make those kinds of sacrifices for my family. Something Dale Hancock, BHS '57 wrote makes me think that *I could have* though, had God guided me in that direction. You see, I grew up in Bisbee and this is what Dale had to say about those of us who grew up in Bisbee:

"When people who are not from Bisbee ask me why so many people from Bisbee in so many different walks of life are so successful, I have an answer for them. I think it is because people from Bisbee come from a stock and an environment where work, effort, dedication and being responsible has been modeled for them by those who have gone on before. Those of us who grew up in this special town have lived with that legacy every day of our lives. That legacy has crossed over into every facet of Bisbee; and that legacy began with the miners."

I have to agree with Sam Borozan. The Iron Man should be restored to his original weathered condition. He looks out of place "all spruced up"!

BISBEE'S REAL WAR HEROES. CONTINUED.

2nd Lt. Leonard **Douglas Davis**, BHS '60 was the first. Others would soon follow, but Doug Davis was the first BHS graduate to die in Vietnam. He had graduated from West Point just months before he died. He was to be married on his first R and R (Rest and Recuperation) in Japan, which was coming up shortly. His fiancé had her bags packed ready to fly to Japan to meet Doug. They had a brief honeymoon planned. They were going to tour the Japanese islands and possibly make a hurried trip to Hawaii. The young lady received word of Doug's death the night before she was to depart. JAJance, BHS '62 met Doug's former fiancé several years ago and found out that her only memories of Bisbee are going there for his funeral.

S. Sgt. **Richard Allen Thursby** and Lance Corporal **Leonard Carabeo** were killed sometime after Doug Davis; as were Sgt. **Robert Nathan Fiesler,** Air Man 1st Class **Willard Wesley Lehman** and Lance Corporal **Richard Lynn Embrey.** Rod (Robert) Sheets knew Ricky Embrey well. The two young BHS '64 graduates joined the Marines shortly after they said "goodbye" to Bisbee High. They went in on "The Buddy Plan". They took basic training together. They went on weekend passes together. They went on leaves together. They probably even went home to Bisbee together just before leaving for 'Nam. The two, Rodney Sheets and Ricky Embry were buddies *from Bisbee*. Rodney was in Vietnam when Ricky was killed. Rodney said there isn't a day goes by that he doesn't think about his buddy, Ricky Embry. Rodney, if you read this, please accept **my personal thanks** for your service to America. You didn't get many "thanks" when you got back from 'Nam. The media, war protestors, and the Hollywood elite saw to that. You guys were portrayed as "baby killers" and "mass murders". Somehow America was *brain washed* to forget you who fought and gave your lives in a war in which you had very little support. Whether you should have been there in the first place or not is beside the point. You were there. You deserved America's full support; you did not get it. In retrospect, many of us are saddened by that.

Junie Hamrick Schaub, BHS '65 remembers standing on her front porch in Briggs and crying as she watched Ricky's long funeral procession go by on its way to Memory Gardens across from Lowell Grade School. Family and friends joined Junie in expressing grief over the death of Ricky Embry. My guess is that *The Bisbee Daily Review* had nice write ups on Ricky, Richard Thursby, Leonard Carabeo and the other Bisbee boys who died in that ugly war. Rodney, I would be interested to know if there was anything written about *you* when you came home. I hope there was, but I would not be surprised if there wasn't. You Vietnam veterans were our *forgotten heroes*. I am saddened by that.

There just were not many emails circulated regarding BHS boys fighting in Korea and Vietnam. We seem to have just closed our minds to that part of America's history. When I asked for email memories of the Korean and Vietnam wars, and the BHS graduates who fought in them, I received very little response. I got a lot on World War II. I did not receive one faded, yellowed newspaper article or picture referencing the Korean or Vietnam wars. I received many from family and friends of World War II heroes. The American culture fostered by the *decadent Sixties* wanted to forget Korea and Vietnam.

One BHS *Puma* who had not been forgotten is my good friend and former track teammate, Bill Owen, BHS '52. At our fiftieth class reunion in 2002 at the Warren Country Club, Bill tearfully told us of his stint in Vietnam and how "God had his hand on me". Bill was one of the first American Air Force "advisors" to be sent to Vietnam in 1964. At that time the United States was putting Air Force personal on the ground with the American Special Forces who had been there since 1963. Bill was assigned to a Special Service unit in the Southern

Vietnam Delta with twelve other American "advisors". Bill remembers how close he was to the "front". The first night there he could see artillery flashes in the sky and hear the thunder of the exploding shells. Bill prayed at that time, "Lord, you know the number of hairs on my head. You will not call me Home until my work for You is done here on earth." The very next day, Bill thought his "work here on earth was done"! Bill was sent "up country" on a reconnaissance patrol. He was in a jeep with one Special Service officer, and two South Vietnam soldiers. They were followed by another jeep with two Americans and two Vietnamese. They spent most of that day observing the progress of the war from a distance. On their way back to the base camp, Bill's jeep detonated a land mine on the narrow jungle trail they were on. The concussion from the explosion broke both of Bill's eardrums and a piece of glass from the shattered windshield penetrated Bill's right eye. Immediately upon reaching base camp via the second jeep, Bill was air evacuated to Saigon. The glass was removed from his eye, but his broken eardrums required skilled surgery, which was not available in Saigon. Bill was then air evacuated to Clark Air Base in Hawaii and then on to Wilford Hall Hospital in San Antonio, Texas. Bill received the Purple Heart for his wounds but since he was *only an advisor* he did not receive "combat pay"!

Bill was later sent back to Vietnam where he flew supplies into the combat zones. A grim task Bill had to oversee was the removal of American bodies from the area and flying them back to the American bases for shipment "home".

Bill retired in 1976 as a major. He then finished college at Texas State Technical College at Waco, Texas. Before entering the Air Force, Bill had completed several years at The University of Arizona and one year at Bob Jones University in Greenville, South Carolina. Bill taught *automotive air conditioning* at Texas State Technical College for twenty years.

Bill had entered the Air Force in 1955 and while stationed at Harlingen Air Force Base, he met and married Leslye Lee Keys. They have two daughters, Dawn Elaine and Dana Lee.

While at BHS, Bill had an outstanding track career. He was undefeated in the 440 yard run his senior year. I remember being so excited for him when he won the 440 at the State Meet at The University of Arizona. That was a proud moment for Bill.

I was proud of Bill for his service in Vietnam, in May of 1952; but even prouder of him in July of 2002 when he proudly stood before many of his 1952 Bisbee High classmates at a class reunion wearing his Purple Heart and giving praise to God for the life he has had.

Bill Owen. God had His hand on him.

"...WELL DONE, GOOD AND FAITHFUL SERVANT..." JIM QUILL

"Some people spend their entire life wondering if they made a difference. The Marines don't have that problem." President Ronald Reagan.

Jim Quill was a Marine.

Naval Lieutenant Commander, C.C. Piepergerdes, was crawling for his life shortly after he had landed with the first wave of Marines to hit the beach in the battle for Guam. The Bisbee ophthalmologist had been assigned to the Marine Third Battalion as a technical advisor. Lieutenant Commander Piepergerdes' immediate objective was a low abutment of a bombed out Japanese bunker. The abutment would give him some protection from the massive wall of bullets the Japanese were pouring down upon the embattled Marines. As Piepergerdes inched forward on his belly, he was not aware of someone crawling beside him. The first inkling that he had a comrade nearby was when he heard someone whisper "How you doing, Doc? Remember me? Quill from Bisbee?" Needless to say, with all the bullets flying around, Sergeant Jim Quill and Lieutenant Commander C.C. Piepergerdes did not take the time to hug, shake hands, and slap each other on the back. A lull in the battle several hours later did provide the two Bisbeeites time to have a long chat together. Once again, that old Bisbee proverb was realized: "You run into someone from Bisbee wherever you go!" (I wonder where Max Spilsbury was at this time? Max's records show he was in the neighborhood!) Soon after the lull, Quill and Piepergerdes were separated due to the chaos of combat. They didn't meet again until the end of the war in 1945.

With the possible exception of Art Benko, Jim Quill saw more combat in World War II than any other Bisbee veteran. In September of 1944 *The Bisbee Daily Review* carried this article about Jim Quill:

NARROW ESCAPES FEATURE LIFE
OF BISBEE MAN

GUAM (Delayed)-Marine Sergeant James J. Quill, 26, of Bisbee, Arizona, figures he's living on borrowed time. A bandsman, he acted as a stretcher bearer throughout the Guam campaign, and twice had the narrowest of escapes with death.

He and three other bandsmen carried a wounded Marine from the front to the beach through wide patches of mortar fire late in the morning of D-Day. When they reached the beach, Sergeant Quill went looking for an amphibious tractor to take the wounded man back to the ship. The other three stretcher-bearers stayed by the patient, who had been wounded by a Jap grenade. Sergeant Quill found a tractor, but before he could get back to the stretcher, a cluster of Jap mortar shells whistled towards it. The three bandsmen couldn't get the patient to cover, so they stayed with him. A shell killed all of them.

Later that evening, Sergeant Quill and four others were sent with stretchers to pick up wounded men in the front lines once more. Three of them escorted three walking wounded back, while Sergeant Quill and the remaining Marine said they would carry the lone stretcher case.

Two men to a stretcher aren't enough. They were exhausted by dark, and by 8:30 p.m. had to stop. The trail was narrow and lonely. The company was still half a mile away.

Something in the brush moved. Sergeant Quill asked for the pass-word. Shots came in reply. It was too dark to go on, so the bandsmen stayed with their patient throughout the long night, with Japs moving in the brush around them.

The Japs didn't attack, however, and the stretcher bearers reached the aid station just after daylight.

In October of 1944, Sgt. Jim Quill had made *The Bisbee Daily Review* front page once again:

MARINE BANDSMAN OF BISBEE NOT FAZED BY WOUNDS

SAN FRANCISCO, Oct. 2 (Special to The Review)-Sergeant James J. Quill, Bisbee marine bandsman who served heroically as a stretcher bearer during the battle for Guam, is a hard man to put out of action, according to Marine combat correspondent, James Hague.

The Bisbee leatherneck was hit by Jap shell fragments while helping erect a medial aid station near the front lines and was evacuated for treatment.

A few hours later, he had talked doctors into letting him return to his unit and resume his work.

A Jap counter-attack that afternoon left 30 marines wounded in the field, and Sergeant Quill worked with other stretcher-bearers. Only then did he consent to return to the hospital. Doctors found that in addition to his wounds, he had been serving in the front lines with a 103 degree fever.

Battlefield blood transfusions were not common in 1944; however, Jim Quill was the first recipient of what would become a common life saving procedure.

Jim suffered a serious head injury when a Japanese mortar round blew up near him and sent a large chunk of shrapnel into his head, penetrating his brain. After very delicate brain surgery in a *MASH* (mobile army surgical hospital) unit on the battlefield, Jim was in critical condition. He would not live unless he could receive blood. Here is how the *International News Service* reported the story and how Jim's name and hometown was made known world wide:

TELLS AIR TRIP OF BLOOD
Accompanies Gift To Wounded Yank in Far Pacific

Just back from a whirlwind flight to American bases within 1500 miles of Tokyo with his own and other San Franciscans' blood, Call-Bulletin Staff Writer Jack S. McDowell yesterday told how he watched this same blood flow into the veins of a wounded service man. In this, the second of a series of exclusive stories, McDowell, the first person, so far as is known to have flown across the Pacific with his own and others blood, takes the reader aboard a trans-Pacific plane to a blood recipient in a tropical hospital.

By **JACK S. M'DOEWLL**
Call-Bulletin Staff Writer. Distributed by International News Service.

SAN FRANCISCO, Dec. 6.

The big Coronado flying boat's four husky motors chewed into the fine midnight drizzle. Her tons of metal slowly began to lift from Alameda's inky offshore waters-and seven cases of whole blood drawn from the arms of 112 Californians but a few hours earlier now were on their way to the fighting fronts of the Pacific.

On each of the square plywood containers lashed in the cargo holds of the Naval Air Transport Service plane was stenciled: "**Human Blood—Priority 1-000**"

In these boxes—which take precedence over munitions, mail and admirals—was the blood other San Franciscans and I had donated at the Red Cross Blood Center, 2415 Jones Street that same day, together with similar bottles from the centers in Oakland and Los Angeles.

We had had our last look at San Francisco and North America and headed for the forward combat area with our traveling companions, those seven boxes of liquid life for Leyte and the Marianas.

Morning brought the most beautiful sight I had ever seen—sunrise from 8,000 feet above the mid-Pacific.

Later, after another plane had landed us at a forward area air-strip within 1500 miles of Tokyo, *a bottle of the blood was taken at random* from one of the containers and speeded to an advance base hospital. (emphasis mine). The bottle that was removed from the container bore a little white tag with the name of Mrs. Ruth M. Pickall who lives in San Francisco.

With Lieut. Herbert R. Brown, Jr., medical officer in charge of the advance blood bank facility and one of the pioneers of the whole blood program, I walked into a Quonset hut to find **Technical Sergt. James J. Quill, 27-year old marine from Bisbee, Arizona.** (emphasis mine)

His head was swathed in bandages and the doctors said he had just undergone a delicate brain operation as a result of shrapnel wounds.

"**The Japs were firing from concealed positions and we couldn't get at them,**" **Quill said as the blood of Mrs. Pickall flowed slowly into his arm, replacing that which he had lost, revitalizing the body he had spent on the beachhead. "I was hit in the first 15 minutes."**

"**This blood is wonderful stuff,**" **the wounded man said. "Tell the people back home we really appreciate it—and to keep it coming. And tell the young lady who donated this pint for me that I am very, very thankful, too, will you?**" (emphasis not mine)

Accompanying the article were four large pictures. The first picture has this caption: *"This is the picture story of how whole blood reaches men overseas, told exclusively in The Evening Herald-Express. Here Mrs. Ruth Pickall, gives blood at a San Francisco blood donor center."*

The next two pictures show Mrs. Pickall's blood being packaged in a container and then it is being shown taken off the plane after arrival in The Marianas forty eight hours after Mrs. Pickall donated.

The last picture shows Jim Quill in a bed with his head completely wrapped in bandages. Looking on are two naval medical officers. Jim is hooked up to a plasma bottle dripping Mrs. Pickall's live giving blood into the vein in his right arm. The caption under the picture reads: *"Finally, Technical Sgt. James J. Quill, of Bisbee, Ariz., in a field hospital in the Marianas, 6000 miles from San Francisco, gets the blood donated by Mrs. Pickall, wife of a navy lieutenant. Quill suffered head wounds from Japanese shell fire. He is shown with Lieut. Hunter J. MacKay, and Lieut. Comdr. Paul K. Cullen."*

I knew Jim Quill for many years. I knew he had been in the Marines. I heard him say once that he had been in The U.S. Marine Band. Big deal! My vision of *Jim Quill, U.S. Marine Band* was of him all dressed up in his Marine "Blues" marching though the street of San Diego, toot'en on a tuba, enjoying the "ooh's" and "ahh's' of all the pretty girls, and soaking-in the sun and the sights of the San Diego beach on the weekends.

I wept as I read the newspaper accounts of Jim's World War II exploits. I had no idea he was such a war hero! He was wounded twice. He saved numerous lives. He wasn't toot'en a tuba; he was toting stretchers carrying wounded comrades through the jungles of Guam. He was face to face with death more than once. Jim asked himself on numerous occasions "...why me?" Why was he spared when buddies all around were being killed? Jim knew there was only one answer. He had heard it preached from the pulpit of The First Baptist Church in Bisbee by Pastor Hubert Verrill; and taught in his Sunday School classes by Mrs. Ruby Haynes: Jeremiah 29:11, "For I know the plans I have for you," declares the Lord, "plans to prosper you and not to harm you, plans to give you hope and a future." Jim knew when that Japanese mortar shell killed four of the men he had just been with and spared him, his only hope was in The Lord. Jim knew, too, that when Mrs. Pickall's blood flowed into his body, The Lord had plans for him. God was not through with him, yet.

When Jim received his Honorable Discharge from the Marines in 1946, he took with him two *Purple Hearts* for wounds suffered in combat, and *The Silver Star* for "gallantry in action while disregarding his own safety."

Jim returned to Bisbee upon his discharge from the Marines, and spent several months recuperating from his head wound and regaining lost strength. Jim suffered from excruciating headaches from the piece of shrapnel, which was still imbedded in his head near his brain. Brain surgery was still in its infant stage in 1946, so Jim decided not to undergo further surgery. He would "just live with it." Jim's mother tells of hearing him in his room beating his head on the wall to try to alleviate the pain. She recalls both his eyes being black from the bruising. Jim also suffered some paralysis of his arms and had to exercise with a rubber ball to strengthen his grip. He eventually got over the paralysis, but his headaches never did go away completely. Ann Humphreys Quill, BHS '55, Jim's wife of thirty-two and a half years, tells us that Jim's headaches decreased the last several years of his life. They both agreed that God was slowly edging him into Eternity where there would no longer be any pain!

But, Jim Quill was one tough *hombre*. He had grown up as a fighter. His younger and bigger brother, Fred, was not reluctant to encourage a fight knowing that his "big" brother, Jim, would finish it. They were known as "the Quill boys" and had the admiration and respect of all Bisbee. Both boys were excellent musicians. Both were in the First Baptist Church Choir for many years. Jim was accomplished in several musical instruments including the piano; he had a preference for the baritone horn though the bugle/trumpet was a close second. Jim taught music at Ft. Grant Boys' Industrial School before going into the Marines and he organized the school's first drum and bugle corps.

While at Bisbee High, Jim was a starting guard for the Pumas football teams all four years and was named All-State in 1936 and 1937. Fans and coaches voted Jim to the *All-Time Puma Grid Team* in 1953. Those who saw him play and who played with him, say Jim Quill was one of the toughest linemen the Pumas ever had. Jim's coach, Jack Wilson, said of Jim, "...the tougher it got, the tougher Quill got."

After Jim had recuperated in Bisbee for several months after being discharged from the Marines, he took the train to Flagstaff and enrolled in the Education Department at Arizona State College at Flagstaff. Jim had decided he wanted to be a teacher. His own educational experience at Bisbee High School had been less than fulfilling. He was determined he would not treat any student as he had been treated in Miss Rosamond Shreve's Freshman English class! For some reason Miss Shreve and the rugged, tough little Irishman (Jim's ancestors were from The Isle of Man, near Ireland) did not see eye-to-eye. Miss Shreve would not give Jim a passing grade in Freshman English. He passed each of the other three English classes, but he *never* did pass Freshman English. Jim had to come back a fifth year to take the class and try to pass it. Finally, in complete frustration and resignation, Jim walked out of her class, vowing never to return. He walked to Principal Rouse's office and sought advice. Mr. Rouse, knowing that two "bulldogs" had been battling each other for five years, relented and gave Jim credit for Freshman English. The rest of the story though, is that when Jim was hired as music teacher and coach in the Bisbee School District, the two of them, Miss Shreve and Jim Quill, got along famously. Because of his experience with Miss Shreve, Jim always treated his students with the utmost of respect. The student always got the benefit of the doubt in Jim Quill's class. He wanted to have a positive influence on student's lives. He wanted to make a difference. And, based on the testimony of former students, Jim Quill was one of the most influential teachers BHS ever had.

Susan Ridgway, BHS '67 says:

"I was so glad to see Mr. Quill mentioned as one of the best of Bisbee. Other than my parents, he was the biggest influence on my decision to be a teacher. As the elementary band director, he allowed me to join band a year earlier than most and I stayed in band for eight years. I loved his sense of humor, the way he encouraged kids to be their best (he broke many batons over the music stand until we got the piece perfect) and the 'insights' about life that he shared with us. In high school Health Education his lessons on sex education, as we call it today, came down to one phrase, 'nature will always cross you up!' He was one of the most inspiring teachers I ever had. I tried to model my approach to teaching after his way of always giving the students the benefit of the doubt and a voice in what mattered to them."

Paul Renner, BHS '56 remembers Jim Quill as a firm disciplinarian. Renner recalls seventh grade:

"The other teachers that really stood out were in the seventh grade where I had Jimmy Quill as our music teacher. Talk about the *board of education!* He had it in the form of a board about eighteen inches long and about three inches wide and could he swing it! All the smart guys in class had to try it; me included. I only tried it once as I was a quick learner. All he would do is snap his wrist and stand you on your head. Boy, that hurt! He was also a great teacher in the class room and on the football field as our line coach he was great! We loved him."

"'Fiddle Sticks!' that was the term I can remember James Quill using when he was not happy with our performance or our effort in music or at football practice" wrote Dale Hancock, BHS '57. "He sure changed a lot of attitudes about the Arts and athletics not mixing. He was a talented teacher of music as well as a talented teacher and motivator of football skills. I tried the trumpet in elementary school and I had to give up physical education in order to take music lessons; but, after my parents had used hard earned money to by me a trumpet, I found out quickly that I did not have any musical talents at all. I was totally tone deaf. Throughout my years as an educator I would cross paths with James Quill occasionally and he always seemed so proud of me and showed pride in me as one of his former students; the feeling was more than mutual. What I now know about quality teaching skills and talent, he ranks among the best I have ever been associated with."

Another Bisbeeite who remembers "Fiddle Sticks" as Jim Quill's swear word is Tom Fulgham, BHS '56:

"One of the most meaningful relationships and people in my growing up days in Bisbee, was Jim Quill", Tom wrote recently, "He was my football coach and my music instructor. He was a 'go to' person in my life that I could call on at any time. He never took lightly my growing up concerns of problems, and he always had wise advice. He was a true mentor and a great example to all of us who knew him well. I remember during football practice, when the other coaches would use more colorful language, he would just say, 'fiddle sticks', and make his point just the same.

He influenced my decision to go to the college I attended because of its good academic reputation. I have never regretted that decision. He was a hero of real stature. He never spoke of his heroism medals earned in wartime for the rescue of others on the battlefield while wounded him self. He was a guy who was an athlete, a musician, and a marine hero who loved and cared for people and who cared for his mother until her death.

I have always been glad he was a part of my growing up as a Christian, because he taught me a lot about how to live. Later, after I graduated from Wheaton College, he recommended me to take his job as Jr. High band teacher. That was a wonderful job I enjoyed to the full for two years before my wife and I went to the mission field in Ecuador where we stayed for most of the last 37 years. I am sure Jim had a similar impact on many others."

Jim Quill was always very discerning when giving advice. To those who were highly disorganized, he gave most practical advice. He told George Hershey, BHS '57 and Ronnie Sanders, BHS '57 that they both needed to get organized. He told them that the first thing they needed to purchase after graduating from college was a *filing cabinet*! Hershey said it was among the best pieces of advice he ever got. He now has seventeen of "the damn things!"

Jimmy Quill may have been part Serbian. Remember Pete Vucuevich, BHS '47 saying what a smart man his dad was because he married a girl twenty years younger than he. Pete told us that it was common for the Serbian men to marry younger women. Well, Jim Quill did the same! His wife, Ann, was twenty years younger and one of Jim's former students. I don't know how quickly the Serbian men put the moves on the ladies, but I have it from a reliable source that Jim *KISSED ANN* on their first date! But, just to keep Ann in line and not to give her the "big head", he *stood her up* the next date they had! He had told Ann that he would pick her up for church on Sunday; but, he was a "no show"! Jim did have a good excuse though; his mother was having medical problems and Jim had to care for her. Jim was very devoted to his mother and cared for her many years before she died.

Jim came back from college on weekends when Ann was in seventh or eighth grade and to her he was just another "old man" who sang in the choir and sometimes even directed it. She didn't really notice him until later in life when she was in nurses' training at Good Samaritan Hospital School of Nursing in Phoenix. When Ann would come home on weekends she began to notice the choir director who was always looking at her when she looked at him. This was not part of the Baptists' code of conduct, so they kept their thoughts to themselves…for awhile.

Besides his teaching and coaching duties, Jim also had the responsibility of managing the *Quill Motel* due to his mother's illness. When Ann graduated from the School of Nursing in August, she knew that Jim was a very special person. To make up for "standing her up" that time, he was on hand to help her move back home. They dated all that summer while Ann was working in the PD hospital in Douglas; they were married on December 27, 1964 and you could hear the *shock waves* all over Bisbee! Serbians may marry younger women, but good Baptists were not expected to do so. After all, Jim had been a bachelor for many years; he was forty-seven years old; too set in his ways; he would be too hard to get along with. The Baptist marriage manual said so.

Well, here is how tough it was for Jim and Ann to get on the same page. For their honeymoon they went to The Rose Parade and Rose Bowl Game in Pasadena, California. Ann loved football. When they got back from their honeymoon, Jim told Ann that she was in charge of their finances and all he wanted was $10.00 every two weeks for spending money. Jim hated church pot-lucks; Ann loved them. Jim went with her and soon loved them as well. Being an efficient nurse and wife, Ann loved green salads knowing they were good for one's health. Jim's mother told Ann years later that Jim had always hated green salads. He had never complained to Ann. He was agreeable to eat what ever she prepared. So much for a bachelor of long standing being too hard to get along with!

Jim and Ann had one son, Jamie, whom they doted on! Jamie graduated from Liberty University with a Criminal Justice degree and is a policeman in Tempe, Arizona. Rumor has it that the kid has the toughest abs. on the force! Jamie has two sons and his oldest, Kyle, got to spend a lot of time with Grandpa Jim the year and a half before Jim died.

The last time I saw Jim was in 1992. My wife, Nancy, and I had been visiting our daughter, Susie, in Camp Verde, Arizona. On our way back to Kansas, we stopped in Flagstaff to go to our former church, Flagstaff Christian Fellowship. We got there a bit late and were seated two rows behind Jim and Ann Quill! There are people from Bisbee everywhere! Jim and Ann were spending the summer in Flagstaff as Ann was working on her EdD. in Educational Administration. Between services we had a good chat with Jim and Ann. A very enlightening chat! I have already told you that I did not know a lot about Jim Quill. When I was first really aware of him, I was a senior in high school and Jim was our Junior Varsity coach along with Jack Miller. I knew he had been a Marine. But, that is about all I knew about Jim Quill. Other than that he was a *good* guy! He was an encourager. He always had a good word for us along with that perpetual little grin on his face. Our chat after church that day in 1992 told me all I wanted to know about Jim Quill! Jim made it very clear to me that he was a Christian. His relationship with Jesus Christ was the most important thing in his life. He had made a commitment to Jesus Christ as a teenager at First Baptist Church in Bisbee. He told me that he heard it very clearly one day when the pastor was preaching from the Book of Romans; one can only be saved from Hell by a trust and faith in Jesus Christ. It isn't being *good,* or being a Baptist, or a Catholic that gets one to Heaven, it is having trust in Jesus Christ and *believing in Him!* That explains all there is to know about Jim Quill. Was he scared that day on Guam when he crawled up next to his Bisbee buddy, Lt. Commander C.C. Piepergerdes, and said, "How you doing, Doc.?" as Japanese bullets whined over head? Was he scared as the Japanese rained bullets and mortar shells down on his position, and was he scared when he and two buddies spent a sleepless night on a lonely jungle trail with Japanese all around them? You *know* he was scared! And you know he was scared when he was in the MASH unit preparing to under-go brain surgery. He was scared, but you know what? He had "that peace that passes all understanding." He knew *for certain* where he would be should he die. You see, Jim knew that should he die, he would hear his Lord say to him **"Well done, good and faithful servant; you were faithful over a few things, I will make you ruler over many things. Enter into the joy of your lord."**

Jim Quill. Entered into the joy of the Lord on June 28, 1997.

U.S. Marine Band/Stretcher-bearers Guam 1944. Jim Quill front right.

4

GLEANINGS

◆

(Webster dictionary: "gleanings. To collect or gather anything little by little. Gatherings")

MY MOST POIGNANT MEMORY. POST SCRIPT

The headlines on the front page of the Schulenburg, Texas newspaper on April 18, 1944 boldly proclaimed:

MR. AND MRS. LOUIS BEDNAR AND DAUGHTER LOSE LIVES IN CRASH

The accompanying obituary helped put closure to *My Most Poignant Memory*. The "cutest girl in St. Patrick's Grade School", 4th grader Patricia Jane Bednar, was killed in a head on collision with an ambulance near El Paso, Texas. For sixty years I had not even known Patty's last name. I had not known much of anything about Patty except that "she was the cutest girl in St. Patrick's Grade School"; and that Sister Anthony Louise had announced to our 4th grade class on Monday, April 14, 1944 that Patty would not be coming back to St. Pat's because she and her dad and mom had been killed in an automobile accident over the weekend. I had not known any more than that. But, I had a very precious memory which came back to me every so often over those sixty years; Patty had blessed me with *a beautiful smile* just a few hours before she was killed.

With the aid of Stella Wasser, BHS '55, and Kathy Phillips, BHS '52, I was able to get news accounts of the tragedy. Kathy knew that Stella was somehow related to Patty and was able to put me in touch with Stella. Stella, in turn, was able to get me the newspaper account and the funeral notice.

Here is what I now know; quoting from the Schulenburg, Texas newspaper:

"Three members of an Arizona family of four, en-route to La Grange for a visit with relatives, were killed instantly when their car was in collision with an army ambulance, near El Paso Friday night just before midnight.

The dead:

Louis Bednar, 35, of Lowell, Arizona

His wife, Mrs. Frances Bednar.

Their nine-year-old daughter, Patricia Jane Bednar.

Bodies of all were badly crushed by the impact.

Another daughter, Kay Beth, who will be five in June, was slightly injured and suffered principally from shock.

Also in the Bednar car was Sgt. Lad Bednar, who sustained a fractured leg and fractured skull. He was taken to an El Paso hospital where his condition at first was reported as critical. However, Sunday night his condition was reported as much improved, having regained consciousness and was able to talk to his brother, Ben, of Houston and brother-in-law Adolph Piwetz, Baytown, who left for El Paso Saturday night.

Sgt. Thurman E. Norman of Biggs Field, driver of the ambulance, was also reported to have been seriously injured.

The accident occurred near Fabens, about 20 miles east of El Paso. No details were learned here, other than that the two vehicles met in head-on collision.

The bodies arrived at Schulenburg Sunday night and were brought to Koenig Funeral Home here. They were accompanied by Mr. and Mrs. Alvin Bednar, nephew and niece, also of Lowell, and little Kay Beth.

Funeral services were held at the Koenig Funeral Home chapel Monday morning at 9:30, followed by solemn requiem high mass at 10 o'clock, Rev. F. D. Urbanovsky of Fayetteville, officiating, with Rev. A.W. Nesvadba of Wallis as the deacon, and Rev. S.A. Zientek of La Grange as sub-deacon. The Rev. Zientek delivered an English sermon and Rev. Nesvadba a Czech sermon.

Mr. Bednar was born at Latium, near Brenham, on December 8, 1908. He had lived in Lowell for the past 10 years, where he was employed in *the copper mines...*" (emphasis mine hh)

Attached to the funeral announcement was an old copy of a newspaper article, which featured four faded pictures. The headline read:

VICTIMS OF RECENT AUTOMOBILE ACCIDENT NEAR El PASO

The caption under the pictures read:

"Shown above are members of the Louis Bednar family of Lowell, Arizona, three of whom were killed instantly, and Sgt. Lad Bednar, passed away several days later..."

In the first picture, Patty is shown sitting on what looks like the trunk of a large tree, beside her sister, Kay Beth. Mr. Bednar is standing in front of the tree-trunk.

The second picture is of Mrs. Louis Bednar dressed in what appears to be church attire, standing in front of a bush.

The third picture is of Sgt. Lad Bednar, Mr. Bednar's brother. Lad is standing tall and proud in his Army dress uniform.

The last picture could have been left out. It shows the mangled wreckage of the car the Bednar family was riding in.

Mr. Bednar was from a family of eight children. They were Czechoslovakian. I found it interesting that part of the funeral service was spoken in the Czech tongue. There must have been a number of first-generation Czechoslovakians in the family. It was also interesting to me that Mr. Bednar had worked for the PD for ten years as a miner.

I don't know if it is my imagination or not, but in the picture of Patty sitting on the tree-trunk, she has that *same smile*. The picture is so faded, I can't tell for sure. I like to believe she was smiling.

BOB BROWDER STILL *KNOWS THINGS*

I knew from the way Bob Browder handled our arrest on VJ Day that he was going to be a good lawyer. Bob graduated from the University of Arizona Law School in 1956; he passed the Bar Exam the same year. His law career spanned over four decades, from 1958 to 2002. Bob was a trial lawyer. He specialized in Litigation cases; injury and malpractice cases. His law firm, *Browder and Kinney*, was one of the most respected law firms in Arizona.

As a high school football player, Bob was a tough, little nose guard. He weighed, soaking wet, 130 pounds. In those days, it was against the rules for a center to come over the football and move it, even to the slightest degree, without asking permission from the official. Bob was our starting nose guard; he lined up directly on the point of the ball. Coach Dicus gave Bob a specific duty. He was to be ready when the center came over the ball and if the center should move it, Bob was to immediately pounce on the ball. If the official deemed that the center did indeed move the ball, it was ruled a "fumble" and that Bob had recovered it. *Pumas* ball! However, if the official said the center had not moved the ball, Bob was ruled "off-sides". Five yard penalty on the *Pumas*! Bob had to be absolutely certain the center moved the football. Several times each season, Bob would recover "fumbles" that way. Once, however, Bob was called "off-sides". We were playing the Nogales *Apaches*. Their center came up over the football. Bob thought he saw the ball move. He pounced on it. The official called "off-sides". Immediately, Bob's lawyer instincts took over. As the official was marking off the five yards, Bob could be heard loud and clear arguing his case. "HE MOVED THE BALL, DAMMIT!"…."DAMMIT, REF. HE MOVED THE BALL!!" Bob lost his case.

Bob married his high school sweetheart, Charlene Cobb. Charlene passed away in 2002. Bob and Charlene had a daughter, Becky, and one grandson. Bob is retired and lives in Phoenix. He stays in the Cobb home on Arizona Street in Warren when he visits Bisbee, which he does often. Bob can be found at most BHS reunions. For those who have known Bob over the years, he will be hard to recognize now; he recently gave up his ever-present cigar, which he chewed on for years. "Nasty habit" he said. Bob and I had dinner together in Bisbee over the 2004 Memorial Day weekend. Bob bought. All lawyers worth their salt will spring for the check.

OWANDA BIN TALLEYBAN

The date was 9/11/42. A date which will live in infamy. It was on that date that the peaceful playground of St. Patrick's Grade School was savagely attacked by a gang of terrorists bent on destroying a way of life. It was exactly 12:30 p.m. Most of the peace loving students had finished lunch. Kathy Phillips and Pat Cardwell were testing each other with their multiplication flash cards. Bill Monahan and Joyce Andrews were practicing their Catechism lesson Father Howard had assigned. John Taylor, Valeria Dugie, and Rosalinda Yungaray were studiously involved it their inductive Bible study on The Book of Romans. Barbara Riggs and Jim Halstead were loosing up for their daily mile run on the lower play ground. Other students were finishing lunch, while still others were in private prayer. It was a typical noon-period for the gentle students of St. Patrick's Grade School. Suddenly, this tranquil setting was changed forever!

The student's first indication that something was amiss was when Sister Mary Godfrey suddenly appeared on the top landing of the steps leading inside. She was wildly clicking on her ever present *clicker* and yelling, "Attack! Everybody inside. NOW!!" Before she could say any more, golf-ball sized rocks started pummeling down from the brush laden hillside south of the play ground. The first victim was Jimmy Spivey. He received a gash on his head by a well placed rock. Sylvester Dugie was the first student to react to the attack. He immediately put his arm around Bernice Uhls, and started yelling, "Boys, protect our girls!" Sylvester's gallant cry fell on deaf ears. All of the boys, led by Bob Browder, had already fled into the safety of the lower class rooms. The attack lasted about three minutes; time enough for Father Howard and Sister Mary Godfrey to determine that the attack was a well organized assault. In later testimony, Father Howard said that just before the attacks commenced, he saw the attackers scurrying to get into position. Father Howard said that at that point, the attackers were empty handed. This was an obvious indication that the weapons of mass dispersion had been placed in position ready for the attackers. They knew where they were. The WMD had been there all the time. This was not a spontaneous attack. It was a well planned declaration of war.

The immediate task was to be sure that the attacks didn't continue. Father Howard formed a "Play Ground Security Force" and appointed Clarence Dupnik as the head. Dupnik had proven his mettle in securing the Jiggerville ball field several months before. As Dupnik began to intensify his investigation, several factors were revealed. Number one, several of the terrorists had been trained *on the St. Patrick's playground!* That's right. Two of the terrorists, George Ducich and Chuck Cunningham had been visiting St. Patrick's every afternoon for months learning how to choose the correct size of weapon to throw and how to accurately aim the weapons. One of the kindly nuns at St. Patrick's, Sister Colombiere, unknowingly had assisted the sneaky terrorists. Sister Colombiere bought hook line and sinker the terrorists' claim that they wanted to learn how to throw rocks because squirrels had become a nuisance on the Horace Mann playground.

The second piece of information that Dupnik's investigation had uncovered was that the terrorists had a direct tie to the notorious Owanda bin Talleyban. Dupnik could not prove the tie. There was no proof that Talleyban had participated in the sneak attack of 9/11/42. However, when seemingly unrelated attacks on the St. Patrick playground during the winter occurred, it became obvious to Dupnik that Talleyban had been the brains behind the attacks. For years Talleyban had terrorized all of Bisbee with WMD. The WMD that Tallyban had used was unique and hard to detect. When Dupnik first noticed that the snowballs used in the winter attacks fell with a greater velocity than the ordinary back yard type snowball, he examined one. It was a golf ball size rock packed inside a snowball! Cunning! And deadly! Only a mind like Owanda bin Talleyban would conceive of such a lethal weapon.

Suddenly, as quickly as they had begun, the terrorists attacks ceased. Years went by and never another attack. Soon people forgot that they had ever happened. Though the gash on Jimmy Spivey's head had long ago healed, and WMD had been eradicated from the hillside and the playground of St. Patrick's, the damage to the sensitive psyches of the victims of 9/11/42 continued. Some of the victims were known to suffer spells of violent quaking at the slightest hint of snow. The memory of that day would forever haunt those victims. For this very reason, Clarence Dupnik never, for one moment, relented in his investigation to prove the attacks had a tie to Owanda bin Talleyban. His soul goal in life was to put the terrorist away for life. Tallyban, feeling the heat, and suffering from great guilt, went underground. Sixty-two years passed and because of the intense pressure of the 24-7 surveillance that Dupnik kept up, Tallelyban finally confessed!

In a letter dated March 30, 2004, Talleyban wrote:

"My name is Wanda Talley Owens, BHS class of '52...as a student just across the court house from St. Pat's, I must make a confession. Jealousy was rampant with me and some of my little friends...one of our favorite things to do...was to throw rocks at the over-privileged students at St. Pat's...it had nothing to do with religion, or the fact that St. Pat's was a private school...it was strictly class warfare...they had a playground and we didn't." Talleyban, aka Wanda Talley, in another note written April 4, 2004 said that she was so heartless and eager to inflict harm on the privileged St. Pat's kids that on one occasion she "...ate an apple while throwing rocks..."

Owanda bin Talleyban signed another note of confession very simply, "Wanda' 52, ex-Horace Mann thrower of rocks at St. Pat's kids."

Owanda bin Talleyban aka. Wanda Talley.

Due to the unrelenting surveillance and pressure applied by Clarence Dupnik and his *Play Ground Security Force*, Talleyban has lived an upright and exemplary life the past sixty some odd years. Her confessions came too late. The statute of limitations had long ago expired. She can no longer be punished. Some of the families of the victims wanted revenge; but most were able to forgive and let by-gones be by-gones. Wanda is now a grandmother who will not let her grandkids go near a rock. She makes sure her grandkids have the nicest playground in the neighborhood. She and her husband, Mac, are avid square dancers; obviously an activity that does not lend itself to acts of terrorism. *Owanda bin Talleyban* has indeed "paid the fiddler."

Because of his superb work in eliminating the terrorists attacks led by Owanda bin Talleyban, aka Wanda Talley, in the early 1940's, Clarence Dupnik found he had *law enforcement* in his blood. He has served for years as the very successful and popular sheriff of Pima County in Southern Arizona.

HOW TO PERFORM SUCCESSFUL HEMORRHOID SURGERY ON YOURSELF.

Dr. George Yard, former Flagstaff physician and Bisbee High graduate is one of the *all time Great Guys!* To know George Yard is to love him. To know George Yard is to laugh. His laugh and smile are contagious. I wish I could describe his voice. It too, is contagious; when you hear it, you automatically break into a huge smile trying to match the one George has on his face.

On May 28, 2004, my wife, Nancy, and I were seated in the Camp Verde High School football stadium waiting for the graduation ceremonies to begin. Our granddaughter, Megan McDonald was graduating that evening. All of a sudden the lights got brighter! The mood of the people became more jovial! George Yard and his lovely wife, Sharon, had just walked in! That's what George's presence does to any crowd. I hadn't seen George in over twenty years. He was older of course, his walk not as spry, his beard had more gray, but his voice and smile were the same. I couldn't help myself when I saw him; I yelled out loudly, "GEORGE YARD!" He stopped and looked up to where I was seated; probably five rows from where George and Sharon were standing. His face broke into that wonderful smile and he yelled back, even louder, "HADLEY HICKS!" People sitting near by got the impression that we knew each other.

Hadley Hicks and Dr. George Yard. Camp Verde, AZ 2004.

I first became aware of this Bisbee icon named George Yard when I was a sixth grader. It was 1945 and George was a member of the *Puma* football team. I was messing around with some of my buddies on the sideline. The *Pumas* were getting ready to end practice by running their customary wind sprints. It was always fun to watch this particular bunch run because they had one guy who could not run. I don't mean he was slow. He was, but what I mean is, he *couldn't run*. He didn't know *how to run*. George Yard thought he was running, but he wasn't. All he would do was kind of pick up his feet an inch or so off the ground and quickly move them forward three or four inches. All the time his knees never bent. He ran stiff legged, if you could call it "running". Coach Fuzzy Warren usually lost patience with George. Fuzzy was the back field coach and George was a tough lineman who didn't have to run as well as the backs. We always loved to hear Fuzzy "get on" one of the *Pumas*. He could get upset. He'd yell at George, "Yard, when are you going to learn how to run?" George would just smile and reply, "I am running, Fuzzy. Going as fast as I can!"

Years later, when my family and I lived in Flagstaff near George, he told me that it was Fuzzy who had finally showed him how to run. George said that one day at practice it all came together for him. Fuzzy ran beside George the length of the field yelling, "YARD, COPY ME! DO WHAT I DO!" George realized as he copied Fuzzy's high knee-pumping motion that he, George, was learning how to *run!* George said how amazed he was to find out that all these years he had always thought he had been running. He thought that he just wasn't as fast as all the other guys. After running like Fuzzy showed him for a few days, George said he tried to talk Coach Dicus into making him a back. Coach wisely said "no". George was too tough a guard to move him to the backfield. Besides, he still wasn't *that* fast.

In 1975, my family and I moved to Flagstaff, Arizona from Prescott, Arizona. I had accepted the head football coaching position at Flagstaff High School. I soon found out that Flagstaff at that time was "Bisbee-North". Quite a few Bisbee people lived in there including George Yard. George had been a successful and popular M.D. in Flagstaff for many years. He and George Hershey, also a successful doctor in Flagstaff, were the first two Bisbeeites to welcome us. Wally Quayle was among the first, but I can't count him as he just came by looking for a free meal.

After a year or so, my family and I were looking for some acreage out side of town. George owned a bunch of land about five miles up Mt. Eldon Look-Out road and he sold us two and a half acres at "reduced Bisbee price" as George said. We built a nice home there, only a gully and a couple dozen pine trees away from George's barn. It wasn't long before George had converted that barn into a lovely, comfortable house. He said he had always wanted a home where his horses

could look into his bedroom to wake him up every morning. He designed his
home so his horses could do just that. They could stick their heads in anytime
they wanted, not just in the morning. George was truly a "cowboy doctor". He
and his wife, Sharon, were great neighbors. Once George's son, Mike, started a
fire, which burned several trees on George's property and was contained before it
did much damage to trees on my property. Several of our trees were scorched,
though not enough to really hurt them. A couple months late George came to
our door with a check for five hundred dollars. He said he had insurance on all
his trees and the money was our share for the "damage" done to our trees. He
said, "Those damn insurance companies can afford it."

Pat Harris Flick, BHS '58 and her husband, Mike had been living in Flagstaff
for quite a few years before we got there. Mike was an administrator in the school
system. Pat relays this "George Yard" story:

"George was my doctor when I had my daughter, Pam. Of course, it had to be
in the middle of the night in a Flagstaff blizzard. The nurses kept calling for Dr.
Yard, telling him to hurry; that I was going to have this baby without him. Well,
he finally got there in his old trench coat and floppy rubber boots that came to his
knees. He looked like 'Colombo'. He made it just in time to catch her head. All
the while he was sewing me up he was telling me all about dating my Aunt Zona
when they were in BHS together. George's bedside manner was the best."

Pat goes on to tell another "George Yard" story: Pat's daughter, Pam, grew up
to be quite a lover of horses herself and was most able at treating them when they
were sick. One 4th of July, George's horse that he was running in a race, became
ill. The PA announcer called for Pam to come attend George's sick horse. A large
crowd had gathered around Pam and the sick horse. When it looked like the
crowd was large enough, George proudly announce in his booming voice "I SAW
THIS GAL NAKED BEFORE ANYONE ELSE EVER DID!" Needless to say,
Pam was embarrassed to tears!

The "George Yard" stories are many and varied. Like the time George, Edie
Kelly, BHS '47 and several others climbed the Shattuck Denn mine shaft after
their Senior Prom. in their formal attire. Maybe if I ever write a sequel to this
book, I will include some more about George.

The one story I want to make sure the readers read now is the one about
George using mirrors to direct hemorrhoid surgery **on himself. In the middle of
Lake Powell! On the deck of a fishing boat! While under the influence of
adult beverages! And performed by some buddies who were as snokered as
he was! And who used** *Old Granddad Whiskey* **as the anesthetic!**

You, the readers may not believe this story. If you know George Yard, you will be more inclined to believe it. I heard George proudly tell the story. George is a true Bisbeeite; he does not lie. Here is how I remember George telling it:

On a fishing trip to Lake Powell with several of his fishing buddies one weekend, George anchored the boat in a windy cove after the guys had decided the fishing was over for the day; it was time to begin partaking of the "nightcaps". Since their camp was several miles away and nighttime was still hours off, it seemed like a good idea to relax, down a few, and "shoot the bull" for awhile. George was never one to mince words and when the subject of *physical ailments* came up, George mentioned that he had been hampered greatly by hemorrhoids all his life. He confided to his close buddies that he had never, ever, had a smooth bowel movement! He was in agony every time. He had learned to live with it. One of the men on the trip with George had acquired a degree of Bisbee compassion via osmosis. Lee Hutchinson had married a Bisbee girl, Til French Hutchinson. Til was the daughter of Bisbee physician, Dr. French. The more detailed George got in telling his sad tale, the more Lee wanted to fix the problem. George had performed numerous hemorrhoid surgeries on others and Lee felt confident that George could direct his buddies during the procedure while George lay still on the deck of the boat. Finally, George decided, "What the heck. Let's do it!" Only one problem; in order to direct their hands in the surgery, George had to be able to see what they were doing. This is where Bisbee-ingenuity came to the rescue. George and his buddies dug through their fishing gear and came up with several mirrors. By rigging the mirrors up to several lengths of fishing poles, a *Rube Goldberg* gismo was put together allowing George to lie on his belly and hold the ingenious invention in front of him to watch and direct the surgery behind him via the mirrors. The first procedure in any surgery is to completely shave and sterilize the area involved. Lee got his razor out and shaved the area to the best of his ability. Then he sterilized his razor because it would have to be used as the scalpel. The part George and his buddies hated the most was pouring most of a full quart of *Old Granddad* on George's rear end to insure a sterile working area. That done, the "doctor" and his assistants were ready to proceed under the watchful eye of their instructor, the patient, George Yard. Now, if they could only calm the waters. The lake seemed extra rough. The boat seemed to be rocking more than usual. The "doctor" decided one more swig of *Old Granddad* would steady his hands and possibly the boat. A new bottle was opened and each of them, including the patient, had another swig. Between swells lifting the boat up and down, the surgery was completed. "Doctor" Hutchinson boasted for years that it only took one slash with the razor blade between swells to make a clean cut. The troublesome hemorrhoid was cleaned out and according to George, he has been "as smooth as a baby's bottom" ever since.

P.S. On George Yard from his good friend, Dr. George Hershey, BHS '56 dated Monday, April 26, 2004: "He had five vessel by-pass surgery on Christmas Eve and did well. Unfortunately one of the vessels closed and he had to have two stints put in about four weeks ago. I talked with him last week and he is interested in the *Bisbee Memories*, but has no access to the internet. He said it is too expensive to use 'box phone' and he doesn't have a TV. He said Julian Courteol called him recently. He does enjoy phone calls.

Yes, he is a true cowboy. Still runs cattle from Perkinsville nearly to the top of Mingus Mountain. Sharon and he built a beautiful ranch home in Perkinsville. Home telephone number: 928-308-1365
Address: P.O. Box 847, Williams, Arizona 86048"

THERE ARE PEOPLE FROM BISBEE EVERYWHERE

The troop transport ship returning from Europe with a load of battle weary GIs that was totally blacked-out. German UBoats still patrolled the waters in this area of the Atlantic Ocean on a regular basis. John "Buddy" Gabrilson, a former BHS *Puma,* was too exhausted to sleep. Since DDay, June 6, 1944, when he parachuted into Normandy with the 82nd Airborne, Gabrilson had had very little sleep. That was over a year ago. Now, in the darkened hold of the transport ship, Gabrilson was too exhausted to sleep. The darkness seemed oppressive. Almost like it could grab hold of you; surround you, and force you to remain awake. Total quiet was insisted upon by the ship's commander. The German UBoats' sonar was able to pick up laughter and normal conversational vibrations a good distance away. The troops had been instructed to speak only in whispers. Several hundred combat veterans were crowded into the hold, laying in bunk-beds stacked three high. The body stench, in addition to the darkness and the quiet, kept all, except a very few, awake. Many thoughts went through "Buddy" Gabrilson's mind. He thought of going home to Bisbee. He thought of his months of combat; the death, the violence necessary to free a people from the grip of German tyranny. He thought of his buddies that he had seen die. He especially thought of his Bisbee buddy, John Pidgeon. The two of them had enlisted in the paratroopers together over two years ago. They had gone through basic and advanced training together. They had both parachuted into Normandy the same day, though from different planes and with different outfits. "Gabe" wondered if" Pidge." had come through the invasion and subsequent advance into German occupied territory alive. They had not seen each other during that time.

As "Gabe" lay in his bunk just letting his mind wander, a subdued cough came to his ears from several bunks away. The cough was familiar. "Gabe" sat up. He whispered, "'Pidge.'! Is that you?" A voice whispered back "Yah. 'Gabe' is that you?"

Two Bisbee buddies, both war heroes, meeting in a darkened troop ship somewhere in the Atlantic. There are people from Bisbee everywhere!

In the foreword to this book, I enumerated the different places I have "run into" people *from Bisbee*. I will get more specific here:

My entire military "career" was spent at Fort Ord, California. The same Fort Ord where seven valiant Bisbee High students had served so faithfully as reservists in the summer of 1950. One day toward the end of my regular tour of duty in the summer of 1956, I was watching a new batch of "recruits" that had arrived the evening before. It was always fun to watch the new guys. The expressions on their faces were worth a month's pay to watch. Their clothes did not fit. They were all totally bald. They were "recruits". In the very first platoon was my Bisbee buddy, Bob Butler, BHS '51! Not "Bob Butler" anymore. Now he is *Private Butler, sir!* I knew it would be pointless to yell out "Hey, Butler" because half the first platoon would respond. "Butler" is a popular name. So, being a seasoned GI who had little time in "this man's army" remaining, I did a bold thing. Looking back on it, it was a dumb thing. I could have spent some time in the brig and thus delay my discharge date. I returned to my barracks, got out of my fatigues (army work clothes), put on my "class A" uniform (dress uniform) so I would look somewhat important. I then walked back to the Reception Center where Bob Butler was still going through orientation. All the newly arrived recruits had assembled in a large auditorium. Bob Butler was somewhere in the midst of all of them. Even though Bob was a Bisbeeite, he was just as fearful and insecure as the rest. I walked into the back of the auditorium and waited for an appropriate time to do what I had come to do. When the lieutenant who was giving that portion of the orientation address was finished, I boldly marched up the aisle and approached the stage. In my best military manner, I saluted the officer in charge, and said, "Sir, Private Robert Butler is wanted in the Orderly Room immediately, sir." With that, the officer said over the loud speaker "Private Robert Butler, please stand up." Bob stood. I wish I had the expression on his face preserved on tape! He was scared to death. He had no clue who wanted him in the Orderly Room. Then the expression on his face when he saw and recognized *me*! It was priceless! I winked at Bob and said "Follow me, Private Butler." He did. We marched out of the auditorium and went to a Post Exchange (PX) and had coffee and donuts for an hour or so; then I marched him back to his company and we went our separate ways.

I began my teaching and coaching career at Carmel High School, Carmel, California in the early 1960's. Ocean Avenue, the main street through the middle of Carmel, is known world wide for its very unique and very expensive shops. Carmel itself, as well as its shops, is extremely extravagant, to say the least! Carmel was the kind of place where it was not at all uncommon to bump into Bing Crosby, Frank Sinatra, Joan Baez, Richard Boone, Clint Eastwood, Al Rochin, and other famous people…wait a minute! Al Rochin? Yep, Al Rochin, the former mayor of Naco, Sonora, Mexico. I was walking down Ocean Avenue one day in the early 1960' and ran into Al Rochin! He was on vacation. No doubt spending some of that "gringo money" which had energized the economy of Naco for years.

One morning during my "prep." hour at Carmel High, I had occasion to walk into our counselor, John Graham's office to check on the eligibility of one of the football players. Mr. Graham was busy with a visitor, so I just stuck my head in and went back to the faculty room to wait until Mr. Graham was free. Within just a few minutes, Mr. Graham came into the faculty room with his visitor. Mr. Graham said, "Hadley, this gentleman says he knows you." The guy had evidently recognized me when I had stuck my head in Mr. Graham's office, but for the life of me, I could not place the guy. The man said "Hadley, we grew up together. I am Bill Callison." Holy Cow! One of the family members Bill Plumb had tormented so many years before! He had survived! Bill Callison was a recruiter for U.C.L.A. and was checking out some of Carmel High's students. We spent an enjoyable half hour or so reliving "old times". And, yes, he did remember Bill Plumb!

While I was teaching at Carmel High School, my family and I enjoyed spending weekends in San Francisco. One of the favorite things we liked doing was riding the trolley cars up and down those renowned streets of San Francisco. On one such occasion, we were headed down one of the hills and not more than sixty feet away, headed up the street on foot, was Bosco Verbica, one of the original

Goat Row Gang! Of course, I yelled "BOSCO" as loud as I could. He heard me and turned around. I waved, but by then the trolley was too far away for him to see me, much less recognize me. I'll bet to this day, Bosco is wondering who *from Bisbee* was calling him. Nobody in San Francisco knew him as "Bosco". He was Robert Verbica.

In 1987 my wife and kids and I had made a summer trip to Myrtle Beach, South Carolina to visit Nancy's family. I had to come home early due to football practice starting at Sterling College. Nancy and the kids stayed to come home with Nancy's mother, Norma. One day after I had left to drive back to Sterling, Nancy took the kids to a frozen yogurt shop. Nancy and I had owned Flagstaff Frozen Yogurt Shop in Flagstaff, Arizona shortly after we were married. We never passed up an opportunity to eat frozen yogurt! While Nancy and the kids were enjoying the frozen yogurt, Nancy got to talking to the friendly young college age girl who was behind the counter. Of course, Nancy told her we had owned a yogurt shop in Flagstaff and that prompted the girl to tell Nancy she had been born in Bisbee. Her parents were Bisbee natives. Nancy, you need to understand, is a wonderful lady. But, she *is not from Bisbee*. She did not understand the necessity to get the young girl's name, or to tell her my name. Nancy missed a great opportunity to partake in some highly stimulating and meaningful dialogue. Instead, she passed the time with, "Oh, that's nice. Bisbee is a fun place. I just love the weather there." etc., etc. I have no clue who that young girl's family was.

In 1988, I took our Sterling College baseball team to Florida to play in the Christian College Baseball Tournament, which was held for many years at Dodger Town, Florida. On an off day, I took the team to visit Busch Gardens, a truly tropical paradise. As we ate lunch in a hotel restaurant, I struck up a conversation with an elderly gentleman who was with a group of tourists. When I asked him where he was from he replied, "Tucson, Arizona". Well, you know what happened next! I told him I was *from Bisbee* and I introduced myself. "Hadley Hicks!" he exclaimed, 'Why, I used to watch you guys play football. I lived in Bisbee for two years. I worked for the PD. I never missed one of the *Pumas*' games. I was at the Tucson game with relatives in 1951 when you beat THS!" This guy was an exception to the rule. He did not mention seeing me loose my contact lens!

The meeting of someone *from Bisbee* that I get the biggest chuckle out of was the time I was in the crowded Los Angeles Train Depot. I was on my way to Bisbee on leave from the army. It was in 1955. I had some time to kill so I wandered over to the postcard rack to look them over. It was one of those rotating kind. You stand in one place and turn the rack so the postcards rotate towards you. I was slowly turning the rack when it suddenly wouldn't rotate towards me. Someone on the other side was trying to get the rack to turn his way, opposite my way. We resisted each other for a few seconds until we both got slightly irritated. I stuck my head around the rack and looked eye-ball to eye-ball at Bobby "Harpo" Windsor, my BHS football teammate! I yelled, too loudly, "Harpo, you old s.o.b.!!" I got several disgusted looks from some elderly ladies nearby. Harpo was on his way to an assignment with the army. We had a good visit.

One more. I was with the Sterling College football team in Ottawa, Kansas for a game with Ottawa University. The team was going through pre-game warm ups and I was standing on the sidelines at about the five yard line. A man came up to me and asked if I was "Coach Hicks". Since it was my first year as head coach and hadn't lost too many games as yet, I answered "Yes". He handed me a note and said an old friend from Bisbee wanted to say "hello". I opened the note and it read "Hadley. Just wanted to say hello. Hope I can get by to see you. Your old Bisbee friend, Tommy Byrd."

Tommy Byrd never did get by to see me. I wonder if his mother was still worried about him catching tuberculosis from me!?

That wasn't *a person from Bisbee*, but it was *a message from a person from Bisbee*. Close enough.

Ellen (Snider) Stringer and Steve Stringer, both BHS '65, share this story of a chance meeting:

"It is so strange how people from the little town of Bisbee just show up everywhere. We were on Main Street in Ridgeway, Colorado a couple of years ago with Cheryl and Henry Smith of Bisbee. We were shopping and dining out. We ran into John Wasser and his son. I recognized him instantly and he knew us right away. His family were good friends with the Henry Smith family up in Old Bisbee...so it was like *old home week*. I believe that the "Bisbee Spirit" lives on in all of us and no matter where we go we still have that connection between all of us. I think it is unique and wonderful. Just keep those sweet memories of our little town coming. It makes us feel so lucky to have lived those years in that special little town with all those special people."

"HONDRO". WORLD CHAMPION BEAN-BAG KICKER

Alejandro Morales was a fixture in Greenway Grade School's eighth grade classes. I don't know much about him. His nick name was "Hondro". He had a smile on his face that never went away. I went to Greenway Grade School for my sixth, seventh and eighth grades. "Hondro" was there in the eighth grade all three of those years. As I have already explained, I started school in the first grade at Greenway; took a year off, then went to St. Pat's for my second, third, forth, and fifth grades. For all I know, "Hondro" was in eighth grade each of those years. I know he was in eighth grade when I came back to Greenway in the sixth grade. Now that I think about it, I don't remember "Hondro" actually **in** my eight grade class. He was there for every recess/physical education class and every lunch recess. I don't remember him ever sitting in the class room. I don't remember him ever answering a question. In fact, I don't remember "Hondro" ever speaking. All he ever did was smile. And kick his bean bag! Boy, could he kick that bean bag! Often we'd see him walking on to the playground kicking that bean bag and he'd kick it all the way to the other end of the playground where a game was in progress. Only then would he put his bean bag in his pocket. Now, when I say he kicked the bean bag all the way from one end of the playground to the other end, I mean just that. He kicked it, kept it in the air, from one end to the other. We see a lot of kids today playing "hackey-sack". They *buy* this fancy sewed leather ball-like thing and kick it around. "Hondro" invented the game! And, he didn't *buy* his sack, and he didn't have beans in it. Any beans his family had, they ate. "Hondro" used an old tobacco sack, filled it with sand and *we* called it a "bean bag". I don't know what he called it.

Now, try to picture this shaggy haired kid in baggy Levi's with worn out knees, coming across the playground seemingly on one leg. His right leg was in perpetual motion; he kicked the bag in the air with the inside edge of his right foot, brought the leg down to the ground quickly, hopped once and kicked the bag again before it hit the ground. All the time he is doing this, he appears to be in deep concentration with his eyes glued to the bean-bag. He never misses a stride and he never misses the bean-bag. And, he is smiling the whole time, just having the time of his life.

"Hondro" is another person I wish I would have gotten to know. I know he lived behind the center-field fence of the Warren Ball Park across the copper water ditch, across from the Benavidez family. I wonder if he had any brothers or sisters? I wonder if he could speak English? I wonder if he could speak? I wonder what his father did? I wonder if he ever got out of eighth grade? I wonder what ever happened to him? I wonder if he would have come over to my house for dinner if I would have invited him? I wonder if any of the kids ever invited him over to their house? I wonder if he ever quit smiling?

WES WRIGHT, SHERIFF

One day Wes Wright just showed up. I don't believe he was born in Bisbee. I don't know where he came from. One day he was just there. I must have been in about the fifth or sixth grade when I first saw him. I was sitting on the window ledge of the Warren Drug Store talking to a bunch of my buddies when Wes rode up on his bicycle. He parked it across the street from us, up against Browder's Variety Shop. Roy Hudgins said, "Who's the new kid?" Bob Browder said "He's no kid. Hell, he's an old man!" And, he was. Wes appeared to be at least thirty years old. Maybe even older. It was hard to tell. Somehow Wes was *different*. It wasn't just his dark, scrubby growth of a two day old beard that was different. It wasn't just the old tattered hat. Nor was it just his unkempt appearance. I couldn't put my finger on it; he was just different.

What Wes did next was *really* different. Without a word, without saying "hello", without asking permission, Wes just went out in the middle of the road and started **directing traffic**!

There was already one *stop* sign where Congdon crossed Arizona Street. But, Wes didn't seem to worry about that. When a car stopped at Congdon, Wes just waved him on through. After a half an hour or so, Wes got back on his bicycle and rode back up Congdon the way he'd come. He didn't even say "good-bye". He just rode on up Congdon.

From that day on Wes was always just *around*. He'd show up at the least expected places. Tony Carretto lived on west Black Knob down by the bus barn. Tony woke up one morning and went out to get his milk off the front porch. Must have been about 6:30 a.m. Wes was out in the middle of Arizona Street stopping a car from going south. Tony said Wes was directing the car to go north on Black Knob instead of south towards Naco. Most people in Warren knew Wes by that time and so the driver just slowed down and drove around him continuing on south. When people disobeyed Wes' orders he could fairly well let loose with some cuss words! That's what got Tony's attention; he heard a bunch of cussing and the looked to see what was going on. Wes was letting the "law-breaker" really have it!

It wasn't long before Wes was just *of one us.* He was different, but he was still *one of us.* My mother had told me that Wes was "mentally retarded". That he was just *born that way.*

That didn't make any difference to me; or to any of us. Wes was just fun to have around. He would talk to us and tell us all the latest happenings in Warren. He knew who won the game on Friday night. If the *Pumas* had lost, Wes always referred to the Pumas as "those damn *Pumas.*" I believe it was after a particularly disappointing loss that Wes started the tradition of giving Coach Dicus a "play" to use in the next game. Wes told Coach Dicus that the "play" would go for a touchdown. His "play" was always drawn on a piece of scrap paper; it consisted of a bunch of X's and O's connected by a series of squiggly lines. Coach Dicus made sure that when they ran the "play" in practice that it always went for "a touchdown".

We could expect Wes to show up for most of our football practices. The first several that he showed up for, Coach Al Ridgway had to tell Wes that Coach Dicus didn't want him to get in the way and possibly get hurt. From then on, Wes always stayed well out of the way. The players and the coaches were always very good to Wes. Doug Knipp, BHS '60 remembers Wes proudly wearing an old gray sweater with a red "B" sewn on the front. He wore it all football season. One of the coaches wives had made it for Wes. One year when Al Ridgway was coach, Wes was allowed to ride the team bus to the big Turkey-Day game in Douglas! He was tickled to death.

Dale Hancock, BHS '57 remembers "…how well Max Spilsbury dealt with Wes….once we were loading up the bus for an away game. Wes came up to Max and handed him some paper. Max asked Wes if the papers were the special plays Max had asked for. Wes said they were. Max looked at one and told Wes it would be the first one he would run in the game that night. Wes went away happy."

George Hershey, BHS '56 says he remembers Wes very well. Wes would even be allowed to come in to huddles at some practices when Spilsbury and Ridgway were coaching. Wes would always have some plays for them to run. Hershey speculates that somehow the NFL Arizona *Cardinals* must have gotten hold of some of Wes' plays. According to George some of the *Cardinals* plays look just like the ones Wes used to draw up. George also commented that the movie *Radio* epitomizes the *Wes Wrights* of the world.

Even though Wes will go down in *Puma* football lore as an offensive genius, it was his *law enforcement career* in Bisbee, which has earned Wes his reputation as one of Bisbee's all-time favorite sons. I believe it was Lee Bodenhamer who first talked Wes into running for sheriff. The way Wes handled a bus loaded with tourists headed for Douglas was the deciding factor in Lee talking Wes into running. Bennie Hamrick, BHS '47 told his daughter, Junie Hamrick Schaub, BHS '65 the following story:

One time Wes was directing traffic in Warren by the Warren Drug where he was almost always on duty. Wes was wearing his sheriff's badge. His trusty bike with a siren was near by. Suddenly, a Greyhound Bus loaded with tourists appeared from the west on Congdon coming toward the intersection where Wes was on duty. This was rather out of the ordinary. Wes stopped the bus and the driver told Wes he had missed the turn off to Douglas somewhere in Lowell. "Which is the best way to get to Douglas?" the driver inquired. Without blinking an eye, Wes directed the driver **straight ahead** up Congdon! Now, Congdon Street is up a pretty steep hill. And, it dead-ends at a narrow path leading to Cochise Trail, better known as "Necker's Knob". The driver followed Wes' directions. After all Wes had his badge on. He *looked* official. When the driver got to the top of the hill and found out he could not go forward, and he could not turn around, he was pretty upset. Somebody had to guide the bus back down Congdon. It backed up the whole way. When the bus got down, Wes was "off duty" and some kind soul directed the driver down Arizona Street towards Douglas.

When that story got around, Wes was a shoo-in for a spot on the ballot. When the next election rolled around, Warren had a "WES FOR SHERIFF" sign nailed to every light pole. I.V. Pruett, long time Cochise County Sheriff, was Wes' opponent. Though Wes was not on the ballot officially, he garnered many write-in votes. Pruett won a hotly contested battle. Wes was narrowly defeated. It is said that the election went Pruett's way because some ballots from Lowell were discounted because some there could not read the instructions. There were also a number of "hanging chads" in the Tin Town precinct. Regardless, Wes' supporters would not give up. Wes was proclaimed *unofficial* sheriff for as long as he wanted it. Wes's supporters were so impressed with the clean campaign Wes ran that they got Wes a spot in the 4TH of July parade in Bisbee. He proudly rode his bike and displayed his "WES FOR SHERIFF" sign on his back. He got the biggest hand from the crowd of any of the other participants; bigger even than when the Ft. Huachucha Drum and Bugle Corps marched by.

Sam Moore, BHS '56 relates a little known aspect of Wes' importance to the daily life of Warren. The Bendarack brothers who owned the grocery store next to Browder's Variety Shop, recruited Wes' to inventory their store on a fairly consistent basis. Lee Bendarack gave Wes a note book and a pencil, and taught

Wes how to go up and down the aisles determining what needed to be re-ordered. Wes would then scribble it down and Lee would "order" it.

Sam said, "My dad liked Wes and was always teasing him. Wes would always greet my dad with 'There's that g.d. Tex Moore'…and he always called me 'that g.d. Tex Moore's son'".

Nobody seems to know what ever happened to Wes Wright. One day he just wasn't there anymore. And, he hasn't come back.

SCHOOLS ARE ONLY AS GOOD AT THEIR TEACHERS

Next to Waldo Dicus, **Martha Woundy** was the teacher who had the biggest impact on me. I don't mean that she impacted me with *knowledge* because she didn't. To be perfectly frank, few of the teachers at BHS impacted me with much *knowledge*. The *knowledge* was available to me as BHS had many outstanding teachers. Sadly, I was not in school to get *knowledge*. If there was such a thing as a *high school major* at that time, it would be safe to say that I *majored in eligibility!* I did just enough to stay *eligible* for sports. What Martha Woundy impacted me with was **wisdom.** Good old, down to earth, common sense, *wisdom.*

When I walked into Miss Woundy's senior English class the first day in 1951, I made sure I sat in the first row and I made sure I sat next to Kathy Phillips, BHS '52. I sat in the first row because the "skinny" on Woundy was that she wouldn't call on the "brains" who sat in the first row; she tormented those in the back rows. I sat next to Kathy Phillips because she let me copy off her papers. When I walked in and was seated two desks away from Miss Woundy's desk, she sweetly smiled at me and said, "Good morning, Hadley; it is nice to have *the star* sitting so close to me." Well, so Miss Woundy knew! My reputation had pre-ceded me! After all, I was a senior and I had already lettered in all the sports. I was *the star!* I liked Miss Woundy already! I would stay eligible in this class, no sweat! As I left class at the end of the period, Miss Woundy stopped me and said, "Had-ley, for your information, a 'star' according to the dictionary, is **'a self-inflated mass of gas'.** Have a good day. See you tomorrow." That popped my balloon for awhile.

Miss Woundy was full of pithy comments like that. I wish I had written all of them down. I wish *she* would have written them down! She would have given Mark Twain a run for his money! She stopped Bill Monahan, Howard Loper and myself one time in the middle of a conversation about two of our class mates. We were discussing what we thought went on between the two the previous evening. Miss Woundy said, "Gentlemen, **unless you held the lantern** don't ever guess about another's conduct."

Many of her *jewels of wisdom* would come back to me at various times over the years. One which I have recalled many times and which has had the most profound impact on me was offered to me by Miss Woundy shortly before graduation. It was one of my last class periods in senior English. I had recently accepted *The Phelps Dodge Scholarship* and a football scholarship to The University of Arizona. As I left her class that day, she stopped me and said, "Hadley, I hope things go well for you at The UofA. Just remember that **you have been a big fish in a little pond.** At the UofA you will be **a little fish in a big pond!**" How true, how true! The Bible says it another way, "To him who thinks he stands, let him take heed lest he fall."

As an aside, Miss Woundy had probably the ugliest dog I have ever seen! Every now and then, she would bring the dog to class with her. The dog would sit obediently at the side of her desk, cross his paws, lay his head on his crossed paws and mostly sleep. Miss Woundy loved that dog. She would even **kiss the ugly thing on its lips!** And, she didn't even seem to mind the dog's occasional **emissions of flatulence**. That was a big draw-back to sitting in the front row! The dog was gross! But, Miss Woundy loved him.

Jack Miller, our U.S. History teacher, went by many nick-names, mostly behind his back; but he had two he was proud of: "The Rock" and "I Was There." We called him "The Rock" because he spent a lot of time in his history class talking about The Rock of Gibraltar. It was one of his assignments when he served in the U.S. Navy during World War II. It seemed like every place of historical importance that would be discussed in his class, he would proudly tell us "I was there."

Jack Miller was also proud of his ability to name all the U.S. Presidents in order. At one of our reunions he even named them backwards. He didn't miss a one!

Jack Miller was an excellent history teacher. He must have been because he was one of the few teachers who "got through" to me. I liked his class so much that I entered the UofA fully intending to become a history teacher. Why I didn't is another story. To this day, though, I wish I had taken more history classes in college.

Ron Sanders, BHS '56, brought to mind one of Mr. Miller's most prominent, yet most unappreciated, traits. Mr. Miller would have made an excellent "campaign manager" for a politician! He was the one who selected Ron Haynes, "Hooty" Howell, "Lefty" Weld, Bill Wagner and me to represent BHS at the yearly *Boys' State* convention held at Arizona State College in Flagstaff the summer between our junior and our senior year. When he called us together one lunch period to tell us we had been chosen, he also told us to what degree of involvement in the political realm we were to have while at Boys' State. He informed me that I was to run for the office of *Governor of Boys' State!* I had no clue what that meant, but I did know that it was the highest office one could achieve at Boys' State. Mr. Miller said "not to worry" that he had it all planned. And, he did! Mr. Miller had had **Mr. Mitchell**, our talented graphic arts teacher, design some "Hicks for Governor" pamphlets and business cards. He even told me the strategy "we" would employ. Mr. Miller was pretty astute. He knew that a boy from one of the "big schools" such as Tucson High, Mesa High, Phoenix Union, had won the Boys' State governorship just about every year. It seemed the "big schools" were more organized going in. This year, Mr. Miller informed us, the "little schools" were to be better organized. And, here is how we were to do it. Mr. Miller knew that our Class B Track and Field Championships were to be held at the UofA in a week or so. All the "little schools" would be there. Douglas, Nogales, Safford, Winslow, all the little schools would be represented. Our job, the five of us, Haynes, Wagner, Weld, Howell and myself, was to intermingle with all the other Class B athletes there and start talking it up. This year a "little school" candidate would win *Governor of Boys' State!* Well, that's what we did and when we all got to Flagstaff the "little school" juggernaut was off and rolling!

The last thing Mr. Miller told us before the five of us left the meeting was to keep his plan *confidential*. Nobody was to know that he had printed out the publicity pamphlets ahead of time. It was illegal. He winked as he said it and scrinched his chin and neck around like he had the habit of doing.

My first and last fling at politics was a success, thanks to Mr. Jack Miller!

In bringing all this to my memory, Ron Sanders reminded me that Jack Miller was his neighbor on Campbell Street in Warren. Ron said that Jack had often told him about his work behind the scenes in getting a Puma elected Governor of Boys' State. Ron was a big fan of "The Rock" as were we all!

We had twenty four teachers at BHS when I graduated in 1952. As I look at their pictures in the *Cuprite* (our yearbook) I can truthfully say that I don't see a "weak link" in the bunch. Granted, I did not have all of them in class, and I knew some much better than others. I recall my peers complaining about how tough **Miss Shreve** was, and how mean **Miss Smith** was, and how much **Mr. Strang** would flirt with Wanda Talley and Marlene Harris, and I agreed with most of what they said. But, I believe that each one of them in their own unique way, made BHS an outstanding educational institution. I will only mention a few of them. It would take several volumes to write about each one!

In my preparation for writing this book, I accumulated the numerous emails and categorized them by the topics I wanted to write about. The "teachers" file was by far the thickest! We had over one hundred participate in the email sharing and it seemed that every one of them had something good to say about one or more of their teachers. Sure, some of the names came up more frequently than others, but I do believe that all twenty four of the teachers were mentioned in a positive light more than once. Most of our respondents said they didn't realize just how much a particular teacher influenced them until, sometimes, years later. Again, I will only mention a few.

Sam Moore, BHS '56 said that about **Mr. Joe Payne**, the choral director at BHS. "I never appreciated how good he was until after I left school. Joe was a small man and carried one shoulder lower than the other due to having a lung removed as a youth. Of course, being the sensitive and politically correct kids of that day, we nicknamed him "one lung Joe". Mr. Payne was not a strict disciplinarian and the students took advantage of his kindness; but he knew choral music and he loved his students. I, along with Ted Sorich, Neil Barnett, Tom Fulgum and others were selected to sing in a Madrigal group. I guess Joe was trying to enhance our musical horizons and we met in his home it practice. I don't know how Sorich ever made the choir…he sounded like a bull-frog in heat. But, Joe turned out a good product in spite of who he had to work with!" Sam ended by saying "It is a shame that we didn't realize how good our teachers were until we left them. Maybe we would have been kinder to them at the time."

Margaret Holt was our women's physical education teacher and quite a few of the women had very fond memories of her. I remember Miss Holt as an outstanding athlete. At various times she held the women's Warren Country Club golf championship. She and Mrs. Waldo Dicus at one time were ranked state wide in the top ten women golfers. Each of her former students alluded to her firm but fair discipline that she insisted upon in her classes. Even Miss Holt's niece, Margaret Downs Bemis went to Douglas High School because she was intimidated by being "Miss Holt's niece". Margaret Beamis lived in the Sulfur Springs Valley and could have attended either BHS or DHS. Mrs. Bemis knew how strict her aunt was and was afraid students would give her trouble over it. So she opted to be a *Bulldog* rather than *a Puma*.

It is really a shame that a "Title IX" wasn't in vogue in those years. Miss Holt would have been an outstanding coach for the girls.

Junie Hamrick Schaub, BHS '65, loved being in the play *Our Town* directed by **Miss Barbara Reavis**. Almost eighteen years earlier Junie's mom, Shirley McGuire Hamrick, BHS '47 was in several of Miss Reavis' productions as well; *Junior Miss* was her favorite. Junie commented "It is interesting how many classes Miss Reavis influenced!" Almost two decades of students! Wanda Talley, BHS '52 was another former student influenced by Miss Reavis. Wanda credits Miss Reavis for Wanda's winning the "Juliet Award" at the Kern County Drama Festival in California in 1956.

Mona Baldwin, BHS '57 wrote a long article for *The Bisbee Daily Review* quite a few years ago extolling the virtues of **Mr. Fred Corrin**, BHS tennis coach, and Mona's favorite teacher at BHS. In the article, Mona tells about being sent to BHS by her parents who worked in Cananea, Mexico. They wanted Mona to be educated in America. Mona credits Mr.Corrin with taking her under his wing and making Mona's transition from Mexico to America less painful. Mona also developed a love for tennis that has never left her. Mona concluded the article with this "I thought I was his favorite, but I found out that every student he had thought *they* were his favorite. I love Mr. Corrin and I will never forget him."

Ann Hawkins Bird, BHS '63 refers to Fred Corrin as "the best math teacher and tennis coach around. I used his style of teaching in my thirty plus years in the classroom; he was the best." In her email, Ann also mentions **Miss Medigovich** and **Molly Bendixen.** She said "Molly Bendixen saved me from going down the wrong path." and that "Miss Medigovich convinced me I could make it in college." Butch Lynn, BHS, '? sheds some light on little known facts about Miss Medigovich's personal life. He tells us that she was a "Mrs." and not a "Miss". According to Lynn, Mrs. Medigovich was married to a Reno, Nevada gambler. Lynn and his family were close to Mrs. Medigovich and spent quality time with her before she moved to Reno to be with her husband. Mrs. Medigovich gave Butch her personal collection of William Shakespeare's works. He said he cherishes that collection to this day. Butch says she is the wisest person he ever had the good fortune to know. "She probably taught more of us about the basics of communication than we'll ever know." said Butch.

Those two, Medigovich and Bendixon, were mentioned by many more of the email respondents, as were the **Big and Little Regan sisters** who were grade school teachers for a number of years. I did not know them, but those who did, loved them both. There were so many more mentioned at least once, usually more than once: **Sullivan, Dye, Riddle, Watkins, Ribic, Nelson, Van Scoy,**

Woodmansee, Rosewarne, McKereghan, Parrish. So many who touched so many lives! It is sad that we didn't fully appreciate them *at the time.*

Larry Brockbank, BHS '56 pointed out to me recently that one of the reasons the Bisbee School District always had such good teachers is because of the ties Phelps Dodge had with eastern schools. Phelps Dodge was headquartered in New York and thus, could recruit heavily at Columbia Teachers College, Northwestern and other east and north east schools. Check your Cuprites and see where a large number of our teachers in the 1940's, the 1950's and the 1960's were educated.

DOUGLAS *BULLDOGS.* A WORTHY OPPONENT

There was a rich Saudi oil man who had three sons. He wanted the best for his sons; he decided that in order for them to have the best education possible, he would have to send them to The United States of America to go to college. He called his sons to him. "My sons" he said, "I am going to send you to the United States to go to college. If, after the first year, you have distinguished yourselves with good grades, I buy you anything in the world that you want." And, with that promise, he sent them off to the United States. One he sent to New York University. One he sent to the University of Florida. The third son, he sent to U.C.L.A. in California. At the end of the first year, he called his son in New York. "Son" he said, "How did you do your first year of college in America?" The son replied "Father, you will be so proud. I got all A's my first year!" To which the father said "Son, I am so proud. I will buy you anything in the world. What do you want me to buy you?"

"Father, there is a beautiful statue in the harbor on New York called The Statue of Liberty. I would like to have that statue" son number one replied. "Say no more" the father said. "I will buy you The Statue of Liberty." And so he did.

Then he called son number two in Florida. "Son, how did you do your first year of college in America?" Son number two said, "Father you will be so proud. I got all A's." The father said "Son I am so proud. I will buy you anything in the world. What is it you want?" To which son number two said "Father, Florida has the most beautiful beaches in the world. I would like one of their beaches." "Son, I will buy you the entire coast line of Florida!" And, he did.

He next called son number three at U.C.L.A. "Son, how did you do your first year of college in America?" Son number three answered "Father, you will be so proud. I got all A's." Again, the father said "Son, I am so proud. I will buy you anything you want. What is it you would like?" Son number three replied "Father, just down the road from school they have the most enjoyable place called *Disney Land...*" The father said "Son, say no more. I will buy you Disney Land!" "Oh, no father, I don't want all of Disney Land. But when I was last there, I saw the cutest little *Mickey Mouse* outfit..." The father interrupted again "Son, say no more. You want a Mickey Mouse outfit? I will buy you the *biggest Mickey Mouse outfit* in the world! I will buy you *Douglas High School!*"

That story was always good for a few laughs at some of our BHS class of '52 reunions. But, the truth be known, Douglas High School was anything but a *Mickey Mouse* outfit!

I am sure they had excellent teachers as did BHS, because Douglas, thirty miles from Bisbee, was also a PD town. In this brief section I want to concentrate on the athletes I personally knew from Douglas High School. The ones I knew were quality guys. They always gave us all we could handle. Only one time do I remember beating a Douglas team decisively and I have already written about that; the 1948 whipping we gave Douglas in football. I don't remember any other athletic contest with DHS that was a "blow out" either way. There were no doubt a few, but I do not recall them.

Of course, **Gib Dawson** was head and shoulders above the other *Bulldogs* athletically. I have already mentioned him. He was a good guy, too. I got to know him fairly well over the years. He would always talk to us whenever he showed up at a track meet we were having with Douglas and he was home from the University of Texas. He even wrote me a nice letter when I made all-state my senior year. I have not seen Gib Dawson since I graduated from BHS.

My freshman, sophomore, and junior years we had to put up with a guy named **Arthur Lawrence**, a jumbo sized running back. He is listed in the football programs as weighing two hundred fifteen pounds. I know he was bigger than that. He had to weigh at least two hundred thirty. He was a tank! I got to know Arthur well when we played them in baseball. He pitched and *played center field!* And, he could cover a lot of ground in center field. He could run!

One of the best defensive backs I played against in high school was **Artie Rodriquez**. He was not big; maybe one hundred forty or fifty. But, he was quick and I could not get away from him in the open field. He took the best moves I had and nullified them. I don't ever remember him missing me when he attempted to tackle me.

The *Bulldog* who had more sense than any of them was **Ivan Huish**. He married Betty Pomroy, BHS '52. Ivan was a tough end in football, a better than average forward in basketball and a good high school catcher in baseball. I got to know Ivan at many of our BHS '52 reunions. He always took our "Douglas jokes" with a smile on his face.

Ivan, **Robert Falls** a very good basketball player from DHS, and Gib Dawson came up to Bisbee several times in the mid1950's to play with some former Pumas on an all-star basketball team we put together. Charlie Leftault, "Hooty" Howell, Danny Vucurevich, sometimes Bill Wagner, and myself, along with the Douglas guys, played all-star teams from around the state. We very seldom lost. Once we played an all-star team comprised of former UofA basketballers and we beat them!

Probably the Douglas guy I got to know the best was **Dan Pollack.** I hung around Dan quite a bit in the summers and when we were at Arizona State together. Dan and I played golf with **Jerry Floyd** a couple times one summer. Jerry and I became friends when we attended Boys' State together. I ran into Jerry at a restaurant in Palm Springs, California in 1981 when I was at an insurance convention. Jerry had on his military uniform and if I remember correctly, he was a major and was living in a beach-side resort. He invited me over to go for a cruise on his yacht. I couldn't make it, sorry to say. Jerry was always fun to compete against in track. For some reason he was always entered in the *broad jump* event. He wouldn't mind me saying this, but he was pitiful! On a good day, Jerry would jump fifteen feet. Everybody else was over eighteen feet. Just to break the monotony, on his last jump he would turn a flip in mid-air and land on his feet. On those occasions Jerry only jumped twelve feet. Jerry loved a good laugh even at his own expense.

Douglas had some good coaches as I recall. The most note worthy was football and basketball coach **Otis Coffey**. He always put a good team on the field and court. He too, was very friendly to us. I talked to him a bunch at track meets. He always had something encouraging and complimentary to say. Douglas kids told us stories about Coach Coffee's memory. One time, they say, his wife came to pick him up after a practice and he walked out to the car in his underwear. He had forgotten to put on his pants! Most of the Douglas athletes I spoke with about Coach Coffee had nothing but good things to say about him as a coach and a man.

Coach **Barney Lay** was the *Bulldog* baseball coach and was always most friendly to us. He too, put a good team on the field. They always hustled and were well coached. *However, Bulldog* baseball teams always had the worst looking uniforms of anybody we played! They were a bleached out gray with faded yellow lettering. I never could figure that out. Everything else about DHS athletic teams was pretty much standard and stylish.

Bisbee-Douglas. What a great rivalry! When PD ceased operations in Bisbee that all went by the wayside. Barry Sollenberger, Sports Information Director of the Arizona Interscholastic Association has written an excellent article cataloging the long rivalry of Bisbee-Douglas. You can acquire a copy if you are interested, by contacting Barry at the AIA office in Phoenix.

"DOONIE"

Layton "Doonie" Ducote was one of Bisbee High's most talented and unpredictable athletes. "Doonie" did not play by the rules. He would often do what he *shouldn't do;* and what his opponents knew *he couldn't do;* yet, that's what *he would do.* As an example I saw him play a Thanksgiving game against Douglas in 1956. He was the starting quarter back and holder on extra-points for the kicker. The *Pumas* had scored and "Doonie" got ready to hold for the extra point. The center snapped the ball low; it bounced to "Doonie" too late to put it down for the kick. "Doonie" picked the ball up and started running to his *left.* Several Douglas *Bulldogs* were in hot pursuit. "Doonie was *right* handed and he was carrying the ball in his *left* hand running to his *left.* He suddenly spotted a *Puma* teammate free in the end zone. "Doonie" threw *left handed* to the receiver for a *Puma* conversion.

Also in 1956 "Doonie" and the Max Spilsbury-coached BHS basketball team were playing in the Southern Conference basketball tournament at Benson High School. The Benson High gymnasium was fairly new and they had a brightly painted logo of a fiercely growling Benson *Bobcat* in the center of the court. The *Pumas* were playing host Benson in the first game. The gymnasium was packed with rabid *Bobcat* fans. Late in the game with the score tied, "Doonie" was bringing the ball down court after a Benson basket. As "Doonie" got to mid-court, he stepped directly in the mouth of the fierce *Bobcat.* He came to a screeching halt. The *Bobcat* had "grabbed" 'Doonie's" foot and held on tightly! "Doonie" passed the ball off to Charlie Lugo to keep the ball in play, and he continued to try to his pull his foot out of the *Bobcat's* mouth. "Doonie" pulled on his "entrapped" foot for a few seconds before the *Bobcat* "let go". He caught up to the ball and continued as though nothing had happened. The crowd loved it! Max Spilsbury was in stitches.

In the summer of 1950 "Doonie" and I became pretty close friends even though he was several years behind me in school. We wanted to go to Flagstaff that summer to watch the all-star high school basketball and football games. My dad said we could use his car if we would paint the roof of the house. It was a typical Bisbee summer where the temperature hovered around the one hundred degree mark. Painting the roof was slow, hot and tedious work. At one point "Doonie" thought it was going too slow. We might not be through in time to go to Flagstaff. So, picking up both his gallon of paint and mine, he proceeded to slosh both gallons in a wide swath across the roof. Needless to say, we couldn't paint fast enough or even enough to spread all that paint over the entire area. When my dad came home he was livid! He had a pretty hot temper and when he saw the mess we had made, he started kicking at me, which is what he often did if he couldn't reach me with his hand. "Doonie" had gone home by this time. He missed dad's tirade. Dad bought two more gallons of paint and "Doonie" and I continued painting the next day. We didn't complete the job in time, but we went to Flagstaff in dad's car anyway. I think dad completed the job. My dad was a "softy".

"Doonie" was an excellent all-around athlete. His best game was baseball. After graduating from BHS, "Doonie" went to Arizona State University on a baseball scholarship. After a few years as a *Sun Devil,* "Doonie" signed with the Chicago *Cubs.* He played in the *Cubs'* organization for several years and had moved up a step or so away from the *big leagues* when he quit for reasons only "Doonie" knows. "Doonie" has had a very successful career with the Scottsdale, Arizona fire department since he quit baseball. Layton "Doonie" Ducote was indeed one of Bisbee High's greatest all-around athletes.

MOTHER.
CONTINUED

Margaret "Peg" Hicks, my mother, loved her beer. She was an alcoholic as I have mentioned. She was also very benevolent and shared her beer with any that came calling. There were a group of Mexican nationals who made the rounds of Warren frequently looking for yard work. My mother became a soft touch for those guys. She not only gave them a good wage, but her tips were often a cold bottle of beer and good conversation around her kitchen table. She loved to try to speak Spanish with them and could usually hold her own. I can't count the times I would come in from school only to find one or more of them around the kitchen table laughing and having a blast with her. Of course mother wouldn't offer beer without something to snack on, usually home-roasted almonds. When dad or I would complain to her about these guys "mooching" off of her, she would always just say "But, they are such sweet boys".

Dad tried several things over the years to get her to stop drinking. He sent her to an alcohol rehabilitation center in Wickenburg, Arizona, which did her some good. The rehab. center suggested dad buy a gift shop for mother as further therapy for her. Mother was a very accomplished knitter and loved to teach young ladies how to knit. "Peg's Gift Shop" became very popular in southern Arizona. She had ladies from as far away as Nogales come to her to learn how to knit. After a year or so mother's lack of financial managing skills came into play and she had to sell the shop.

Next, dad bought mother a monkey. I was in the military, my sister, Cathy, was in seventh or eighth grade, and my brother, Bill, was a toddler. Dad figured that a monkey would be just the thing to keep mother occupied during the day when she was alone with Bill. Mother and "Siam" became great buddies. The monkey would nap with mother every afternoon. He would go through her hair making sure she didn't have lice. "Siam" was quite a "hit" with the community. Dad had rigged up a long wire going the length of the front yard to which he would chain "Siam". "Siam" pretty much had free reign of the front yard. Cars would pull up at all times of the day and the people would feed him peanuts and play with him. Young kids loved to play with "Siam". He would chase sticks and sycamore balls that the kids would throw. One weird little kid, Sammy Moore, BHS '56, would actually talk to "Siam". Sammy and "Siam" would sit for hours just chattering away and enjoying each other's company. They seemed to have a lot in common.

My uncle, Forbes Fergus, was visiting from San Diego one time when "Siam" swiped one of his cigars! Forbes was smoking a cigar out on our back patio when "Siam" suddenly leaped and grabbed the cigar out of Forbes' mouth. "Siam" then climbed up on the roof of the house where he sat contentedly trying to smoke the cigar. When he tried to put the "hot" end in his mouth, he threw the cigar back at Forbes.

Our neighbors to the south on Oliver Circle, were Bert, Ruth, Pat and "Tinkey" Whitehead. One morning Ruth was sitting at her kitchen table enjoying a cup of coffee and reading the paper when she heard the door open behind her. Thinking that it was one of her family, Ruth continued reading. She was startled when "Siam" suddenly jumped on the kitchen counter and began to rummage through the dirty dishes left over from breakfast. "Siam" had somehow gotten loose from his front-yard chain, which he often did. He scared Ruth to death!

One day "Siam" got loose and he was never found. Mother was grief stricken. She had lost her "buddy".

I don't know what the reason was but all of a sudden mother just quit drinking "cold turkey". It was probably a combination of things, but I always considered it an answer to my prayers. I was married at the time and living in Carmel, California. My wife, Joan, and I had had Susie, our first child. It became obvious to mother that we couldn't and wouldn't trust her to be alone with Susie. I am sure that had something to do with her quitting. When we moved to Prescott, Arizona, we noticed that mother was not drinking. She did not say anything about it, but it was obvious to us. The next thing we knew mother was going to Cochise College to get her nursing degree, which had been a goal of mother's since her high school days. When mother graduated with her nursing degree she was hired immediately by The Copper Queen Hospital. Some said she was the best nurse they had. We were very proud of her.

Those were the happiest years of my mother's and dad's life. Bill was in high school and was a blessing to them both. Cathy was married at that time, so Bill was their only kid at home. The three of them went on fishing trips and vacations together. Mother and dad even got away for a few extended vacations; something they never could do when mother was drinking. After five wonderful years, mother contacted cancer. Within eight months she had died. Several times over the years after mother had died, dad commented that when she quit drinking they became the best of "friends". Though dad and mother had a very stormy marriage until the last eight or so years, divorce was never an option in their minds. God blessed their obedience by granting them much happiness at the end.

LES FENDERSON.
DEFINITELY *UPPER-VISTA.*

Working with Les Fenderson was an **Experience!** And, please notice the capital *E.* I believe I could write another book just on my experiences working as Les Fenderson's assistant baseball coach at Prescott High School in the mid-1960's. Les and his lovely wife Shirley had both graduated from Bisbee High in the late '50's and had been at Prescott High School since graduating from the University of Arizona. Shirley was our sons' kindergarten teacher. Susie, our oldest, missed Shirley by a year. Shirley and Les are both outstanding teachers. The big difference between Les and Shirley is that Shirley did not *chew!* Les had the nasty habit of chewing *RED MAN* chewing-tobacco. He did not chew in the classroom, I don't believe. But, he did chew up a storm on the baseball diamond! He always had a stream of brown liquid dribbling down his chin. I told him on a number of occasions that if he ever choked on that stuff I was not going to dig around in his mouth to pry the wad out. If he ever had a heart attack, I was definitely not going to give him mouth-to-mouth. Smoking and chewing was forbidden by the school administration for the students AND the faculty. Les' coaching buddies were afraid Les would get caught and reprimanded. We tried several tactics to get him to quit chewing. He would never carry the RED MAN pouch in his pocket to baseball practice. He would load up his mouth ahead of time with the nasty stuff and leave the pouch in his locker. Once we put sand in the pouch. Once we put ground-up oregano in the pouch. We put ground-up leaves in it. We tried hiding the pouch on numerous occasions. Once, we even urinated in it! Les said that only enhanced the flavor. He said it tasted a little like "copper-water". It was after that attempt that we gave up trying to break him of the habit.

The closest I ever got to getting Les riled up over his bad habit was when I told him "Chewing tobacco is strictly *lower Vista.*" Understand now, Les was most proud of his Bisbee roots. Les grew up in Warren and to him, *upper Vista* was *class! Lower Vista* was *nowhere*; definitely, *low-class!* When Les wanted to bestow the ultimate insult to anybody, he said they were **lower Vista.**

Les was an outstanding high school baseball coach. His players loved him. They loved his intensity. They loved his demand for excellence. They loved his humor. The players did not understand, but they also loved Les' *Al Ridgway modus operandi.* Al's coaching philosophy was well engrained in Les. The *spark of greatness, which was passed from Waldo Dicus to Al Ridgway,* was caught by Les Fenderson. Les had outstanding baseball teams while at Prescott High School. One of his players, John Denny, played twelve years in the major leagues and won the "CY YOUNG AWARD" in 1983 while playing for the Philadelphia *Phillies.* One of Les' teams, a group he labeled *The Golden Boys,* was voted into the Prescott High School Hall of Fame. Prescott's colors are blue and gold. *The Golden Boys* wore mostly all-gold uniforms! Strictly **upper Vista;** depending on one's view point!

Prescott High School at the time I was with Les, did not have a practice or game baseball field. We had to bus from the high school down to The Prescott City Park for all practices and games. Usually, most of the team rode to and back from practice in an old Prescott School bus driven by Les. If the team had had a particularly good practice, or if Les was hungry which he *often* was, he would sometimes let the players stop for ice-cream at an ice-cream parlor across from City Park. Of course, the deal was, that the team had to buy Les and his trusty assistant ice-cream. One day, Les and I came out of the coaches' locker-room to get on the bus to drive the players to practice. When we got to the parking lot, the bus was gone! And the players were gone! As Les' so eloquently phrased it "Those little @X *^!!# s took the damn bus!!" It didn't take Les' fertile mind long to decide what to do. He said, "Hell. Let's just take the day off and go *watch* practice." So, that is what we did. We got in Les' old 1941 Jeep and drove to the City Park. First, however, we stopped at the ice-cream parlor and we each got a milk shake. We then went across the street and took a seat at the top of the stadium. We were not surprised when we got there. The players were a disciplined bunch. They were just finishing warm ups and were getting ready for infield practice. We just sat and watched. Of course, the players knew we were there, but they ignored us and went on with practice. We knew that the whole time, the players were wondering what we were going to do. When would we step in and take over practice? Les and I sat there the entire hour and a half of practice. The team leader, Bob Manriquez, conducted practice just as Les would have. Les nudged me when he estimated that they only had half an hour of practice left. His scheming mind had concocted a plan! We left the stadium and went back to the school. Les had a master key to each of the players' lockers. He had a devilish smile on his face as he informed me what the plan was. We took all the players' clothes out of the locker, including shoes. We hauled it all up to the flag-pole in the parking lot and tied each piece of clothing to another piece of clothing. Then we hoisted all of it **up** the flag pole! Les said he wanted the players to know how he felt when *his pants* got hoisted up the flag-pole on his first day of school at BHS! Then Les did a very *upper Vista* thing! He went down to his office and called the sports desk at the *Prescott Courier* and told them to get a photographer up to the high school at once! Les and his loyal assistant then went around back of the school and used a ladder to get up on the roof. We wanted to be hidden when the team-bus got back. Soon we saw the bus chugging up the hill. The players got off having the time of their lives. We could tell what they were thinking: *Boy, we sure put one over on the old coaches! Wait until this got around school the next day!* We were thinking: *Wait until the picture gets around town!* Les and I could hardly contain our glee as the players went in the gym to go to the locker room. They were down there for five minutes or so before they all came running out the door yelling and screaming and cussing. "Those s.o.b.s!! Where did they put our clothes?! I can't believe they did this!" Half of them were in their jock-straps and tee-shirts, half of them still had their practice uniforms on. Finally one of them saw the clothes hanging from the flag-pole. The photographer got there just in time to get a good shot of them hauling the clothes down. It was **fun** coaching and playing for Les Fenderson.

My favorite *Les Fenderson* story centers around the movie *Patton*. Les and I went to see the movie together and we loved it. Les, was especially enthralled with the scenes where George C. Scott as *Patton,* was preparing for his show-down battle with German General *Rommel, The Desert Fox. Patton* had read every book he could get his hands on which discussed *Rommel's* battle-field strategies. The one *Patton studied* the most thoroughly was the book written by *The Desert Fox* himself. If you saw the movie, you may remember the scene, which had Les on the edge of his seat. *Patton* had set the trap. *Rommel's* tanks were chewing up the African desert behind a huge cloud of sand. *Patton* was on his belly, eyes glued to his binoculars watching *Rommel* slowly lead his tanks into the teeth of *Patton's* hidden tanks. The trap was sprung! Suddenly, on *Patton's* command, his tanks came out from their hiding places behind sand dunes. *Rommel* was completely caught by surprise. As *Rommel's* tanks retreated in confusion and chaos, *Patton* stood up, shook his fist and shouted at the retreating *Rommel "ROMMEL, YOU MAGNIFICIANT BASTARD, I READ YOUR BOOK!!"* Les loved it! He was clapping and shouting as *Rommel* fled for his life, completely defeated.

A week or so later, Les' had an opportunity to emulate *General Patton.* Prescott High's baseball team was preparing for a game with arch rival, Flagstaff High School. Flagstaff's coach was veteran Gilbert Corona, a personal thorn in the side for Les. Coach Corona was known as a "bunter". He would bunt in all kinds of situations. He would not wait until a bunt was expected; he would often bunt when it wasn't expected. Les had played against Corona for several years. Les felt he knew the strategies Corona would employ and when. Les said he had a good "book" on Corona. All that week of practice, Les drilled and drilled the team on how to defend against the bunt; and how to expect it at the most unexpected times. Finally, game-time arrived. It was a crucial conference game. The game was played at The City Park. The stadium was filled with Prescott faithful. Sure enough, Coach Corona bunted early in the game. But, Les' team was ready. They executed perfectly and the Flagstaff bunter was thrown out at first base. Les was so jubilant that he jumped up, shook his fist at Coach Corona and yelled loud enough for everybody in the stands to hear *"CORONA, YOU MAGNIFICANT BASTARD, I READ YOUR BOOK!"* The Flagstaff coach and players must have been thinking that Coach Fenderson had to have a few "screws loose". Not at all, Les Fenderson was just **upper Vista.**

THE MECHANICL WOMAN

Times have changed. It is inevitable. In my view many of those changes *are not* good changes. One change, however, which I feel is for the good is how society treats and cares for our *mentally and physically handicapped* citizens. I call them "God's special children." We have special schools for them now. We have trained professionals who are skilled in caring for them. They are no longer treated as outcasts and shunned by society. Families no longer feel shame at bringing their handicapped loved ones into public. I sadly recall seeing Gladys and Henry Jewell's handicapped sister riding in the back seat of the family car. She would be looking out the side window staring in awe at "the outside world". I would guess that the girl had Down' syndrome, but I don't know for sure. At any rate she did not "go public" as far as I know, except to ride partially hidden in the back seat of the car.

Don Wolslagel, BHS '53 tells another touching story. He tells of *The Mechanical Woman:*

It was the darkest, most inhumane, uncaring, un-secret we ever harbored in Warren. I had heard about *The Mechanical Woman* even before I saw her. All us kids joked about her. Later, when I was grown and more aware of what the real situation was, I was so upset that we had treated the family the way we did. I was disgusted with myself and the stupidity that I passed off as being young and dumb. I really think our (my) parents should have been more open and instructive about the truth.

I started delivering the *Bisbee Daily Review* when I was in the 4th grade...my route included the house where *The Mechanical Woman* lived. I was terrified going there to collect for the paper the first time; but, it had to be done. The first couple of months, the only contact I had when I knocked on the door was with an old lady; grandmotherly and matronly in appearance. She was nice, but brusque and business like. I eventually saw the *Mechanical Woman* standing behind the older lady one time. In today's jargon, I'd say she had cerebral palsy or something similar. Her body and limbs were twisted and distorted. Her mouth was open with saliva drooling down her chin. She was ambulatory, but just barely. She made vocal sounds, but no talking. Grunts and whines. No matter how many times I saw the disabled lady while collecting, I was never comfortable with the situation. I wasn't scared, but I didn't like it. I never knew their names and to the best of my knowledge, neither one of them ever left the house. It seems that no adult I ever talked to knew their name. They were seemingly just not a member of the community; unknown, uncared about, and ignored. I feel shame in myself for being part of the cover up. I now go out of my way to help mainstream handicapped individuals and try to have them become a part of the community at large. I volunteer with an organization here in Bozeman, Montana that works with disabled people. I work in the therapeutic gardening program in the summer. It is just great helping them plant a seed and watch their amazement as the seed sprouts and grows. I watch in pure joy when they harvest the vegetable, clean it off, and eat it right on the spot. Most times they never even get it out of the garden patch before they finish it off. They have the same joyful enthusiasm and astonishment, year after year as they go through to whole process again."

This poignant letter from Don Wolslagel touched a tender chord with Mona Baldwin, BHS '57. Mona responded to Don with this brief note: "I read your description of the Mechanical Woman. It touched my heart and I say we need more Don Wolslagel's in this life. We have a son who is 35. He was born deaf and has Tourette Syndrome. He has totally isolated himself from the world. I am sure the kids in his neighborhood think of him in much the same way you did the Mechanical Woman. Kelly does not have any speech and makes weird sounds and noises. He depends solely on sign language to communicate. His tics drive him crazy and he is constantly in motion with his jerks and grimaces. I applaud you, Don, for the effort you are making to include the handicapped in every day life. Thank you for making the world for those who are 'different' special."

As Mona wrote about her son, I was reminded about two other Bisbee "personalities" that some of the email respondents wrote about. One is the elderly gentleman I would see on the bus at times. He would always get off the bus at the stop where Congdon intersected with Bisbee Road; where he went from there I have no idea. He either went up to The Terraces or else he walked down Cochise Row. He walked in that direction. He was a sad individual. He, too, had horrible tics as does Mona's son. He would hit himself violently in his head, over and over again. He would not utter a word, but was obviously in much pain. As a kid, I just sat and stared at him; too uncomfortable to do anything else. I don't remember ever talking about him to my parents, other adults, or my friends. He was just there. We accepted the fact that he was different.

The other "different" individual was "Sonny", the deaf life guard at the city swimming pool "up the canyon". I only remember him being around for a year, or maybe two. In that short time he made a profound impression on me! We called him "Deaf and dumb Sonny". He was deaf for sure, but I doubt that he was "dumb". He may have been the finest gymnast in all of Bisbee. He was built like a Greek-god. "Sonny" was maybe six feet tall and his muscles just rippled. He wore a skimpy bathing suit and his blond hair was always meticulously combed back on his head. "Sonny" would sit for hours in his life-guard's stand alertly watching all the swimmers. Every now and then, when he got the urge, he would get up on the high-dive and put on a diving exhibition that had us all aghast! The rumors of his exploits were many. One which I heard several times was that "Sonny" had climbed up on the cross-piece of the tall swing set at the deep end of the pool; then like a tight-rope walker, he had walked to the middle of the cross-piece and dived into the city reservoir. The reservoir was down hill from the city pool and in order to dive into it, "Sonny" would have had to clear the low fence, which was all around the city pool, plus a fairly high fence around the reservoir. Many people said they saw him do it a number of times. I never did, but I would have loved to! I never talked to anybody who knew anything about "Sonny". He was just there.

The Mechanical Woman; the gentleman with the horrible tic; and "Sonny"; three more "different" people who, along with Wes Wright, Miss Patty, and "Hondro", crossed our paths and touched our lives in special ways. As Dolly Adams, BHS '52 said "So many questions…"

NECKERS' KNOB,
A FIGMENT OF THE IMAGINATION.

I am here to tell you that the term "Neckers' Knob" is a misnomer. The email respondents who lived in Tombstone Canyon (upper-Bisbee) lay claim to having the original *Neckers' Knob* just because they lived close to the divide (the pinnacle of the mountains down which the road through Bisbee ran) and had an observation point; a nice place to pull onto and watch the lights of Bisbee. Plus, they bragged they had a few side canyons they could drive into. Come on! Get real! I drove up there myself a couple of times to check out what all this "Neckers' Knob" talk was about. Let me tell you, nobody in their right mind would go up there to "neck". It was much too public. Sure you could get ten to twenty cars parked side by side, but why? There was no privacy! And, those side canyons? Only one car at a time could go down any one of them. And, to leave, they had to back out the entire way. Nope. The *divide* "Neckers' Knob" was good for only one or two cars on a "first come, first serve' basis. It would never do as a "Neckers' Knob" which serviced a whole community.

Warren kids claimed they had the original "Neckers' Knob" which was located at the top of Cochise Trail. Not so! Wes Wright put a stop to that before it ever got off the ground. Ever vigilant, Wes would make his nightly rounds up to Cochise Trail and "ticket" anybody who was parked there. It was absolutely a "no parking "zone in Wes's mind. Besides it was just a one-way road that did not offer any privacy, either. Pat Jay Lake, BHS '54 circulated a rumor in the mid-fifties that Warren had a sign designating "Neckers' Knob. Warren Kids Only." Pat's rumor claimed that a huge spot-light operated by Sheriff Wright would zero in on any car from Bisbee, Lowell or Douglas, which foolishly intruded into Warren territory. When the spot-light was turned on, sirens all over Warren would be activated, according to the rumor. That was all a lie. It was also a lie, Pat admitted, that if a Warren guy was able to talk his girl into going to "Neckers' Knob" with him, he could cut a notch in the wooden pole holding the sign. It was just one big lie to make Warren kids appear more in tune with the times.

Truth be known, Warren kids were much more advanced, much more *imaginative* than either Bisbee or Lowell kids. Take Don Mangham for instance. Don didn't even bother to drive up to Cochise Trail. And, why drive all the way up *through* Lowell and through Bisbee to the top of the divide? It was such a waste of gas. Don merely drove in behind Ed Plumb's used-car lot in Lowell and parked next to one of the cars on the lot. If Don was feeling he and his date wanted to really be "upper Vista" he would pick out a Cadillac or a shiny late model Ford to park next to. Don and his date spent many a night parked there observing all the traffic going through Lowell both ways. His was just another "used car" on the lot.

Then there was that weird little kid, Sammy Moore, BHS '56. Sammy was the only kid Wes Wright would allow to park for more than a few minutes on Cochise Trail. Wes admired Sammy because Sammy rode a bike. Sammy was so into bikes that when he first heard the rumor about "Neckers' Knob" when he was a sophomore, he rode his date up there on his bike. Sammy had gone to Greenway Grade School so he was smart enough to realize that a date on a bike wouldn't cut it; so he advanced to a car. The car was perfect for Sammy's purposes. He took his dates to "Neckers' Knob" because he found it to be a very conducive place to *study*. Sammy took his school books and homework with him so his time wouldn't be spent foolishly. When Wanda Talley Owens, BHS '52 heard about Sammy's claim to be the only kid who used Cochise Trail, aka "Neckers' Knob", as a study-hall, she wrote him this scathing reply "Sam, Sam, Sam!! *Homework* was what all of us were doing on 'Neckers' Knob'. The constant turning of the text book pages was what fogged up those car windows." Sadly, neither Wanda nor any of those Horace Mann graduates knew the meaning of the word, *homework!* In fact, if you looked at their grades, you'd see there were a lot of words they didn't know the meaning of!

I think the evidence is overwhelming. Warren kids cornered the market on imaginative places to take a date. I won't even lower myself to use the word "neck". We took our dates out for a variety of reasons to a wide variety of places. Weird Sammy was not the only Warren youth interested in growing intellectually. I am sure Don Mangham and his date studied the new styles of automobiles on the market. Ted and Sam Sorich devoted their date-time to discussing sports and politics. Both Hersheys, Jack and George, didn't worry about it too much. When they had a date, their time was spent in rejoicing at their good fortune. *Canasta* was always big in Warren. Many of us would spend the date-time around our date's kitchen table playing *Canasta* with our date and her parents.

So many of the email respondents wrote about "Neckers' Knob". I am afraid it was as Shakespeare said, "Much Ado About Nothing". It was one of those terms, which grew in stature over the years due to wishful thinking. It was only a figment of one's imagination; unless, of course, you were from Warren where very active imaginations were always at work. To Warren kids, "Neckers' Knob" was always just around the corner.

SAMMY WAS A WEIRD LITTLE KID

"SORRY ABOUT THE MINOR ACCIDENT KID... HERE'S YOUR BIKE BACK I STOLE."

Yes, he was. Sammy Moore, BHS '56 was a weird little kid. It has already been pointed out to you how he would sit and talk to a monkey for hours. He did lots of other stuff, like taking his date to "Neckers' Knob" on a bike; which only solidified my contention that *Sammy Moore was weird*. He was weird in so many ways. I will delineate just a few.

The first of these "Moore" characteristics I need to bring to the table is a long standing myth that Sammy has perpetuated. In spite of my being completely exonerated by a jury comprised of my peers, Moore has maintained that I **destroyed his new bike**. He has written poetry, which has maligned my character. He has drawn pictures of me *supposedly* in the act of returning his bike in less than "mint" condition. Much like O.J. Simpson's distracters, Sammy Moore continues to vilify me and insist I was guilty of that wicked deed. Here is the truth of that myth Sammy has kept alive:

Cochise County Court records reveal that in 1950 Sammy Moore brought a law suit against one Hadley F. Hicks for "willfully and maliciously destroying a new Schwinn bicycle belonging to Samuel Moore". Those same court records show that after hearing the testimony of the defendant (me), Judge Frank Thomas threw out the allegations Moore brought against the defendant. In his statement to the jury, Judge Thomas said "Hadley Hicks has been my next door neighbor for eight years. His honesty and integrity is impeccable. He has never once stolen pomegranates from my trees. He has mowed my lawn, washed my car, taken my wife, "Sissy" to town when she broke her leg, and countless other charitable acts of kindness. Hadley did all this without pay! Hadley is 'the Good Samaritan of Warren'. Case dismissed!!"

Before I tell you exactly what happened to Moore's bike, let me tell you one more complaint he has lodged against me. He has accused me of "jury rigging". Sammy maintains that the "jury of my peers" was hand-picked by my lawyer, Bob Browder. True, they were all my friends, but hey, they were supposed to be. They were my peers. Judge Thomas appointed Wes Wright as bailiff and "Hondro" as jury foreman. I had nothing to do with that. The jury comprised of my six Fort Ord buddies, Jim "Lefty" Weld, "Red" Bradshaw, Ruben Leon, Tony Silva, Jack Hershey along with my lawyer, Bob Browder, did present a formidable obstacle to overcome, I admit. They made up a great jury. It was just "the luck of the draw" as they say.

The *true* story of Sammy Moore's "destroyed" bicycle is duly recorded in the records at The Cochise County Courthouse. It is as follows:

It happened on a warm Saturday afternoon in 1950. The evening before the BHS *Pumas* had won an exciting game against the Safford *Bulldogs*. That afternoon, I was totally exhausted after giving it "my all" for my teammates and the people of Bisbee the night before. In every game my total focus was *always* on my teammates and the loyal Bisbee fans. Never on myself. As I sat under the huge evergreen tree in my front yard contemplating the many mistakes I had made in the game and how best to remedy them before next week's game, Sammy Moore came riding up on his new Schwinn bike. As he rode down Cole Street and turned on to Oliver Circle, he saw me lying under the tree; as little kids often did, when they saw one of their heroes, Sammy got overly excited. He over-corrected his bike and wrecked! Fearing the worst, I jumped up and ran to his side. I was relieved that he didn't appear to be injured. I made sure he was ok. I even took him inside and cleaned a scraped area on his knee. After putting a Band-Aid on the scrape, I offered him cookies and milk. As we sat and talked, I tried to give him pieces of wisdom that may carry this young, impressionable boy through "the hard times" that come to all of us. When we had finished the cookies and milk, Sammy politely thanked me for my obvious concern for him. He excused himself, got on his slightly scratched new bike and rode off. I forgot all about the incident because little kids were always hanging around us older, more mature guys. It wasn't until several weeks later when I realized the true nature of kids like

Sammy Moore. I received a letter from The District Attorney of Cochise County, Mr. Fulsome Moore. He was subpoenaing me to appear in court for "stealing and wrecking a new Schwinn bicycle belonging to one Samuel Moore, shirt-tail relative to District Attorney, Fulsome Moore." I immediately called my lawyer, Bob Browder and explained the whole thing to him. He just laughed. "Hadley, don't sweat it. Just don't say a word. We'll beat this rap. I know things and I have lots of connections in the right places."

So there you have it. The real story. You would think that after all these years Sammy Moore would just let it go. But, oh, no. He continues to send me anonymous notes and poems. He is still vilifying my character. I have saved the last two poems he has sent me. Two years ago he sent me this one on my seventieth birthday. These two poems will further testify that Sammy Moore is weird:

ODE TO HADLEY

HADLEY WAS A SUPERSTAR
AT GOOD OLD BISBEE HIGH
PEOPLE ALL ADMIRED HIM…
BUT THEY REALLY DIDN'T KNOW THE GUY

ALL THE GIRLS ADORED HIM
AND LOVED TO KISS HIS MUG
BUT THE TRUTH ABOUT THIS SUPERSTAR
IS THAT HE REALLY WAS A THUG!

FOR WHEN I WAS A LITTLE BOY
(A CUTE AND HARMLESS TYKE)
HADLEY MAULED AND MUGGED ME
AND WRECKED MY BRAND NEW BIKE.

NOW HADLEY'S IN HIS GOLDEN YEARS
HIS HAIR AS WHITE AS SNOW

I WONDER WHO HE'S MUGGING NOW?
I'D REALLY LIKE TO KNOW!

HAPPY BIRTHDAY HADLEY
SAM MOORE

Sure, he signed his name and even wished me a "happy birthday". But, the poem just reeked of sarcasm. I can spot a phony a mile away. What hurt really bad was that my entire family was gathered around the table when my daughter read Sammy's poem. None of them thought it was at all funny. My young grandsons were in tears to think that someone would be so low as to call their "papa" a *thug!* It caused them nightmares for weeks.

Here is the poem I received this last birthday. It is much shorter and yet, we still sense Sammy's anger and bitterness:

ANCIENT, ANTIQUATED
NO MORE FUN
DESCRIBES A PERSON
WHO IS SEVENTY-ONE

Happy Birthday!....Sam

There! See what I mean? The "Happy Birthday" has an exclamation point after it. This is an obvious sign that he said it without the slightest hint of sincerity. He didn't even bother to capitalize the *s* in his name. Don't you just feel the indifference? I sure do!

But, you know what? He did offer to draw the **GREAT CARTOONS, which** appear throughout the book. So I guess I can overlook the seething anger he has vented on me all these years. I am more than willing to elevate his status to **upper Vista!**

WALLY RE-VISITS NACO

Some wise sage once said "You can never go home again." Wally Quayle, BHS '53 found this to be true. It was a very traumatic experience for him! I am even hesitant to write about it for fear of rekindling memories which will only serve to frustrate Wally and others who were at one time respected and much welcomed guests in Naco. As I read this anguished note from Wally, I could visualize him weeping as he wrote it: "Several years ago Wanda and I took her sister and our brother-in-law across to Naco. I had spent the past fifteen years telling them how important I was in Naco. I told them about my good friend Al Rochin who was the mayor of Naco at one time. I told them about my Naco credit card, which I still had in my wallet. Since it was out-dated and no longer valid, I had it gold-plated. Al had told me that it would always be proof of my good standing in the Naco community during his regime. I was certain one of Al's grandsons would be the current mayor. When we drove up to the boarder guards' station, I flashed my gold-plated credit card with *Mayor Al Rochin* pretty well highlighted and drove right across just like I used to do. Much to my surprise and chagrin the *federales* (Mexican police hh) started yelling and waving their automatic weapons at us for not stopping at the red light which was newly installed since I had been there last over forty years ago. They used to have a sign which read "ALTO" which we all knew meant "stop". I never used to have to stop. All the boarder guards knew me and treated me with respect. These new guys didn't know who it was they were treating like a common criminal. They had their guns pointed at us and were in the process of putting hand-cuffs on me when a tottering old man came up supported by a cane. He looked at me though cloudy, blood shot eyes and said, 'Wally? Quien es?…Wally, mi viejo amigo!! Como esta!?' The years rolled by in a flash when I recognized my old friend, Jose Manuel deLorenzo Gonzales, the former captain of the boarder guards. We were each shedding tears of joy as we gave each other huge abrazos. It was so good to see my old amigo. I felt good now. I would be able to impress our relatives and take them into one of the bars for a quick drink before heading home. Jose would vouch for me and tell these punks with the weapons just how important I used to be around here. I was devastated when Jose told me he could not help me. I would not be allowed to cross over the line into Mexico!

Evidentially, a few weeks before, an international incident had occurred which caused all the boarder guards to be extra alert. It seemed that Junie Hamrick Schaub, BHS '65 had crossed over and was showing her brother's daughter the places her father had probably frequented as a youth. The young girl was pretty excited to see where her dad had hung out when he was a kid. At one point, she innocently asked, 'Dad didn't go in *there* did he?' The girl was pointing to 'The Gay Nineties Bar' and when Junie said, 'Of course. Your dad probably spent a lot of time in there', the girl screamed "**MY DAD?! AT A GAY BAR??**' This commotion got all the guards attention and they were watching Junie and her niece very closely. Junie tried to explain to the girl the significance of the term "gay nineties", but Junie was not certain she understood. When her niece took out her camera to take a picture of the "Entering Mexico" sign and the Gay Nineties Bar, the boarder guards would not allow her to take pictures. They said they were afraid that some of the guards images would be on the film and that some highly secret establishments in Naco would be shown. A female boarder guard came up to Junie and her niece and confiscated the camera. Junie's niece was in tears. Finally, after much pleading, begging, and tears, the boarder guard relented and gave the camera and film back."

After Jose had told Wally about this international incident which Junie and her niece had caused, Wally understood only too clearly that "it ain't like it used to be." He was now a *nothing* in Naco. His gold-plated credit card was not worth a centavo. Nobody knew him anymore. The current mayor of Naco was some kid named Siqueiros. It was enough to make a grown man cry. Wally cried all the way home.

WAS THERE REALLY AN *INTELLECTUAL VACANCY* AT LOWELL GRADE SCHOOL?

I will swallow my Greenway pride and answer that question with a resounding **NO!** There has been a lot of bantering back and forth over the merits of one grade school over another. We naturally felt that the grade school we went to was superior to all the others. When we were amalgamated (a little mining lingo, there) under one roof we "put away childish things" and bonded into the wonderful high school we all loved so much. We became *one.* We pulled for each other. We encouraged each other. We were all *Pumas!*

We had our cliques for sure. We liked some better than others. We had our petty jealousies. We were kids. But down inside we were foraging a bond that lasted a life time. We were *from Bisbee.* I am not afraid to say it. I will willingly go out on a limb and say **very few high schools had what we had at Bisbee High School in the 1940's, the 1950's and the 1960's!** We left a legacy for others to follow. It has proven *a tough act* to do so!

I will conclude this book by writing about three men who passed this Bisbee legacy on to countless others. I have already mentioned a number of men who have left a legacy: Dicus, Spilsbury, Warren, Ridgway, Miller, and Quill. The three I want to write about now are more contemporary. They were influenced by those I have already mentioned. All three of these men were *giants* in education. One of these men was born, raised, and worked in the Bisbee schools all his career. Just like Al Ridgway and Jim Quill, he gave his heart and soul to the kids of Bisbee.

Bill Taylor is loved, revered, and yes, even idolized by hundreds of former Bisbee youngsters. I was honored to have gone to school with Bill from Greenway Grade School through Bisbee High. Bill was a year behind me, but we were good friends. We were football and track teammates. We were in Miss Parrish's typing class together. We "kidnapped" Jim "Lefty" Weld off the streets of Tombstone, Arizona. We "skinny-dipped" in a St. David, Arizona irrigation pond. We had some good times together.

The "kidnapping of Lefty" caper was brilliantly conceived. "Hooty", Ron Haynes, Bill Taylor, "Lefty", and I were driving around one summer evening. We decided to drive over to Tombstone and see what was happening. Nothing much was, so we decided to inject a little life into the "Town Too Tough to Die". Here is what we did. We let "Lefty" off at the east end of OK Corral Street going in to Tombstone. "Lefty" began to saunter down the street mingling with some tourists. The rest of us drove down and around the block and came up behind our "unsuspecting victim". When we got abreast of "Lefty", we screeched to a halt. "Hooty" and Ron jumped out, grabbed a screaming and kicking "Lefty", and dragged him back into the car. We rapidly drove off headed for Benson leaving behind some startled tourists.

We got a Dairy Queen in Benson and headed back towards home. It was a warm summer evening so when we drove though St. David, we decided to go "skinny dipping" in one of St. David's large irrigation ponds. Since it was almost mid-night, we ignored the "no swimming" sign as we climbed over the fence surrounding the pond. We stripped and hung our clothes on the fence and snuck down to the water's edge. None of us had the guts to dive in, but rather we gingerly stuck our toes in to test the temperature. It was cold. Before any of us could get all the way in, flood lights suddenly illuminated the entire pond-area! You should have seen us fly out of there! We fully expected to feel the sting of buckshot at any moment. Nothing happened. The farmer was probably laughing too hard watching those five fluorescent-white rear ends climb over his fence!

Bill Taylor graduated from Arizona State University and went back to his beloved Bisbee where he and his high school sweet-heart, Yvonne Featherman were married. They have six children. Five of them are in education. The one who isn't owns two *Good Egg* restaurants in Tucson.

Bill Taylor is a legend in Arizona track and field circles for the outstanding track program he built at Bisbee High School. He was honored by the Arizona Interscholastic Association by being inducted into the prestigious Arizona

Coaches' Hall of Fame. Bill joins his former Bisbee High football coach, Waldo Dicus in that august group. Earlier, Bill had been inducted into the Arizona Track Coaches' Hall of Fame. BHS, under Bill Taylor's coaching, never lost a conference championship and won an unbelievable seven state titles!

Junie Hamrick Schaub, '65 sums up the feelings of so many of Bill's former students. She writes "My favorite teacher of all time was Bill Taylor, eighth grade teacher at Lowell Grade School. When we moved to the high school the next year, Bill moved with us. He taught us a lot more than just English, though he did that very well. He taught us about life and what we could expect in the future. He gave us so much self-confidence and inspired us to try harder and to always strive to do our best. He was a great coach, too! Just a great guy!" I strongly concur with Junie!

Bill's life long buddy, Wally Quayle, BHS '53 reminds us just all Bill did for Bisbee even after he had retired from teaching and coaching. Perhaps Bill's largest contribution to the community was in leading a drive to get new lights for the Warren Ball Park. Bill organized raffles, bake sales, and car washes in addition to soliciting money from businesses in Bisbee. In all, Bill helped raise over $50,000 towards the new lights. Bill was instrumental in getting grade school kids to spruce up the Vietnam Memorial on several occasions. Wally reminds us that Bill served on the Bisbee School Board for several terms as well as serving as president of the Bisbee Kiwanis Club. Bill Taylor's entire life has been consumed by his two main concerns, his love for his family, and his love for Bisbee.

Jerry Loper's life and lustrous coaching career was cut much too short! Shortly before Jerry's life was snuffed out in a tragic automobile accident, Jerry told his life-long pal, Dale Hancock, BHS '57, that he would coach forever if he could. Hancock at that time was Jerry's immediate boss. Dale served as Assistant Superintendent of Chandler School District and had hired Jerry away from another high school. Dale explains how he brought Jerry to Chandler to revive their football program, which was in shambles:

Jerry had won state championships at every school he served; first at Antelope High in Wellton, Arizona; from there he went to Amphitheater High in Tucson; and then to Westwood High in Mesa. Westwood had been a football powerhouse in the 1970's under the legendary Coach Mutt Ford. Dallas *Cowboy* great, Danny White had played for Ford at Westwood. Jerry soon restored Westwood's winning tradition and he had a football dynasty in place at Westwood when Jerry's Bisbee buddy came calling. Dale Hancock made Jerry an offer he could not afford to turn down. Dale reveals he made Jerry "…the highest paid coach in

Arizona. He made more than the principal when everything was added up. He and I had a performance contract of three years to allow me to justify to the Board my hiring of Jerry." Dale goes on to delineate some of the "perks" that Jerry received: "...first of all he was paid $10,000 more than his former school was paying him. He was given credit for all his previous years in education (he didn't have to go *back* on the pay scale like most districts required for a transferring teacher-hh). He only had to teach two classes. He was paid to run a summer program. He was allowed to bring in three assistants from outside regardless of teaching areas, and two more assistants from inside...just for the varsity level...and of course new uniforms, equipment and upgraded playing fields. A year later, Chandler High School's field was named the 'best high school field in the state' by a poll of coaches and writers."

Dale Hancock, who had known Jerry Loper since their Jiggerville days, was amazed, but not surprised at how quickly Jerry got the Chandler program turned around even *before they had played a game.* Loper hit town running! He met all the potential players and their parents. He met with community leaders. He met with school personnel. Dale said that the support the high school teachers and staff gave Jerry was remarkable.

That first year, Jerry led the team to a 5-5 record. After that season, Dale informs us, "...we never lost more than two games." It should be said that Chandler was in what many called the "toughest league in the state". The likes of Mesa High School, Mountain View High School and Dobson High School were all in the league and each was a perennial power-house.

After Jerry was tragically killed half way through the 1996 season, the players and coaches vowed to win the state championship for Jerry. They almost did. In an article in the *Arizona Tribune*, political columnist, David Leibowitz, wrote this article after Chandler High School lost a triple over-time game to Dobson High School in the state semi-final game:

> The dream died 10 yards short of destiny, on a fumble. Before that, the boys from Chandler High School had you thinking Hollywood, thinking of touchdowns and tackles on toward a 5A state championship, ending scripted in Technicolor blue. You started to want it, and badly. For them, those stoic men in boys bodies. And for him. The coach you met only with his death. The coach named Jerry Loper. That was Friday night on the gridiron at Dobson High School: simple as a paper cut, beautiful as a tornado tearing through a field. Nothing less than the best high school football game this state has ever seen. Three overtimes in the semi finals of the state championship run.
>
> Loper liked best efforts, you see; honest sweat more than kudos and headlines. He would have beamed is the thing—you know it—would have

admired his kids for the fact that they came to the field without an ounce of quit in them.

Hell, he knew it all along.

"I didn't believe him," said Assistant Superintendent Dale Hancock, Loper's childhood friend, "but, he told me the first game of the season that we would be here. Mentally and physically, he said these kids were where the program needed to be."

And they were.

So the season ends, and the kids go home. The book closes on the man called Loper. They'll tell you he won 224 games in 33 seasons. That's a lie. He won 225 including one of the greatest football games ever played in Arizona. Sometime the scoreboard lies. And sometimes, denied dreams aside, a man never stops reaching out, even past death. For Jerry Loper, Friday night was one of those times.

Jerry's football coaching resume stands at 224 wins, 106 losses, and 10 ties. He stood number three in the list of most wins by a high school football coach. Jerry coached for thirty three years. Previous to the year Jerry died he had told Assistant Superintendent Dale Hancock that he would never retire. He said he would die coaching; doing what he loved best. That year Jerry did not have classroom responsibilities. He only coached football and was Director of Football for the Chandler School District.

I was very touched when I read Dale's account of the memorial service for Jerry, which was conducted at Chandler High School's Austin Field. Many of Jerry's former players from every high school he coached, his former teammates from high school to NAU, in addition to many of his former coaching colleagues and coaching opponents were on hand to pay their last respects to Jerry, Jerry's wife, Patti, and family. A number of Bisbee people were there as well; Max Spilsbury was there, as was Jerry's mentor and role model, Al Ridgway.

Several years ago a new high school was built in Chandler. It was named Hamilton High School. The school's football stadium is appropriately named *Jerry Loper Stadium.*

Prior to the dedication service for the new stadium, Dale Hancock had driven to Bisbee; with the aid of two Phelps Dodge administrators and Jerry's former *Puma* teammates, Bob Ballard and Nick Balich, BHS '58, selected a large boulder from the Lavendar Pit in Bisbee to serve as a memorial to Jerry. The boulder sits at the entrance to *Jerry Loper Stadium.* It is meaningful that the boulder was chosen from the area of Lavendar Pit where Jiggerville once stood. The Chandler School District paid to have the boulder shipped via a trucking firm to be placed at the entrance to the stadium. The boulder has a metal plaque with a picture of

Jerry and a nice eulogy written by Jerry's son embedded in it. It is a fitting tribute to one of Arizona's greatest high school football coaches, Bisbee's own Jerry Loper.

These last few words will be my way of paying tribute to the man who is largely responsible for me undertaking what has been a *labor of love*. **Dale Hancock, BHS '57** encouraged me early last February to write a book based on the memories, which were generated by all the emails. Dale and Ed "Pappy" Swierc, BHS '53 with an able assist from Junie Hamrick Schaub, BHS '65, were the "movers" and "shakers" who got it all started.

Dale Hancock is a manager, an administrator of people *par excellence*. He is a born leader. Dale was recognized by President Ronald Reagan as one of the top fifty public school administrators in America for his outstanding work at Chandler's Willis Junior High School in 1983. It was in 1983 that the study, *A Nation at Risk* done by the National Commission on Excellence in Education task force was released to the American public. The findings of the report were the major headlines of the day and one statement caused much concern: "If a foreign power had done to our educational system what has been done, it would be considered an act of war." Our public schools were in crisis and President Ronald Reagan took immediate action.

President Reagan appointed a Blue Ribbon Commission composed of CEO's of the major corporations and industries in America along with some university presidents to find the best schools in the United States which were "doing it right" so these schools could be offered as models of excellence. This commission immediately started searching the nation for schools whose success on test scores and curriculum met the needs of students as outlined in the *Nation at Risk* report. Once the schools were identified, commission members then visited the schools for several days collecting data and interviewing parents, students, community members and staff. This would lead them to selecting the best schools in America to submit to President Ronald Reagan and United States Secretary of Education, T.H. Bell. Willis Junior High School, from Chandler, Arizona was one of the schools across the country, which received a visit from the Blue Ribbon Commission. The findings of the Blue Ribbon Commission were very favorable to Willis Junior High. The school was presented with the *1982–1983 Secondary School Recognition Program* award. Principal Dale Hancock was invited to The White House along with other school administrators from across the country to meet with President Reagan for further dialogue as to the status of America's schools.

On Wednesday, September 28, 1983 fifty public school principals met with President Reagan and Secretary of Education T.H. Bell and members of their staff. Not every state in America was represented and some states had more than one school in attendance. After serious dialogue for several hours, lunch, and a tour of The White House, the administrators headed back to their respective communities. Their ideas and suggestions were duly noted by President Reagan's committee.

Several days after returning from Washington, D.C., Dale received this note from President Reagan: "Your school is proof of what the National Commission on Excellence in Education concluded in its report last April: 'America can do it.' You know I don't normally advocate busing. But right now I wish I could bus your school team to every school in the country."

On July 28, 1984 Dale met again with President Reagan as a national educational leader. This time it was a very small group which met with The President in the East Room of The White House to discuss how to deal with national educational issues more effectively. President Reagan displayed his famous sense of humor when he addressed the few assembled administrators. He said, "You know I got used to being called to the principal's office when I was a kid. Now, I get to call the principals to my office!"

Shortly after his visit with President Reagan and his staff, Dale received several letters commending him for his work at Willis Junior High School. One letter from Gary L. Bauer, Deputy Under Secretary of Education said in part "American education will, in the final analysis, succeed on the performance of people like yourself on the front line rather than on the performance of us bureaucrats in Washington."

Dale's trips to Washington and his meetings with President Reagan were highlights of his life. He felt very humbled and privileged to be so honored. He felt much pride in his fellow administrators, teachers and staff at Willis Junior High School. Dale had raised the bar to unprecedented heights in the Chandler School District. He would soon be asked to raise it even higher!

In 1988 the Chandler School District asked Dale to take over an elementary school that was in an economically deprived area. Ninety percent of the children coming into kindergarten spoke no English. The test scores in the school were the lowest in the school district and among the lowest in the state. The superintendent and the school board agreed to give Dale complete control of the school. They removed the present staff to a new school just built and allowed Dale to select every staff member who would come on board with him. He was allowed to design the curriculum and to make the school the most technologically advanced elementary school *in the nation*. Dale was even given the authority to change the name of the school so they could start anew and remove the stigma of the past.

San Marcos Elementary School opened its doors in September of 1989 and Principal Dale Hancock and his personally selected teachers and staff went to work! By April 30, 1990, San Marcos Elementary School was named the **top elementary school** in Arizona by the *Arizona Department of Education* and the *Arizona Educational Foundation*. The judging panel consisted of a cross section of Arizona citizens who visited the selected schools once they were narrowed down by test scores, average daily attendance, curriculum and drop out data. San Marcos Elementary School, under the guidance of Principal Dale Hancock, was head and shoulders above the others.

Here is what the *Arizona Department of Education* and the *Arizona Educational Foundation* found out when they scrutinized San Marcos Elementary School: San Marcos was eighty five percent minority students. Ninety percent coming into kindergarten spoke no or very limited English. Yet, test scores indicated that ninety eight percent of first graders had mastered the necessary math units, ninety seven percent had mastered reading units and ninety percent had mastered language units. No student was excused from the testing. *Electronics Learning* magazine recognized San Marcos as one of the nation's most computerized schools. Every student leaving after the sixth grade had to demonstrate skill in doing all homework and school assignments on a computer.

An article in the Sunday, May 27, 1990 edition of the Chandler *Tribune*, Sandy Schwartz, Executive Editor paid tribute to Dale. This is what he wrote:

> "Hancock is a change agent, a catalyst, a mediator, a problem solver and an innovator. In each of these areas his criteria for success is what is good for the community and what is best for the kids. Hancock is credited with turning a troubled south Chandler school into the best in the state. He is not afraid to speak his mind and stimulates discussion as evidenced by his work on the city's *Land Use Task Force*, yet he also has the ability to bring people together to reach consensus."

After thirty seven years of enhancing Arizona education, thirty three of them in the Chandler School District, Dale retired in May 1997. At a district wide ceremony, the new gymnasium at Hamilton High School was appropriately named **T. Dale Hancock Gymnasium.** One can look out the door of T. Dale Hancock Gymnasium and see the large boulder from Bisbee's Lavendar Pit, which sits at the entrance to **Jerry Loper Stadium.** Two Bisbee High School buddies forever honored!

In October 2004, a new elementary school in Chandler will be dedicated. Dale Hancock will be present. The new school will be named **T. Dale Hancock Elementary School.**

A tremendous honor for Arizona's outstanding public school administrator; and...a proud graduate of Bisbee High School **and** *Lowell Grade School!!*

Bill Taylor future member of the Arizona Coaches Hall of Fame.

Jerry Loper Arizona's third most winning football coach.

Dale Hancock.
Would you name a school after this kid?

FINAL THOUGHTS

Writing this book has indeed been a *labor of love*. I have been in touch with my home town as never before. I experienced emotions I had kept under wraps too long. I shed tears writing about Mother, Waldo Dicus, Fuzzy, Al Ridgway, and Jim Quill. I experienced pangs of shame as I wrote about "Hondro" and *Nigger* Patty. I shed tears of laughter as I remembered Bill Plumb. I chuckled as I re-walked the streets of Monterey, California with my Bisbee buddies. I have drawn close to people from Bisbee whom I had only known by name. I feel I *know* Art Benko. My mother knew him well. Now, I feel I do too. I had only heard about Dale Hancock. Now, I know him and am in awe of the many leadership qualities The Lord has blessed him with. I have so much more respect for *The Iron Men* of Bisbee; those miners who worked in the mines for too many years to make a way of life for their families that was better than what *they had before*. I remembered just how heavy Norman Wright *really* was. I just shook my head in disbelief as I mentally looked on the other side of that post-card rack in the crowded Los Angeles Train Station!

There are truly people from Bisbee everywhere!

EPILOGUE

This picture of the B was taken from an airplane piloted by
Rulon Wagner, Bisbee H.S. class of 1950.

THE DIMMING OF THE B

The B began to lose its luster in the 1960's. It was in the 1960's that Madelyn Murray O'Hara took a simple, brief prayer to the United States Supreme Court and successfully got God outlawed from the public schools. A Texas high school girl had delivered that simple prayer and O'Hara was offended. Here is what that young girl prayed: "Our Father in Heaven, we ask Your blessings **on our country, on our families, on our schools and teachers** and **on our fellow students.** Amen."

Just a quick glance at that prayer along with some serious thinking and one can see the subversive impact of The Supreme Court's ruling. What has happened to **our country, our families, our schools, our teachers,** and **our kids** since God was removed is pretty obvious. Multitudes of books and papers have been written since that so called, and misnamed, "separation of church and state" doctrine has been in force. Much research has been done showing how each of those five areas, our **country,** our **families,** our **schools,** our **teachers,** and our **students** have been deteriorating exponentially since the Supreme Court took God out of the mix for the first time since our country was founded. I am not going to get into all that. It is all well documented. I do want to point out, however, how that Supreme Court ruling and the Vietnam war set in motion an attitude that affected every nook and cranny of our great country; **including Bisbee High School!** I will explain my thoughts:

My focus as I wrote this book was on ***THE LEGACY OF BISBEE HIGH SCHOOL.*** A *legacy is history handed down from one generation to another.* It is my contention that when the *original* Bisbee High School was moved from Bisbee to Warren, **the Bisbee legacy was left behind!** I know I lost some of you there! I can almost hear all the books being slammed shut! Those of you still with me, just hear me out. I know that when BHS moved to its present location a number of the *old staff* went with it. I don't know who. I know Al Ridgway did. Maybe Fuzzy? I don't know. It doesn't matter. What does matter is that the *old BHS legacy was left behind.* Not intentionally. Not spitefully. But, left behind nevertheless.

The *Dimming of the B,* as I refer to this loss of our legacy, began for me personally in the late 1960's while I was teaching at Prescott High School with Les Fenderson. It had all begun so slowly and so insidiously. It was like boiling a frog in water. You can't just plop a frog in a pot of boiling water. He would jump out immediately. Instead you put him in a tepid pot of water and get him *comfortable and sleepy* as the temperature is slowly turned up to boiling. The same thing had been happening in our high schools all over America. At Prescott High School, Les and I had watched as "the inmates started running the asylum". Here are two examples of administrative indifference. One time as per administrative policy, I walked a student down to the vice-principal's office for having cigarettes in his shirt pocket. I couldn't just tell the kid to go down; I had to take him down. No big deal. I took him down. I told the vice-principal that the kid had cigarettes in his pocket, which was strictly against Prescott High policy. It was obvious to the vice-principal, as the kid still had them in his pocket. The vice-principal thanked me and told me he would handle it from there. On the way back to my classroom, I stopped in the faculty room for a couple minutes. When I got back to my classroom, the kid I just taken to the vice-principal's office was back at his desk with a "go to hell" smirk on his face. The kid had beaten me back to the room! He told me the vice-principal had told him to put the cigarettes in his locker and not to have them in his pocket any more. It was against Prescott High policy to even have cigarettes on campus, much less in one's locker. The kid wasn't punished. The administrator just let it ride. He didn't want to "rock the boat".

Another example; one winter a student trampled an obscenity directed toward one of our coaches in the snow on the football field. Les saw him do it. The administration was informed and they made the kid go out and "erase" it. That's all. Just erase it and don't do it again! No punishment. I wonder what Max Spilsbury would have done? Or, Al Ridgway?

But, I am getting ahead of myself. I need to go back a couple of years to when *the water was turned up to boiling*; to when it was too late to turn back.

It was the evening the Prescott School Board was going to vote on the possibility of doing away with the ages old "dress code". Les and I and a few other teachers were adamantly opposed to doing away with a dress code, which had been very effective for years. We knew that kids need and want boundaries. Coaches and effective teachers had proven over and over again that respect had to be earned. It was earned by firmness bathed in love. Les and I had learned that at Bisbee High School. We knew too, that kids would test us. They would compete with each other to see just how much they could get away with. Once they realized that an authority was not going to give in to them, they were relieved to fall in line and be obedient. A minority of Prescott High students and their complacent parents had "rattled the cage" to the extent that the administration of Prescott High School and the Prescott School Board allowed *the Vietnam syndrome* to sway them. They felt a sense of "political obligation" to let youth "redefine themselves". They allowed a minority to dictate to the school district. Since God had been removed from public schools, so too, had His blessings been removed.

Two *Pumas* went down fighting that night! Les and I were the only ones who went public with our concern for how "the youth culture" was progressively eroding the traditional values that had made America great. We probably couldn't have expressed it quite like that at the time. But, we knew that something had gone terribly wrong at Prescott High School. We knew that if the last restraint on the students' behavior was eliminated, Prescott High School would become a "zoo". Les and I got on the School Board's agenda and when we both spoke, we used that term "zoo". We no doubt spoke in less than professional educational jargon. We no doubt seemed to be just a couple of *jocks* who meant well, but who just did not know that "public education was in the process of being restructured." We went down fighting that night; two former BHS *Pumas* who had the *Puma* legacy deeply ingrained in us.

The educational process at Prescott High School was indeed restructured that Thursday evening and on the following Monday Prescott High had become a "zoo". What happened at Prescott High School happened to most high schools around the country; *including Bisbee High School.* We were all victims of "the decade of decadence", the 1960's. And we reaped the chaos brought about by that Supreme Court Ruling Madelyn M. O'Hara initiated. God was removing His blessings. The "Now Generation" was taking over.

In the process of being "restructured" to fit society's head long dive into what some call "trickle-down mediocrity", Bisbee High School **forgot** what had made her a very *unique* school. Bisbee High's **legacy** was left behind in the move to a new building. It has been said that when Al Ridgway retired from BHS that discipline went out with him. As I understand it, the *three-decade* teachers like Ester Louise Smith, Barbara Reavis, Fuzzy Warren, Bill Taylor, and others have all gone. Few of the teachers today in the Bisbee public schools are "in it for the long haul". They aren't there long enough to become *family.* They do not know, nor do they care, what the **Bisbee High legacy is.** If I am wrong about this, I will hear about it. I sincerely hope I am wrong.

Daniel Webster once said "He who knoweth not from whence he came, careth little whither he goeth." So true! I believe it is most important for the students, administrators, and people of Bisbee to know our history. For too many of us, *history* began the day we were born and not a day sooner. We need to see beyond ourselves. We need to understand "from whence he came". We need to understand what "the Iron Men" contributed to our beloved town. We need to understand the sacrifices that B. Hancock, Sam Sorich, Sr., and scores of others made for their families. We need to understand why Sam Borozan stops at the statue of The Iron Man and silently thanks God for his grandfather, Eli Yuksanovich.

The primary purpose I wrote this book was to somehow delineate our legacy. I want my grandchildren to understand why I "tick" the way I do. What went into making me the way I am? I want them to understand that God put me at St. Patrick's Grade School for the main purpose of having some loving, kind, and Godly mentors who would instill "seeds of faith" in me. That is the main reason why I "tick" the way I do; those seeds of faith bore fruit when I trusted in Jesus Christ at age forty one. I want *our* grandchildren to understand that we had fun living in an age that was not based on "instant gratification". We had fun spending days building coasters that lasted only one or two runs down a rocky road in Jiggerville. I want them to understand that our authorities were honored and respected; that they did not compromise their values. We knew Coach Dicus was serious when he said we would be kicked off the team for "messing with the whores in Naco". I want them to understand that we lived and still live in the greatest country in the world. They need to understand that Max Spilsbury, Jim

Quill, "Buddy" Gabrilson and many more *Pumas* fought to preserve our country's way of life. They need to understand that Art Benko, Rick Embry and others died for that same reason.

Howard Cain, BHS '47, wrote a poem in 1990, which captures the nostalgia of being part of a legacy. If you have read this poem before, please read it again….slowly.

COMING HOME

I have a thousand times before,
Passed through that heavy double door;
To stand inside at hallways end
And to my right the stairs ascend.
There's little light, it's hard to see
And a flood of memories pour over me.
Many feet have trod that old staircase;
Oh, this was such a busy place!
Dark, shabby, neglected now
Silent!…and yet…I hear…somehow
Phantom sounds in these empty halls.
Dimly heard echoes from tired old walls
Metallic squeak of a locker door,
Whisper feet on a dingy floor.
Then, from the shadows I seem to see
A host of forms approaching me.
Ghostly shapes with a youthful grace
Brightest eye and fairest face;
Sweaters gray and skirts of red
Wraiths coming on in an easy tread;
Strong young man—slim lovely girl
Pass me by in a happy whirl!
Among them, some with serious looks
Youthful arms and heavy books;
Burst of laughter in the gloom

Behind the door…of an empty room!
Piano clink from a music class
Voices murmur as groups pass.
And then!….thru haze upon the stair
A soft-eyed girl descending there;
As she approaches, I can see
Those gentle eyes are fixed on me.
I want to speak, but lack the will
To call out "I remember still!"
Then a mournful bell in the upper hall
My vision's ending must now call
Her youthful form turns with a smile.
And then, as night fog in a forest aisle
By warmest light of early dawn
Fades…and then is…Gone!
I stand here with brimming eye
I was in that pageant passing by.
The questions came…were they really here
Images of yesteryear?
Has nostalgia played a trick on me?
Was this only what I wished to see?
Where did those lovely young people go?
We changed…and now have hair like snow.
Then comes a thought so mournfully sad
We really knew not what we had!
"Youth and joy and robust health
Of this world's gifts, the greatest wealth."
Now gone like sand between the fingers;
But a sense of springtime strength yet lingers.
Reflections of a time long past
Four years…how did they fly so fast?
Long vanished youthful dreams and fears,
Melancholy!…in his waning years.

An aging man in his reverie

Visits the place of what used to be.

An old high school building on a hill

A half a century gone…and it lives in him still.

By

C.H. Cain

Can those "Reflections of a time long past" be unlocked from behind "that heavy double door"? I honestly doubt it. At least not completely. They are "…gone like sand between the fingers." **But, it is worth a try!**

I am impressed with the present BHS administration. Both Principal Vince Creviston and Vice-principal Fred Giacoletti are former *Pumas*. The **Legacy** has been tucked away in their minds for some time. It is time to **unlock it!** Those two men have established a ground work of discipline that had been absent since Al Ridgway left. They have established a foundation on which to start re-building the **Legacy.** In my opinion the place to start would be to **bring the B back where it belongs!** It belongs in full view of the students of BHS. It has served its purpose on "B Mountain". The **B** has over-looked Bisbee for *seventy-seven* years! My uncle, Robert Fergus, Jr. and Marvin Polley, staked out the first **B** in 1927. It has been many years since that original **B** was painted. Why not put a new **B** on the mountain behind Black Knob Street? It would overlook the entirety of War-ren. Require as part of the freshmen students' "right of passage", that they paint it each year. If need be, get freshmen parents to sign "a parent permission slip". Maybe this has been tried in the past and for some reason it couldn't be done. **Try again!**

WE WOULD.

0-595-32831-8